# SIR BOBBY CHARLTON

In this first part of Sir Bobby's remarkable autobiography he describes his early life growing up in a mining community in the north-east of England and charts his extraordinary career at Manchester United.

A member of the orginal 'Busby Babes', Sir Bobby devoted his career to the club. He played alongside some of the greats such as Best and Law and, in Munich in 1958, was involved in arguably the most shocking football tragedy of all time.

Charlton tasted FA Cup victory in the emotional final of 1963, won three First division championships and in 1968 reached the pinnacle of club success, by defeating Benfica in the European Cup final. Inevitably, such highs were balanced with no less dramatic lows—the 1957 European Cup semi-final, the highly charged 1958 FA Cup loss only weeks after Munich, and the 1969 European Cup defeat by Milan.

Sir Bobby is one of the true gentlemen of football and the legacy that he has given to United is beyond compare.

# MY MANCHESTER UNITED YEARS
## The Autobiography

Sir Bobby Charlton

with James Lawton

**WINDSOR**
**PARAGON**

First published 2007
by Headline Publishing Group
This Large Print edition published 2008
by BBC Audiobooks Ltd
by arrangement with
Headline Publishing Group

Hardcover  ISBN: 978 1 408 41313 5
Softcover    ISBN: 978 1 408 41314 2

All photographs are courtesy of Sir Bobby
Charlton

British Library Cataloguing in Publication Data available

02|16

Printed and bound in Great Britain by
Antony Rowe Ltd., Chippenham, Wiltshire

For Norma, who has always given me her
love and her strength

# CONTENTS

# ACKNOWLEDGEMENTS

I hope that in the following pages I make clear my gratitude to all those who have helped me on my way through life and football. Heaven knows, the cast list is long. If I have had one ambition more than any other in this book it has been to stress that among all my other good fortune I have been so lucky in my roots and all those who have been around helping me to build on the gift to play football that was given to me so generously as a boy.

For any man, I imagine, reawakening his past can bring both pleasure and pain and certainly if this is true I am no exception.

For persuading me that this was a good time to tell my story, after shying away from the task for so long, I must thank the editorial director of Headline, David Wilson—and for his vision and his enthusiastic support. I'm also grateful for the help of my friend James Lawton, who appeared at Old Trafford as a young sports writer soon after I established myself in the United team. In his company I have tried to reclaim the years and make them live again.

In telling my story another hope is that along the way I have conveyed my thanks, above all, to the game of football which has given me so much.

# PROLOGUE

Now, when I look back on my life and remember all that I wanted from it as a young boy in the North East, I see more clearly than ever it is a miracle. I see one privilege heaped upon another. I wonder all over again how so much could come to one man simply because he was able to do something which for him was so natural and easy, and which he knew from the start he loved to do more than anything else.

None of this wonderment is lessened by knowing that when I played football I was probably as dedicated as any professional could be, though I claim no great credit for this. Playing was, in all honesty, almost as natural as breathing. No, the truth is that, although I did work hard at developing the gifts I'd been given, the path of my life truly has been a miracle granted to me. Why, I cannot explain. But in Munich in 1958 I learned that even miracles come at a price.

Mine, until the day I die, is the tragedy which robbed me of so many of my dearest friends who happened to be team-mates—and of so many of the certainties that had come to me, one as seamlessly as another, in my brief and largely untroubled life up to that moment.

Even now, forty-nine years on, it still reaches down and touches me every day. Sometimes I feel it quite lightly, a mere brush stroke across an otherwise happy mood. Sometimes it engulfs me with terrible regret and sadness—and guilt that I walked away and found so much. But whatever the severity of its presence, the Munich air crash is always there, always a factor that can never be discounted, never put down like time-exhausted baggage.

I hope I do not say any of this in a maudlin or self-pitying way—how could I when I consider the lightness of the cost to me when I compare it with the price paid by the young men whose lives I shared so deeply and who so quickly had become like brothers? I confront Munich immediately only because the meaning of it, its implications, its legacy in my spirit, and the unshakeable memory of it, are still so central to my existence.

It would be possible to list a thousand good things that have happened to me before I deal with the moment I regained consciousness and faced that hellish scene at the airfield. With my first glance I saw that one beloved team-mate was dead after suffering injuries I could never bring myself to describe—and then Sir Matt Busby groaning and holding his chest as he sat in a pool of water. I could delve into so much that has been a joy to me before I come to the sight of seven of my team-mates laid out in the snow.

That, however, would be an evasion, a cosmetic device to obscure the truth I have lived with since 6 February 1958: that everything I have been able to achieve since that day—including the winning of the European Cup and the World Cup and being linked, inextricably, with two of the greatest players the world has ever seen, George Best and Denis Law—has been accompanied by a simple question: why me?

Why was I able to run my hands over my body and find that I was still whole when Roger Byrne, Eddie Colman, Liam 'Billy' Whelan, David Pegg, Tommy Taylor, Mark Jones and Geoff Bent lay dead, and Duncan Edwards, who I loved and admired so intensely, faced an unavailing battle for his life? Why had I been picked out to inherit so much of what they, in the first surge of brilliant youth, had achieved so beautifully?

One of the few certainties that replaced my original belief that anything could be achieved in the presence of such great footballers is that I will never stop asking that question—no more than I will be able to shed those feelings of guilt at my own survival which can come to me so suddenly at any moment, night or day.

For many reasons it is not easy to speak of these things, not least because of the sensitivities of those who were left behind by the disaster, all those loved ones whose lives suddenly became so hollow. Even now, when I happen to meet them I suspect they are asking the question, 'How was it that you survived and the others didn't?' But then something I learned beyond all else, after the first shock had been absorbed, was that whatever happens to you, whatever hurt you sustain, and however it is measured, you always have at least two options. One is to submit to the impact of such a catastrophe, the other is to draw strength from those around you, and go on.

That I was able to take the latter course is a matter for gratitude that can never be adequately expressed, though I will do my best as my story unfolds. As the weeks and months extended into years there were so many points of support and inspiration. My team-mates and fellow survivors Harry Gregg and Bill Foulkes were the first to meet the challenge and show the way. They did it with courage and determination and their example taught me one of the greatest lessons I would learn. Then there were so many others. They ranged from my family in the North East, who reclaimed me from the hospital in Germany when I was still stunned and so dislocated, to Jimmy Murphy, Busby's ferociously committed assistant, and my dear friend Nobby Stiles, who would share the supreme moments of my football life at the finals of the World Cup and European Cup. Most importantly, my wife Norma and our daughters, Suzanne and Andrea, gave true meaning to the rest of my life.

Beyond such key figures, the cast which shaped my world—gave me my values and my guidance—is so vast that it touches every moment of my account of the days that were moulded by the first important discovery I made as a boy: that I would never do anything more naturally, or so well, as play football. That was the gift which was retained only miraculously in the horror of that Bavarian night.

I need to go back before Munich now if I am to provide any insight into what was the central drama of my life, something which informed, inevitably, all that came after. I need to try to recreate the sheer, uncomplicated thrill that came with being a member of this young team. A team which, perhaps more than any other in the history of the game, was filled not only with talent but with what seemed a grace which came from some unchartable source, something beyond even the planning and the vision of the great Busby.

We felt nothing was beyond us as we talked so animatedly and laughed on that journey home from Belgrade, where we had played with great maturity to reach the semi-finals of the European Cup. In two days we were to face Wolves in another game of vital importance, one which could well prove decisive in our pursuit of a third straight league title. The sky was low and filled with snow as we landed in Munich for refuelling, but we saw little or no reason to doubt that our own horizons stretched out quite seamlessly.

It was a mood which so cheerfully overcame a long and irksome journey, as most of our travelling was in those days. In less optimistic circumstances I might have been more conscious of my dislike for this particular aircraft bearing us down through the low clouds, a chartered British European Airways Elizabethan. Since the first time I had flown in one, I had been made uneasy by the length of time it took to get airborne. The plane seemed to need an age to get off the ground. The Elizabethan felt like a heavy aircraft, one that needed a long runway and plenty of time to produce sufficient speed. It was all right after you had completed the ascent. You were reassured then by the steady throb of the engines. The first time I experienced a take-off in the plane I found myself saying, under my breath, 'This is a long one.'

When we put down in Munich you couldn't help noticing all the slushy snow on the runway, and as we had coffee in the terminal I imagined they would be clearing it away. Today, I suppose, it would take just a few minutes. There was no tension as we talked eagerly about the days ahead. We were, after all, the team who could apparently do anything. In the last few days we had beaten Arsenal in what some said was the most spectacular game ever seen at Highbury, and in Belgrade we had been equal to anything thrown at us by the tough and skilful players of Red Star. Now we were in the hands of an airline which surely knew, just as we did in our own world, what they were doing.

Even after two aborted take-offs, and a second visit to the terminal for another coffee, as far as I was concerned the spell was scarcely broken. Some players had changed seats, moved to places which they considered safer, but doing that never occurred to me or my companion on the leg from Belgrade, Dennis Viollet. Later, though, when I stood on the cold field in a state of disbelief and shock, I was glad that I had decided to keep on my overcoat. Why did I do that, why was it that I was able to remove the coat and place it on Busby as he waited on the wet tarmac desperately in need of medical assistance?

By the third attempt at take-off, conversation had dwindled almost to nothing. Dennis and I no longer talked about the growth of the team and the possibilities offered by the Wolves game. I looked out of the window and as I did so I was suddenly conscious of the silence inside the plane. Outside, the snowy field flew by, but not quickly enough it seemed. I knew it was too long when I saw the fence and then we were on the house. There was an awful noise, the grind of metal on metal. Then there was the void.

When I came to, I was on the ground, outside the wrecked plane, but still strapped into my seat. Dennis had been pulled out of his seat and was lying beside me, conscious but obviously hurt. Later, I learned that Harry Gregg and Bill Foulkes had helped to get some of the injured out of the plane.

I could hear sirens blaring and then Dennis said, 'What's the matter, Bobby, what's gone on?' Instantly I regretted my reply, which was, 'Dennis, it's dreadful.' He was not in a good condition and at that point I should have protected him from the worst of the truth, but as the horror was overwhelming me, I suppose I was removed from rational thought. I saw the bodies in the snow, though one small and passing mercy was that I didn't recognise among the dead either of my closest friends, Eddie Colman, who with his family had befriended me so warmly in my early days at Old Trafford, and David Pegg from Yorkshire, who shared my roots in the mining community. In addition to my seven, ultimately eight, fallen team-mates, the carnage that confronted my still blinking and dazed eyes had robbed another fourteen, and in time fifteen, souls of their lives—a combination of team officials, journalists, flight personnel and a travelling supporter, who, like us all, had been expected home that evening.

Eventually, I was helped into a mini-truck, one that seemed to have been diverted from its normal task of shifting coal. Gregg and Foulkes came with me as we raced through the blizzard into the city hospital. There, the walking wounded were taken to a waiting room.

Mostly, I stared at the wall. I had one small bruise on my head and I was suffering from concussion. Reality came drifting in and out, but at one of its sharpest points I noticed an orderly smiling, as if to say, it seemed to me, that all this was a routine matter and that the world would still be turning when the dawn came. But of course it wouldn't, not for the football team that was supposed to conquer the world. I was filled with rage and it was directed at this hospital worker who seemed to understand none of that. I screamed at him. What I said exactly is, like much of that night and the days that followed, lost to me now, but I remember vividly the pain that came to me so hard at that moment. Soon after, a doctor stuck something into the back of my neck.

My next memory is of waking the following morning in a hospital ward. In a nearby bed was a young German, who was looking at a newspaper that was spread before him. I could see from the photographs that he was reading about the crash. He spoke little English, but when he looked up and saw me he managed to say, 'I'm sorry.' At that moment I had to know who had gone and who had survived.

The German lad read out the names and then, after a short pause, said, 'Dead.' It was a terrible roll call, and I make no excuse for repeating once again . . . Roger Byrne, David Pegg, Eddie Colman, Tommy Taylor, Billy Whelan, Mark Jones and Geoff Bent. How could it possibly be? It was as though my life was being taken away, piece by piece. I had invited David Pegg to my home for a North Eastern New Year, had spent so many hours in Eddie's house in Salford, where the talk was mostly of football and soldiering; I had shared digs with Billy Whelan, and most Saturdays I would have a few beers at the Bridge Inn in Sale with Tommy Taylor, who would wait for me if I had been away with the reserves.

It was impossible to grasp that these days were gone, that I would never see Eddie swaggering into the ground again, humming some Sinatra tune, walking on the balls of his feet—or have Mark Jones, the kindest of pros, touching my sleeve after a game and giving me some encouraging word. A game never seemed to pass without that tough Yorkshireman taking the chance to say something like, 'Well done, son,' or 'That was a lovely touch.'

There was some relief when I was moved into a ward with a few of the other survivors: the Welsh winger Kenny Morgans, goalkeeper Ray Wood, Dennis Viollet who was looking better than when I last saw him lying in the snow, Albert Scanlon the talented, unpredictable film fan from Salford, who was known to spend most Fridays using his free pass at one of the city-centre cinemas before emerging groggily into the street after gorging on Marilyn Monroe and Rita Hayworth. I wanted to shout, 'At least we're OK,' but then I thought of Duncan Edwards, who was fighting for his life, and the badly injured Johnny Berry and Jackie Blanchflower, who would never play again, and that took away any such urge.

Harry Gregg and Bill Foulkes passed through the ward on their way to what they saw as their duty to the dead, back at Old Trafford. I shivered when I thought how it must be in Manchester. We had been screened from much of the news, but then, as the days passed, you heard of the funerals and something deep inside you was grateful that you weren't there, because it would have been so hard to say goodbye with so many eyes on you. All the time the question came pounding in: why me, why did I survive?

When you heard how Manchester was stricken, how many people were turning up at Old Trafford, aimless in their grief but just wanting to be as close as they could to the team who had so lifted their lives, who they had seen growing up before their eyes, you felt there had to be a match as soon as possible. This was something to try to latch on to, as you might to a piece of flotsam in a wild sea. A match would help everybody, players, fans, the whole city of Manchester. A match would take away some of the horror. It was a small piece of escapism and it didn't take you far. It couldn't, because upstairs Duncan Edwards and Matt Busby were in oxygen tents and fighting uphill battles to stay alive.

Eventually, I was able to see them both. I went up with my heart pounding. Later, I was told that Duncan's fight, which lasted nearly a fortnight, was the result of freakish strength and willpower. The

German doctors did all they could and then just had to shake their heads in disbelief that anyone could fight so hard against such odds.

He was in obvious pain when I visited him, but his spirit was still as strong as ever. When he saw me he threw back his head and said, 'I've been waiting for you. Where the bloody hell have you been?' I whispered my encouragement, feeling my eyes smart while wondering all over again how it could be that this young giant of the game was so stricken while I could prepare to walk down the stairs before packing for home. Big Dunc was more than the admired team-mate and older friend who had looked after me so well when we were in National Service together in Shropshire, who went scouring the camp for a better mattress when he saw that the one I had been issued with had bits falling out. He was the embodiment of everything I admired in a footballer. He had skill and courage and tremendous power. He could do anything, play anywhere, and the world awaited the full scale of his glory.

Once, when I was training with United in Fallowfield, at the same time as England gathered for some work en route to a game with Scotland at Hampden Park, I saw Edwards lapping the field in the company of two of the great internationals, Tom Finney and Billy Wright. The three of them chatted amiably as they jogged and I couldn't help wondering what other teenaged footballer would look so relaxed, so confident, in the company of such stars.

Duncan Edwards wore his own greatness lightly, but he knew it was a suit that fitted him perfectly. Maybe that was one reason why he fought so hard in that hospital in Munich. I could only pray for his survival after Jimmy Murphy took me by train to the Hook of Holland for the ferry to Harwich, where I was met by my mother Cissie and my brother Jack for the drive home to the North East. I didn't say much on the journey back to where everything had started, and where I had to persuade myself, in the company of my own people, that football could once again occupy the core of my being.

Of course I would know it soon enough. What would take a little longer to understand was that nothing would be quite so simple ever again. Some, including Jack, insist that Munich changed me. If it did, I like to think that eventually it was for the better, at the very least in that it told me that even when riding a miracle you still have to remember how easily you can fall. If you are very lucky, you survive, and while you're doing it you fulfil every dream, every ambition, you ever had. This is what lies at the heart of my story, but to tell it properly, first I had to go back to Munich. Without doing that, I know I couldn't begin to define my life.

# CHAPTER 1

## A CAST OF REMARKABLE RELATIVES

Because I was so quickly adopted by Manchester, a place I fell in love with as soon as I got over the first shock of its grimy, soot-covered buildings and whose virtues I have found myself championing in all corners of the world, sometimes I feel the need to dispel a misconception. It is that, somewhere along the way, I forgot who I once was and from where I came. I did not.

The truth is that nothing that has happened to me, good or bad, has come near to preventing me from going back quite effortlessly beyond Munich and the day I first arrived at Old Trafford, a fifteen-year-old dressed, self-consciously, in a beautiful sea-green mac that reached down to my ankles. 'You'll grow into it,' my mother reassured me as she saw me off at the railway station.

Even now, I often return to the deepest of my roots, the ones that I suspect still claim you when all the glory-seeking is done and every game has been played. In my mind's eye I run again in the big sand dunes scoured by the wind and dotted with the concrete pill-boxes left over from the war. Then I sit on the rocks and watch the sun disappear into the night. On other occasions I walk down the promenade where, on a good day, we scrape up the money for ice cream. Or I trail into the fields in the tracks of my big brother Jack when, usually under duress, he agrees to take me in pursuit of rabbits or birds' eggs or to sit by a fishing stream or a pond.

I also go to the pithead again with my father Robert. He buys me milk in a little gill bottle and a meat pie and leaves me in the colliery canteen before going off to collect the wages for which he has worked so hard, even when he is groggy from some bang on the head. While I wait for him I look out and I see the black-faced miners coming out of the cage, singing and joking in their happiness that the shift is over and they have returned safely, for at least another day, to the natural light and the fresh air.

Perhaps, though, it should surprise no one who knows anything about my life, and least of all me, that invariably I stop and linger most affectionately at a moment which seemed to crystallise so much of what lay ahead.

It wasn't one of those small rites of passage that came so regularly out on the football field when, stride by stride, I grasped that what I wanted most was within my power whenever I had the ball at my feet, knowing instinctively it was not so hard to run it by an opponent or hit it low into the wind that seemed always to be blowing. Yet in an unforgettable way it did show me, beyond any doubt, that this indeed was where my future lay.

It was the time James Hamilton, a man of big physical stature and even greater authority, burst into the classroom at North Hirst Primary School, a red-brick building in my home town of Ashington, and shouted, 'Charlton, Bobby Charlton, come with me.'

I followed the headmaster with all the usual apprehension he provoked when, while patrolling his empire, his gaze settled disapprovingly on a boy or a girl who he decided was falling below the standards of behaviour he set for all his pupils.

He was an amiable man most of the time; he

seemed to care about our lives and it was my good fortune that he loved football and realised fully the part it played in so much of the imagination of the North East. However, he inflicted the strictest discipline when someone misbehaved. He especially despised bad language and it was rare that the coarse phrase of a pupil escaped his censure. Only a few days earlier he had imposed what I considered the ultimate punishment on my friend Philip Hazell, who had been heard swearing in the schoolyard. Philip had been dropped from the football team and, as I hurried to keep up as we went down the corridor, I wondered whether I had also done something wrong and was about to share the same fate. This would have been quite ironic in that I had been trying over several days to rouse the courage to appeal against my friend's sentence.

Mr Hamilton stopped at a display of mining implements, picks and shovels and a helmet. I had often wondered about the purpose of this rather grim little tableau. Was it meant to encourage in all those who passed by a desire for book learning and the means to avoid the journey underground that had been forced upon almost all those of my relatives who had failed to make professional football careers? Or was it simply a statement of the inevitable, with options so limited for those who tried to look past the pits and the shipyards?

Mr Hamilton ordered me to pick up the helmet. 'You can put it under your arm as though it is a ball,' he said. Then he unwrapped and handed me the most beautiful thing I had ever seen. It was a bright-red football shirt topped with lace. 'No, it's not red,' he corrected me. 'It's crimson and it's the finest football shirt that's ever been made. It's our new strip.'

Mr Hamilton told me to put on the shirt. 'I want you to run back into the classroom with the helmet under your arm.'

'Run into the classroom?'

'Aye, Bobby lad, run into the classroom. You're the team captain. Go on. This is a great day.'

I had to agree with him as I felt in my hand the fine material of the shirt, and in my pleasure I had no embarrassment at all. Mr Hamilton went ahead of me to the classroom. Then, as he swung open the door and I trotted in, he sang out the signature tune of *Sports Report*. Everyone cheered, even the girls.

When the applause died down, Mr Hamilton announced that one of the teachers, Miss Houston, was already at work converting into shorts the satin black-out curtains which had been made redundant by the end of the war. It was so thrilling to be told we were being given our first custom-made team uniforms. The crimson shirts would replace a ragbag assembly of white ones which everyone had had to find themselves, whatever the state of repair. Our only requirement now was to get hold of red-and-white socks, which we did in various sizes and conditions and designs. In the mood of celebration there was even a pardon for Philip Hazell.

Looking back, I see that either side of that happiest of schooldays there was no special occasion when I realised that I would not have to go down the mines, as Jack did briefly—before he tried out for the police and then signed for Leeds United. There is a picture of him taken afterwards, coming to the surface. He is wearing a helmet and the expression on his face shows how bemusing and dispiriting he had found the experience. For me, the idea that my life would be football was just an assumption that built irrevocably over the months and years, and it was maybe most publicly and explicitly encouraged in that moment when I was told to tuck the mining helmet under my arm. I saw it as the clearest sign of the future—one that would always be reinforced by the fact that I felt so much pleasure and confidence whenever I touched the ball.

Everyone told me I could play well, and I was not so modest that I didn't realise it quickly enough for myself. The game, after all, was so deep in the blood of my mother's family and if I ever forgot that, my grandfather, Tanner, my mother's father, was for a while there to remind me.

Tanner was the head of the Milburn football clan. Four of his sons played professionally, George for Chesterfield, Jack for Leeds, Jimmy for Bradford and Stan for Chesterfield and Leicester, and—shining above all else in family pride—his nephew and my second cousin Jackie was moving towards the height of his career as the greatest legend in the history of Newcastle United.

Long after Tanner died, it was suggested to me that he was not universally popular in Ashington. Some considered him a hard and sometimes ruthless man who made plenty of enemies as a trainer of professional sprinters, a stable that included my Uncle Stan. He was, some said, the toughest of taskmasters if one of his charges disappointed him. However, it was a side he never showed to me. I adored him and was always aware of his presence. He seemed to be at my shoulder constantly, encouraging me, pointing out things I should know if I was going to go beyond mere promise.

His role as an overseer of my life, a protector, was established very early. Though Ashington was hit by only one war-time bomb landing on the ice-rink, which was miraculous when you considered how much industry lay between us and the fifteen miles to Newcastle, we always went to Tanner's home down the street when the air-raid warning sounded. It was a bigger, more substantial house and for me my grandfather's presence was reassuring. When the all-clear came we would grope through the dark back to our house and when we did this I always felt that maybe we were leaving a little safety behind.

I was entranced by Tanner's competitive world, which often involved ferocious betting, and was fascinated by the intensity with which he trained Stan. In the summer I would go with them to miners' galas, when Stan gave away at least eight or nine yards in the handicap sprint. Sometimes in training he would give me a fifty-yard start and let me win. The whole ritual was thrilling as they laid out the string to mark the sprinting lanes. Then Tanner would bring Stan to a fine boiling point, and there would be the explosion of the start.

Along the way there was so much to see in the sideshows, people trying to break free of ropes that had been tied in 'unbreakable' knots and fighting to get out of sacks. As a young man my father had always been drawn to such occasions and it was claimed, though not by him, that he won the money for my mother's engagement ring in a boxing booth at a fair. Certainly I knew he was a strong man and I could easily imagine him faring well in bare-knuckle days. His nickname was Boxer. He was a miner, of course, and that for me has always announced a man's toughness. I went down a pit once, in Salford, long after I had established myself as a player. I descended eight tiers and I hated every minute of it. I was spitting up black

18

stuff for about a week afterwards. Naturally the experience made me think of my father. I was down there for an hour. He went down every day of his working life; once, I remember, he took just one night off after he had been hit by a buggy which left one side of his face twice the size of the other.

Tanner would watch me from the other side of the railings as I played football in the schoolyard and afterwards he would analyse my play; sometimes I would see him conferring intently with Mr Hamilton or the football master, Norman McGuinness. Before he fell ill and became bedridden I always felt his eyes on me when I played. It gave me, I'm sure, an edge of commitment as I tried to maintain the standards he laid down. Famously, my mother is credited with driving on Jack and particularly me in our football careers, and it is true that she was passionate in her desire that we made the best of any talent we had, but some of the stories about her training and coaching me are exaggerated. It was Tanner, weathered by the wind and the rain in which he spent so much time, who painted for me most vividly the possibilities that awaited if I worked hard enough.

He never tired of repeating his most basic message. If you had enough talent, which he repeatedly assured me I did, anything was possible. All I had to do was work at something which I most wanted to do. 'If you are good enough, lad,' he would say, 'there is nothing you can't do—not if you look after yourself, not if you give it everything you have.' Tanner sowed the seeds of my ambition so diligently it would always be one of my regrets that, as I began to find success beyond the boundaries of our neighbourhood, I was never able to take him to a great football occasion, perform well and then say,

19

'Thank you for all that you taught me; today I played for you.'

I was devastated when he died. I missed him most sharply on Saturday evenings, the time when I used to go to his bedroom with the *Newcastle Evening Chronicle* sports pink edition and read him the scores and the reports, starting with Newcastle United and the performance of 'Wor Jackie'. Tanner's sight was failing, but his vision of the game seemed to be as acute as ever. He wanted to know all the details of the important matches. Inevitably some of his last words to me, which I will never forget, were about never letting yourself down just because you weren't prepared to take the extra stride, make that last vital effort to be at least as good as the gifts you had received.

He need not have worried about that as he slipped away. Sometimes on a Sunday I played non-stop for as long as six or seven hours at the nearby Hirst Park. Jack and I would go there hoping for a game and invariably we found one. Lads would come and play for several hours, then go back home for their dinner. Sometimes they would drift back and play again, often, in the case of the older lads, the worse for their time in a pub.

I never tired of kicking the ball and most days I did it until it went dark—and even then we would play under streetlights until we were exhausted or a policeman arrived threatening prosecution. It was the purest pleasure and often I might be the only one left. That was one of the great beauties of football. You could practise on your own. In the end you didn't need anyone to help you polish your skills. You just needed to get hold of a ball, although that wasn't always the easiest of chores. Footballs, like square meals, were not always so readily available. Often you had to go into the street to find someone who had a ball and was willing to come down to the park and start a game. Sometimes I would go into the school field in a gale and practise swinging in corners. I did it with the inside and the outside of my foot and always tried to put some spin on the ball. I never juggled the ball, I had no time for that, I just wanted to improve my game in the most practical way.

Getting hold of a ball was one of twin priorities—that and satisfying the hunger that so often growled in your stomach. Football knowledge was, for me, the one commodity that overflowed, and I never wanted for advice. On the rare occasions when he was slow to offer, I bombarded Tanner with questions. After he died, my uncles faced the same fate when they came home for what they might have hoped was a few weeks' break from the game.

My uncles were the constant, walking, running evidence that, if I followed Tanner's advice, I too could escape the pits and the shipyards. I was proud of my father, his toughness and tremendous work ethic and his lack of self-pity, but he did convey to me, without ever saying it, the benefits of the world my Uncle George first showed me when he took me to Chesterfield to stay while he and his team-mates prepared for a new season.

At the pithead in Ashington I saw the relief of the miners when one day's ordeal was over. At Chesterfield I saw a different kind of life and if, even at my age, I could see there were tensions in the fight for first-team places—and often heard language that would have drained the blood from the face of my old headmaster—there was also a lot of laughter along with the thud of the ball and the cries for a pass or for someone to make a tackle. My annual visits to Chesterfield were a sort of pre-university course in the game which so besotted me. They also provided the signposts to that other life where football was not the weekend escape but, and this always seemed such an unbelievable gift, the centre of your existence.

The life that I would be leaving behind, no one needed to tell me, was rich and warm in so many ways. But no matter how many years passed I would never forget the trials imposed on those who had no way of replacing their existence with something easier, something in which the simple business of putting food on the table—when you had, as in my family's case, one miner's wage and four sons to keep—was not a daily challenge to both nerve and ingenuity.

On Beatrice Street, where we had a house with four bedrooms—grand by mining standards as my parents graduated through smaller, company rented properties with the births of Jack, me, Gordon and Tommy—there was a form of workers' co-operative. Pigs were reared communally and vegetables were grown on the allotments. When a pig was killed it was a kind of fête. I still remember keenly my disappointment when it was first explained to me that the killing of a pig did not mean an instant feast of bacon and ham and pork. The animal had to be cut in pieces and salted and hung for weeks before a careful distribution among the families.

Life could be as hard as nails. I thought this was particularly so whenever our cat had kittens. I was told it would be too expensive to keep them. Usually Tanner would kill them. Once, he showed me how to do it. It involved two buckets, one filled with water, and then the other would go in on top, but I could barely look and there was no question that I would ever do it.

One of the abiding memories is of the hunger, but then I thought it was natural to have that feeling. There were games we played against private schools, when a warm drink and food were provided afterwards, but this represented extraordinary luxury, a rare treat that you accepted as no more than that, and certainly not as a pattern for gracious living. It was much more natural to dream of our lazy whippet rousing itself to catch a rabbit and the ensuing paradise created by the cooking smells back home in the family kitchen.

Poaching was illegal but everyone ignored the law. Often it was a choice between doing that and having nothing to eat. My Uncle Buck was one of the Milburns who didn't become a professional footballer, but he did achieve a kind of stardom. He was a top poacher, so legendary that some locals said that he used dynamite. I had this wonderful image of a river exploding with beautiful salmon. Possibly the claim was just a piece of neighbourhood folklore, but it could have been true because, apart from being known as a dynamite man, Buck also had a reputation for being, in local idiom, a 'cramper', which was another way of saying he was capable of more or less anything that came into his mind.

Whenever I think of Uncle Buck it strengthens my sense that rarely did a boy have such a cast of remarkable relatives. On my mother's side they played football and sprinted and drew allegations of blowing up salmon; on my father's, two of them, Uncle Dave and Uncle Tommy, managed to create a scene that would surely have been seized upon by the scriptwriters of *Last of the Summer Wine*.

Tommy was a kind and gentle man. He bought me my first pair of football boots, Playfair Pigskins, the best you could get, I always believed fondly. He took me to the shop to get them and I'll never forget putting my feet into the boots and thinking, 'This has got to be the best day of my life.'

Uncle Dave had a little boat moored on Wansbeck River. He was a character who I once heard described as a knave, which I thought was putting it a little strongly because as far as I was aware he never did anything illegal. However, he had a certain talent for getting into scrapes and on a day of high family drama he entangled his brother Tommy and me.

We met in the street one Saturday morning when Tommy was dressed for a wedding. His hair was slicked down and he wore his best clothes, including a pair of baggy trousers which were fashionable at the time. Dave said to Tommy, 'I'm just going to throw out a few lines, why don't you join us?' Tommy replied, 'We can't, man. Can't you see I'm dressed for the wedding?' Dave was unimpressed by the importance of the ceremony, saying, 'You'll be fine, boys, I'm not going out to sea—we'll just put out the lines at the mouth of the river.' Tommy thought about it for a little while, then shrugged his shoulders and said, 'Aye, all right.'

Unfortunately, the boat became grounded in the mouth of the river and Dave said we would have to wait for the tide to lift us off the sand. Tommy was upset, pointing out that he was going to be late for the wedding. Dave assured him that we would be off soon enough but Tommy was not placated. 'We can't wait for ever until the tide comes in, man, I'm never going to get there in time.'

Dave was impatient with his brother now, saying,

'For heaven's sake, Tommy lad, the water is only shallow, three or four feet deep, I'll carry you to the bank.' He told me to wait in the boat, he would be back in a few minutes. However, almost as soon as he started wading into the water with Tommy's arms around his neck, the boat started drifting off the sand. I cried out to Dave and he promptly made it quite clear where his priorities lay. He dumped Tommy into the water in his haste to save the boat, and possibly me.

I loved the sea and the rivers and especially those trips down to Newbiggin to the promenade and the dunes, where the wind could be so wild and I could sit for hours on the rocks looking at the changing sky. I cannot argue with Jack's recollection that he was much more of an outdoors man, but I would challenge his memory that I was always happiest in the house near my mother when I wasn't playing football. Maybe Jack prefers to remember it so because, like most older brothers, he wasn't always thrilled to have 'Our Kid' tagging along, getting caught in hedges and other traps, diverting him from the primary quest for rabbits or birds' nests.

My father wasn't a football man, which was probably just as well considering the weight of my mother's attachment to the game through her own family. He had other pastimes: pigeons, ducks, geese and rabbits, and, most valuably for the family income, a little horse. He used to take it down to the seashore to collect coal. Some of the coal came from ships which, when hit by heavy weather after putting out from Blyth, shed some of their cargo. I used to say to my dad, 'Well, you're never going to get that happening on a regular basis.' I thought about it a lot and it concerned me, but my father explained that the seam he worked on went right under the sea and after the shot-firing inevitably some of it would float to the surface and come in with the tide. My father would glean the coal and sell it cheaply to the pensioners.

As the family expanded we moved from Hawthorne Road to Chestnut Avenue and then to Beatrice Street, all mining company houses, all dependent on a man's health holding sufficiently for him to go underground for the coal. Another concession was that the company would dump coal outside your house, a benefit we most appreciated in the terrible winter of '46, when the snow piled so heavily against the doors and the windows. The coal would be loose, and there was a lad down the street called Walter who would shovel it into each of the 'coal holes'. If anyone tried to muscle in on the job, Walter would fight hard for his 'pitch'—sometimes to the point of fisticuffs.

In that way Walter summed up the toughness of the life we all faced. Whatever you got, even if it was only subsistence, you had to work for it, and then defend that right to work so hard.

The men went about their jobs out of need and also pride, and women like my mother were obsessed with the idea that their children do well at school so that they might have more of a chance of gaining something better, something easier in their lives than that which faced them and their menfolk every day. Such pressures no doubt brought strains on marriages, including that of my parents. However, they stuck it out, surviving their difficulties as so many couples did in those days, and if there were times later in my life when I became—as it has sometimes been, for me at least, painfully documented—estranged from some of my family, there has never been a day when I haven't been proud of my roots and deeply appreciative of the support I received when I was a boy.

The pangs of hunger were never accompanied by the impoverishment of not being surrounded by people who cared, passionately, about your wellbeing and, if Jack and I have had our differences, some of them expressed, much to my regret, in public, I am pleased that we have found ways of working them out. It would be tragic, otherwise, because rarely have brothers had such privileges to share, most notably when we played alongside each other on the day that England won the World Cup. As boys we had good times together and also, like most siblings, those when we used to fight. Sometimes we would agree to carry each other when we walked long in the fields; I would support him for a hundred yards, then he would take me for twenty or so before throwing me off. It was, I supposed, the right of the elder brother.

His greatest pleasure was fishing and sometimes you could see his face cloud when he was told to take charge of his kid brother for a few hours. Occasionally there was a flashpoint. Once I watched him play for his team at the Ashington Colliery Welfare football ground. He played well in defence before giving away a daft goal. Later, when he came into the house, I said, 'That was a bloody stupid thing to do.' He hit me hard enough for me to remember that, with Jack, criticism, constructive or otherwise, had to be carefully timed. I knew from that moment that when he was fuming with frustration was not a good time to offer candid opinions.

In our different ways—and some of them are undoubtedly extremely different—both of us have reason to be proud and grateful for our inheritance. From our mother we received the benefit of a brilliant

27

football gene pool—and her passionate insistence that neither of us neglected any talent we had been given. From our father I like to think we learned to be steadfast in what we did, and proud of it.

Many years after I left the North East I discovered fresh evidence that the Milburn football blood had indeed been generously distributed. It was when I was staying for a night with my youngest brother Tommy, who had never been involved seriously in football. He worked in mine safety and lived in a flat above the place where they kept the fire engines. He told me that he and his colleagues were obliged to keep fit for the job and the most agreeable way of doing this, they had decided, was to play two games of football every week. This gave them the required three hours of physical exercise.

Tommy said they were having a match the following day and it would be great if I could play for his team. I could see how much he wanted me to, but I had to point out that I couldn't because it would go against my contract with Manchester United. I told him, 'Tommy, they'd go mad if I got injured in such a game. I would love to play but I just can't. But I'd like to come to watch.'

Tommy was fantastic. I would never have known what a fine natural player he was if I hadn't stayed with him that night. Everything he did was easy: passing, controlling the play, reading defence and attack. He had great balance and natural strength and he struck the ball so comfortably. After the game I said to him, 'Tommy, you have lovely skills, why didn't you ever try to play?' He said, 'Well, Bobby, you know, trying to follow you and Jack, it would have been a bit much.'

The truth is that if Jack and I were our mother's

boys in our ambition, Tommy was his father's. He was more interested in whippets and greyhounds than football and fame. His vocation was to scramble the fire engines and go to fight fires in any of the collieries in his region. I think of him—and my father—whenever I see a news flash of a mining disaster anywhere in the world. I am grateful that when he had a heart attack recently—while playing snooker in Rotherham, where he is now based—one of the top specialists in the country was waiting to operate a few miles down the road in Sheffield. Like the former Liverpool football manager Gerard Houllier, Tommy suffered a burst aorta—and was saved by the speed with which he was taken to one of the few men capable of performing the emergency surgery.

Tommy's current interest is compiling a family tree. He has shown me charts of the 'clans', but has also confessed that sooner rather than later he might have to seek professional advice. This is despite some discouragement, such as 'Tommy, why bother to trace a bunch of sheep stealers.' Well, I tell him, we are more than that. We have had lives of our own and some us could play a bit of football.

My father's gift to his sons was energy and courage and a sense of responsibility to all around him that shaped every day of his life before he died in his early seventies. It seemed to well out of his native soil. He was never drawn to football, and was often embarrassed by the attention that came to him because of the success shared by Jack and me, but if you caught him off guard you might just see his chest swell with pride. Sometimes he would say to me, 'Why didn't you tackle more, why didn't you give that bugger a kick?' but I knew he wasn't speaking from real knowledge. He had heard people talking. He was saying it just to show interest.

He didn't know much about football, but he did know how a man should tackle life. He couldn't be an idler. He couldn't slack, and as he saw it this was as true whether a man clocked on at Old Trafford or Elland Road or the pithead. Absorbing this truth was something that Jack and I always had in common. It was underlined every time our father came home to Beatrice Street with his scars from the colliery, or brought home some coal after walking with his little horse down at the shore.

CHAPTER 2

# BEACONS IN MY PAST

There are days you know you will always keep in the sharpest and warmest of memory, days, it is reasonable to believe, that have contributed significantly to who you are. They stand out like beacons in your past. One of them came to me when for the first time I saw Stanley Matthews performing, in the flesh rather than on some grainy film, skills which pushed back the boundaries of the game I thought I already knew.

One moment he was just another footballer of great reputation in the tangerine shirt of Blackpool. In the next he was utterly separate from any player I had ever seen before. He had taken my breath away, created an aura that I knew, instantly, would never die as long as I ever thought about football.

His movement was both mysterious and thrilling in a unique way and it was a major reason why on at least one issue Jack and I were always united: the importance of earning enough money to go to Newcastle and Sunderland to see the masters of the game.

These were more than day trips: they were the pilgrimages that brought the greatest excitement to our lives. The importance of making them came before any other fleeting pleasure or the chance of free time to laze around. It was in our blood to work at something, and to play football, and so nothing made more sense than trading a little effort for the chance to see the best of the game we loved.

We did odd jobs, most profitably delivering

groceries for Donaldsons' shop. There was an old bike that had a tray fixed in front and we rode it through the rain and the wind on a rota that depended on our various commitments: for both of us playing for our teams, and for Jack the hunting down of wildlife. We told the shopkeeper, 'There's two of us, so we can get the job done between us.' Those deliveries were never neglected because they were an investment in colour and glory and adventure on a Saturday afternoon.

It was such a thrill to get on the bus to Newcastle—the fare was two shillings—and, when the journey was over, to choose between the cafe at the Haymarket bus station where we could get pie and chips, or the Civic restaurant for a wider menu but still cheap rates. Finally, there was the mounting anticipation that came with the walk up the hill to St James' Park. We clutched the shillings that would take us into the ground—and guarantee the greatest bargain a young boy could imagine.

Where we went in the stadium depended on the names that dominated the cast list of that day's theatre. If there was a great goalkeeper on show, a Bert Trautmann or a Bert Williams, we would tend to go behind the goal. That might also be the strong temptation if a Tommy Lawton or a young Nat Lofthouse was leading the visiting attack because that decision would be justified for at least one half of the game by our own Jackie Milburn stretching every defence he faced with the pace that made him a Powderhall sprinter and with one of the most dynamic instincts for striking on goal.

There was one demand above all others, however: to be somewhere near the corner flag if the greatest of them all, Matthews, was playing on the wing. You went to the corner because of the certainty that at least once or twice he was going to be really close to where you stood. Tom Finney of Preston North End was a compelling rival attraction and there were some who pointed out that he headed the ball more often than Matthews, certainly tackled more and that he was just as fast off the mark—but I never thought that last claim was quite true. The genius of Matthews, it was evident to a boy, was that he dominated with his sense of timing, and his awareness of the vulnerability of a defender. This was his supreme gift as he launched himself from a stooping gait. He wrote his own agenda in a language which only he truly understood.

Some years later the greatest teacher of football I would know, Jimmy Murphy, would unlock those parts of the Matthews puzzle that I hadn't worked out for myself. He did it during the several years I spent, reluctantly, on the left wing of Manchester United. Murphy said that, if you had genuine pace, the key to everything you did was the moment you chose to truly challenge the defender. You had to take control, you had to show who was dictating the terms. 'The defender has to turn,' said Murphy, 'and that is your great advantage. You have to exploit it from the moment you knock the ball past him. He's off balance, and if you put it in the right place at the right time you are gone.'

That was the essence of Matthews and it was something I never forgot when I played wide. I thought of what Murphy said but, mostly, I remembered what Matthews did.

As I stood with Jack on the terraces I could not have imagined that one day I would be invited to be president of the National Football Museum in

Preston; infinitely more predictable, certainly, was that the slim, coiled, and then darting figure who so mesmerised us would claim a prime place in the film archives of such an institution. I have spent much of my life admiring the talent of great team-mates and opponents, but nothing has moved me more than the elusive genius of this frail-looking man. Whenever I go to the museum I insist on looking again at the refurbished film of the 'Matthews Final' in the 1953 FA Cup, when he systematically undermined that most formidable of Bolton full backs, Ralph Banks. It still makes the hairs on my neck stand up when he pounces, cat-like, on Banks and then strides into daylight. The Bolton man had a huge reputation for destroying wingers, but you cannot destroy a target that dissolves before your eyes.

When I rode the grocery bike I knew that when I had saved enough there would be some great and unforgettable reward. Maybe it would be Trautmann reaching out to make some improbable save from Milburn, or the young Nat Lofthouse showing the strength and the heart which would earn him the title 'Lion of Vienna' for his overwhelming performance for England.

Sometimes, beyond the thrill and the spectacle there was the pure force of revelation. Even in the longest football life there are not so many times you see something that changes your view of the game, puts it into another dimension and makes you think about possibilities beyond anything you have seen before. Tottenham had this effect when they brought their championship-winning team to Newcastle. I did not realise a team could be so well organised, so filled with coherence in their passing and smooth in attack. They didn't have a Matthews or a Finney, but they had something of rare power: a team which had been beautifully dovetailed. I would remember well enough the big goalkeeker Ted Ditchburn, Alf Ramsey, the polished right back with the slicked-back black hair, and Ronnie Burgess, the captain of Wales, but the most pervasive memory of all was the push-and-run rhythm of an entire team that had found a way to play beautifully.

Len Shackleton was another who went beyond what I thought was possible on a football field. I saw his first game for Newcastle, a 13–0 slaughter of Newport County in a Second Division match, and if it wasn't much of a contest it was still unforgettable. Shackleton scored six times, but more than that he did things which made it impossible to take your eyes off him: flicks and jinks performed in the fine, arrogant belief that he could outplay anyone who faced him. Newcastle had brought in other top players—George Hannah, a clever forward, and Alf McMichael, the Northern Ireland international full back—but they were lost in the crowd. It was Shackleton's day, his greeting to a new and immediately captive audience. He took over the game, shaped every phase of it.

When I first met 'Shack' many years later I was surprised to learn that he came from Bradford in West Yorkshire. I had always thought him a prime property of the North East because of the manner in which the terraces of St James' Park had embraced him so ferociously as one of their own.

In those days football was played in virtually any conditions. They crushed the snow and drew lines in it for the markings and put down straw to try to thaw out the surface, but usually that only made matters worse. It made the pitch treacherously skiddy. For someone like Shackleton, however, it was simply another challenge to surmount. He operated on the principle that if you brought enough imagination to football you could always get something done and, best of all, you could always entertain the people for whom the game was the climax of a hard and often discouraging week. He seemed to understand the public view of football: it was a show that above all demanded a certainty of effort; imagination and skill were the bonuses that made everything worthwhile. The average spectator worked hard in the pit or the shipyard and there was one thing he would never tolerate: indifference on the part of those who had been paid to play the game professionally. If this attitude was identified, the reaction was as harshly vociferous as the praise for some outstanding piece of work could be unrestrained to the point of splitting the sky.

For Jack and me, Shackleton was most intoxicating on a freezing New Year's Day after he had moved on to Sunderland. We were in a narrow little paddock at Roker Park, next to the corner flag, for a game against Wolves. Shack came over to take a corner. To emphasise the conditions, if that was necessary with the snow piled up around the pitch, he had rolled up his socks to his thighs, as though he was wearing a pair of nylons, and the crowd roared with laughter. Fooling around he may have been, but his on-field cabaret acts were almost invariably supported by football substance of the highest quality. The corner kick was stupendous. I shouted to Jack in the uproar, 'Look at that, he's put back-spin on it.' I was wrong. What he had done, in fact, was drive the ball to where the force of the wind stopped it and carried it down into the most dangerous possible position for the defence.

(Shackleton was indeed also a master of the art of putting spin on the ball, chipping down on it with the outside of his foot, as though he was using a short golf iron.)

In those first visits to St James' and Roker, Jack and I were getting a degree course in our future trade. It was on several levels. We could understand more easily what the game meant to the people—and what certain players could bring to it according to their talent and their willingness to push themselves to their limits. We could see the difference between the good players and the great ones and, most clearly of all, those who cared and those who did not.

Bobby Mitchell, Newcastle's left winger, was another of our favourites. There was never any question about how much he cared as he tore his way to the corner flag before putting in immaculate crosses, but in Mitchell there was an example of that separation between the good and the great—the players who could make a big impact on their day, but who might not stand the test of evolving tactics and changing priorities, and those who could survive any new day, any new circumstances. Mitchell belonged, I came to suspect, in the first category and Matthews in the other.

My fear for a Bobby Mitchell of today is that he just wouldn't get a kick. His problem would be that his opposing full back would not be alone in countering his pace and trickiness. There would be plenty of help for the embattled defender, as there is in today's game when someone is obliged to face a Lionel Messi or a Cristiano Ronaldo. Indeed, in my own time, when George Best first became rampant, even a full back as fine and as quick as Bob McNab said the job of marking Best would have been impossible without the help of his Arsenal team-mate Peter Simpson. It was said of McNab that no one contained George better, and indeed I heard that the Arsenal backroom staff felt his effort in one game was worthy of a video defining classic defence, but he was the first to admit it was not a job for one man alone. In Bobby Mitchell's prime no one helped the full back. It was eleven against eleven, number two marked number eleven, number three took on seven, and the best man survived.

Matthews would undoubtedly have received the treatment meted out to Best, but he, too, would have survived. He would have done so because of his awareness of space and where everyone was. Also, he would have the choice of going one of two ways. Each Saturday you would read the same story from the lips of the full back who happened to be marking Matthews that day. The proposed antidotes to genius became so familiar Jack and I could have recited them to each other as the bus wound its way to Newcastle . . . 'I'm going to keep my eye on the ball' . . . 'I'm going to push him on to his left foot, he's not so good with that one' . . . 'I'm going to catch him hard with an early tackle, and we'll see how he likes that.' You would read all that, you would shrug, and then you would see Matthews imposing a quite different reality.

Another reality, the one of economics which touched almost every aspect of our lives, meant that we could go to Newcastle or Sunderland only three or four times a season—but each time was a feast, something you could store against the bleakest of days, and sometimes, too, there was a cut-priced thrill to be had at home in Ashington. Down the years our local team had slipped into the North Eastern

38

League, but from time to time they still drew a good crowd, especially for a cup game, and they could get decent players in an area so filled with aspiring professionals, including our Uncle Stan who played for them before moving to Chesterfield.

One game I remember vividly was after Ashington fought their way into the second round of the FA Cup and were at home to Rochdale. In those pre-floodlit days, games in mid-winter were played in the early afternoon, which meant that two-thirds of the miners were above the surface. So 12,000 fans packed the ground, some of them sitting on the roof of the stand, to see Ashington go down passionately and by just one goal.

However, nothing that I remember lifted the town quite so much as Jackie Milburn's first selection for England, against Northern Ireland at Windsor Park, Belfast. Jack and I were disconsolate because in that time before live television we couldn't see the greatest day of our famous relative. But then, as it turned out, our despair was only temporary. Our consolation came with a sign outside the cinema which announced that before the big picture—Moira Shearer in *The Red Shoes*, a film which in normal circumstances would not have attracted either Jack or me—the Pathé newsreel would show highlights of Wor Jackie's debut for England.

A visitor to Ashington might have assumed that he had arrived in the one mining town in the world obsessed with ballet. The queue was so long that by the time Jack and I claimed our seats *The Red Shoes* had been pirouetting along for at least a quarter of an hour and we'd missed the first showing of the news. When the film ended and the lights went up, an usherette told us we had to leave. We said we had come to see

39

Wor Jackie, but she was unmoved. 'You've seen the main film, now you have to go,' she insisted—but then someone in the crowd said, 'You know, these boys are related to Jackie Milburn,' and we were left in peace as the newsreel began again for the second showing and we could enjoy the great achievement of the man we revered so much, together with all those proud people in the cinema who cheered, along with us, one of their own when the cameras caught him trotting on to the field.

It was, though, the last I would see of Jackie Milburn's first game for England. The rest of the filmed report was dominated by the amazing Stanley Matthews. He sent the Irish full back, maybe the most harassed soul ever seen on a football field, every way but the one which might have given him contact with the ball. Matthews feinted and dummied his way to a performance which would surely have won the approval of the great Moira Shearer, who also—Jack and I had by now established—knew something about footwork. To cap everything, Matthews shimmied his way over sixty yards before scoring.

He sent us dancing our way home to Beatrice Street. Matthews may have worn plain brown boots, not red shoes, but they glittered more brightly than anything a lad who loved football would ever see on the silver screen.

# CHAPTER 3

# BEGINNING THE GREAT ADVENTURE

St Aloysius in Newcastle was one of those few schools which gave hungry lads like me something to eat and drink after the game, but it was the gift I received out on their well-manicured field that I would remember most clearly. My Bedlington Grammar School team-mates lifted me on to their shoulders after I scored the winning goal in a match which we had looked certain to lose. When I think on it now, it was my first 'Roy of the Rovers' moment.

It was as though I was playing under a spell, one that created the feeling that anything I wanted to achieve was within my grasp if I applied myself enough. Before this I had known plenty of success in school colours. Back at North Hirst Primary, the sports master Mr McGuinness had sometimes told me to hold back a little, particularly once when we were hammering in goals against weaker opposition and it looked as if we might go on from a 12–0 lead to a cricket score. He said that it was bad sportsmanship to humiliate opponents— but the match against St Aloysius was quite different.

They had some big strong lads and they could play a bit. They came at us hard and were leading by a couple of goals when I realised, maybe more clearly than ever before, that I could really influence a game, shape it according to my will. The more the St Aloysius players paid attention to me, the more I thrived under the pressure. I felt myself growing with every kick. When I volleyed home the winner it was a perfect climax.

Every game was a challenge to me, I desperately wanted to win every time I played, and it would be false modesty to say that I hadn't realised very early in my life that football came to me more easily than it did to most of my friends. When two big lads picked the teams at Hirst Park, the one with the first choice would almost always say, 'I want Bobby.' It was a natural thing, something I had come to expect, but then what happened at St Aloysius seemed to me to belong in another category. It was a wonderful, dawning sense of the power of my ability. I was determined not to lose, and I told myself I would do anything I could to prevent it. When it happened, when we pulled ourselves back into the game and I sensed the tremendous excitement and confidence building among my team-mates, it became the most important challenge I had faced.

When I scored the winning goal I had never been so pleased on a football field—and then, when the final whistle went, and the boys lifted me up, for once I didn't push them away. I thought to myself, 'Tanner is right. If you try hard enough, if you really want something, you can get it.'

Soon enough there seemed to be no limit to the scale of my adventure. Scouts were beginning to watch me as I made the East Northumberland Boys team and then the Northumberland Juniors. By the time I was picked for England Schoolboys there was no doubt that I would get the chance to join my uncles and Jackie Milburn in the professional ranks.

First though, my future had to be guaranteed beyond the risks of football. My mother was emphatic about this, and looking back I can see more clearly why she would make this point so strongly. Frequently she voiced the question that, because of the background of her family, was never far from her mind: what if you are injured seriously, what, then, do you make of your life? For me such a disaster was not even a speck on the horizon—and nor would it ever be, a fact which, when I think of all the games I have played, is not the least of the miracles of my career. Today I'm walking around with my cartilages still intact and without the nag of any of those chronic injuries which have accompanied many of my fellow professionals so deep into their retirement.

For an example of the risk levels, even many years after I became a pro a cartilage problem still meant your chances of survival in the game could be rated no higher than 50–50. The operation was primitive and was more than anything an act of faith and optimism. They cut into your knee, removed the loose bits of cartilage, drained the fluid and then, when you came right down to it, they hoped for the best. It was a lottery that my mother, for all her passion for football, was not prepared to play on my behalf—and if this threatened to be a serious problem for me when she insisted, for a little while, that I continued my education even as I tried to establish myself at Manchester United, there is no doubt that she was acting as a responsible parent. For me, however, anything that got in the way of football was something between an irritant and an outright nuisance.

The first time the football-versus-education issue arose seriously, however, my mother, with the support of Tanner, fought hard to make sure that my natural talent for the game was not allowed to dwindle in the wrong environment. The problem came when— somewhat surprisingly for a pupil who, no doubt like my brother Jack, would spend a lot of time gazing out of the classroom window daydreaming about football

43

and, in his case, that and other outdoor pursuits—I won a place at Morpeth Grammar School. It was a fine school, but for me it was utterly unsuitable. Morpeth was a rugby school.

My mother enlisted the help of my primary school headmaster Mr Hamilton, who had given me the crimson shirt as though it might have been the Holy Grail. My mother said, 'I'm delighted Bobby has passed for the grammar school, but there is no question about one thing—he just has to play football.' Mr Hamilton agreed and said that he would petition the local education authority. He did so successfully, winning me a place at football-playing Bedlington, and it is something that I've always appreciated, along with my mother's determination to do the best she could for me.

Sometimes the enthusiasm she displayed in supporting my progress as a young footballer of local celebrity could be embarrassing, but I realised that she was from a footballing family and that the game was in her blood, and that however aggressively she went about it, she always had my best interests in her heart.

I wasn't going to break any academic records, but I thrived at Bedlington through the football. It gave me confidence in the new, big school and, if I had doubted it before, the regard of those schoolmates who lifted me on to their shoulders when I scored that winning goal at St Aloysius. However, such a celebration of my football prowess was not always shared in the headmaster's study, where I was refused permission to leave school early to travel to Wembley when I was picked for England Schoolboys. Normally, I was able to fit in my football without too much difficulty. On that critical

44

occasion, however, I had to be saved by the Bedlington games master, George Benson, who took it upon himself to drive me to the station for the London train. His faith in my ability was rewarded quickly enough. I played with great confidence for the England Schoolboys; I was sure of both my talent and my ambition, partly because Manchester United had already made it clear that they wanted me.

I had the feeling that my whole life had turned into a great adventure and that was intensified when I waited for cup draws. I always wanted to be drawn away, and that wish came true when my team, East Northumberland, beat South Northumberland in the English Schools' Cup. When Hull Boys came out of the hat, my first thought was not that they were a formidable team but whether the journey would be long enough for us to stay in a hotel.

We lost to Hull, 2–1, but we did stay in a hotel and for me that was the greatest thing I could imagine. When I graduated to the England Schoolboys team and, all in one year, stayed in London, Cardiff, Leicester and Manchester, I might have been travelling on a magic carpet. The future was golden and without horizons, far more glamorous than I had suspected when I spent those summer weeks in Chesterfield with my Uncle George, which had been such an important part of my early football education. Then, even though I was entranced by seeing professionals at work, I had been a little homesick. Now, though, I thought of myself in the Marco Polo league of travellers and had absolutely no qualms about the days when I would leave both school and home.

One day Harold Shentall, the chairman of Chesterfield and the Football Association, was getting a rub-down from Uncle George, and as he lay on the board he nodded to me and said, 'Has this lad signed for us yet?' and when I shook my head he said, 'Well, at least you can sign our visitors book.' So I did. Later, we ourselves had a visitor, one among many, at home in Ashington, who announced he was a scout for Chesterfield. He said, 'You know you've already signed for us—now wouldn't you like to do it properly?' I said that it was impossible. I had given my word to someone else. I had done it earlier in 1953, on 9 February, when I was fifteen years and four months old.

Joe Armstrong, the twinkling little man who had made a great reputation for himself as chief scout of Manchester United, had come up to me after I had given what I thought was a very ordinary performance for East Northumberland Boys at Jarrow. The conditions had been nearly impossible with the pitch frozen into ruts. Later, though, Joe would say that he had been certain about my ability that day. He would give Matt Busby and Jimmy Murphy a rave report, but here he was, straight after the game, showing the force of his conviction. He said to me, 'My name is Joe Armstrong and I'm from Manchester. I want to know if you would like to play for Manchester United when you leave school this summer.'

In a few months' time, after I had had my spree with England Schoolboys, and scored twice at Wembley against Wales, it seemed league scouts were never away from our door. In all, eighteen clubs made me an offer. They all had different stories, reasons why they were the clubs I should join. The man from Wolves made the most novel pitch, though I have to say it was among the least convincing. He

46

handed me a match programme which had a drawing of the Molineux ground on the front. It wasn't even a photograph, but he pointed to it and said, 'Look, you must join us—you will be playing on pitches like that.' Arsenal came into the running late, but I have to say they did have a lot of appeal for me. They had a wonderfully classic image and so many names that were part of the football legends I had embraced so hungrily: Cliff Bastin and Alex James, Eddie Hapgood and the Compton brothers.

Sometimes there would be two scouts in the house at the same time. One would be in the front room with my father, another in the kitchen with my mother, and I was having to go between the two. Even though I was telling everyone I was going to United, I still had to listen. It was strange because, as far as I knew, there was no money flying around; every player got the same reward in those days. Sometimes I shake my head when I think how it was that someone like Stanley Matthews played for a club like Blackpool for so long.

Naturally, some overtures were more exciting than others. When I played for England in the schoolboy trial at Manchester City's ground, Maine Road, the residing star of City and an England player, Don Revie, spoke to me as I came up the tunnel after the game. I was tremendously flattered because Revie was one of my heroes. I had watched him play and been fascinated by the way he worked with the goalkeeper Bert Trautmann. Revie always made himself free to receive the ball from the goalkeeper— and Trautmann always threw it to him. Revie had tremendous craft and you could see his football intelligence in everything he did. He asked me, 'How would you like to play for us? I know you've maybe promised Manchester United, but you have seen our great stadium and we do have great plans for the future. You could be a big part of that.'

It was perhaps enough to turn a young boy's head, but Manchester United did not neglect to develop their advantage. Joe Armstrong was a man of great charm, and in all the comings and goings of rival scouts he was a regular presence around our house, arguing persuasively that Manchester United had the greatest of futures and that it was at Old Trafford that my talent would best be developed. They had so many fine young players coming through and this was where the club had invested most seriously.

His case certainly did not lack support that day of the England Schoolboys trial. After the game we were taken to lunch in Sale and afterwards, on the way to the railway station, we passed along Chester Road near Old Trafford. I craned to take in the scene as the fans flooded down Warwick Road for that afternoon's United match. There was more than the usual excitement because Tommy Taylor was making his debut after being signed from Barnsley, Busby fixing the transfer fee at £29,999 because, it was said, a little strangely I thought, that he didn't want his new player to have the additional pressure of becoming football's first £30,000 player. What was in a single pound note, I wondered, but more pressingly I wanted to jump off the bus and join in the excitement. However, it did occur to me that I had some time to savour the prospect. All I needed was a little patience. I would be part of this scene by the summer.

It was also true that in me Joe had something of a captive audience. I had lost a little of my heart to his club in 1948 when they beat Blackpool in one of the classic FA Cup finals. I had played with the school team that morning and one of the lads invited us back to his house for his birthday. We were kicking a ball around, inevitably, but the radio was on and we were listening as we played. Everyone was shouting for Blackpool and the great Matthews. No one admired him more than me, but I also liked United and I wasn't convinced that this might be his last chance to win a cup-winners' medal. Anyway, I thought a cup final wasn't just about one man. Twenty-two players had fought to get there, including eleven of United, who ever since the resumption of the league after the war had been playing beautiful football. They had men like Johnny Carey and Jack Rowley, Johnny Morris, Charlie Mitten, Jimmy Delaney and a fine and subtle scorer-creator in Stan Pearson.

I had followed the course of that team with great interest, watched them reach a peak and then noted how Busby was indeed unafraid of introducing new young talent when he felt the timing was right. His boldest move came soon after I had agreed, verbally, to Joe Armstrong's proposition on that freezing day in Jarrow. Busby felt that his ageing maestros were beginning to lose their edge and his reaction was both a dramatic and a swift vindication of Joe's view that youth should not be allowed to grow frustrated, and still less old, on the Old Trafford vine. It was a huge story when he dropped half of his team and picked youngsters like John Doherty and Eddie Lewis. Many predicted humiliation for United, but the new blood flowed strongly, and United announced that they were on the point of launching a new empire. The memory of those exciting days flared again recently when I laid a time capsule in the new quadrant at Old Trafford, fifty years after the team that would forever be known as the Busby Babes won their first championship without the help of the great old players of the post-war years.

When I read about the Old Trafford revolution in the newspaper I felt a great surge of excitement. Not only were they blooding so many talented young players, already they had at the heart of the team somebody who was being described as a phenomenon. He was Duncan Edwards and he was just sixteen years old. I had never been short of confidence, or excitement about my possibilities as a professional, but this seemed like a new dimension to my dreams. Could I be part of this? Could I play alongside this superboy Edwards?

After it became apparent, if not quite official, that this would be the challenge facing me, and when all the rival scouts from other clubs were beginning to accept that indeed I saw my destiny at Old Trafford, I had a visit from the famous relative who had become a huge and inspiring part of my life. Wor Jackie said he was obliged to make the case for his club Newcastle United, but he also said he was doing it without conviction. Newcastle treated their young players without care or thought, he reported. They didn't have a development policy. Instead they operated a kind of lottery. Maybe a young player would survive it, maybe not.

For quite some time Jackie had made me his young companion as he travelled about the North East, making presentations, opening events. He introduced me as 'Our Bobby', saying, 'I've brought a coming football star, one of the England Schoolboys'—and when such a job was done he would hand me four shillings. I protested, saying I was just pleased to tag along with him, but he insisted, 'You've come with me, you're part of the show, take it.'

When he died, in 1988, I saw clearly the impact he had had on the community in which he had played out his life. After the funeral service in Newcastle Cathedral, I was walking through the crowds who thronged the street when Bob Stokoe, the old Newcastle centre half who managed Sunderland to their shock 1973 FA Cup victory over Leeds United, stopped his car and told me to get in. I was very upset. Jackie's death took away a pillar of my life, someone in whom I had grown to feel the deepest pride and affection. He had taken me everywhere. I had even played cricket with him. He had told me about the game, not just the detail of it but how you should approach it in your spirit as well as your talent.

When United had me playing on the wing for a while, he had known I was restive and he once said, 'When are you going to play centre forward?' I said, 'Well, it really isn't up to me.' He replied, 'Well, Bobby, let me tell you something—you *are* Manchester United, and *you* can tell *them* what you want to do.' He wasn't being mischievous. He was trying to make me feel good and better aware of what I had to offer. Now, on that drive after the funeral, Bob confirmed to me that whenever Jackie had something to say to a team-mate it was always encouraging, always a lift of the spirit.

As I drove along with Bob I noticed how solemn were the people lining the route between the cathedral and the crematorium in the outskirts. They were showing respect, of course, but I felt there should also be celebration of a great life—I wanted to hear applause. I said, 'If you do something good in life it is surely a matter for cheers, not just sadness.' A few years later I was delighted to see that other people were beginning to feel this way as bursts of applause accompanied the funeral cortege of that other great hero of mine, Stanley Matthews.

When Jackie had come to our house on behalf of Newcastle he could not have been more honest, but after saying how poor Newcastle's coaching and youth planning was, he also had to tell me the club had promised to get me a job on the *Newcastle Evening Chronicle*. When, at my mother's insistence, I had considered alternative careers, becoming a sports reporter was always high on my list. The job had one supreme advantage. You got a free pass to see the games. It was also something you could do if the worst happened to you, if you broke a leg and had to make a career outside the game. That was always the point being hammered home to me, and not just by my mother. It made me impatient, possibly because if you are ever going to be optimistic, and immortal, it is probably around the age of fifteen. But a boy had to listen to his elders, even if, in the privacy of his own thoughts, he rejected what they said. You could always make a compromise satisfactory to yourself. One of mine came when I asked a relative, a greengrocer, how much it had cost him to set up in business. His answer was very re-assuring. He told me it was around £2,000. That made everything quite straightforward. If I played for twenty years I could easily put away a hundred a year, and then I could face the second half of my life selling apples and oranges. The idea did not fill with me with joy but, as everyone said, you had to plan for the future.

First, though, you had to take the best of what life had to offer and that's what I believed I was doing when my mother dressed me in my sea-green mac and put me on the train to Manchester. I was leaving my brothers and my uncles, and my friends and all that was familiar, including a girlfriend at Bedlington Grammar, who was named, prophetically, Norma— Norma Outhwaite. She was a nice girl, but I was not a victim of young love. We had been good friends but I was a football man and I had to go about my business. At that time of my youth no girl could compete with football. It was both my greatest love and my obsession.

CHAPTER 4

# A NEW LIFE AND A NEW WATCH

When the train came to a halt in Exchange Station, and I looked out through the billowing steam and saw the black buildings and the busy platform, I said to myself, 'Well, Bobby, this is your adventure starting and you don't know what's going to happen.'

For so long I had assumed that my talent for football would give me all that I wanted, take me to fancy hotels and the carefree life that was so appealing in those summer days at Chesterfield when I had my Uncle George to put his arm around my shoulder if I felt a little homesick—but here was the reality, a new world filled with strangers and, for the first time, a sudden feeling of uncertainty. At Chesterfield's Saltergate ground I had known that soon I would be going back to my little empire in the North East, where everyone who knew me patted my shoulder and said, 'You can play, Bobby.' Now, I couldn't be sure of what was going to happen to me. Yes, I could play, but well enough to keep standing out, well enough to survive in this new environment without my own people all around me?

At least some of the mystery of my new life was stripped away, however, even before the taxi pulled up in Birch Avenue, which was just a few hundred yards from an Old Trafford stadium that was still several years away from its first floodlights and a roof to protect the Stretford End loyalists from the rain. Jimmy Murphy had met me at the station, and he made it quite clear on that short journey from the city

54

centre that quite a lot of what was going to happen was Jimmy Murphy himself.

*He* was going to happen as the most persistent and profound football influence I would ever know. *He* was going to happen out on the training field, in what sometimes seemed like a dialogue that would never end and, before long, he was even going to be in my subconscious. One of his sayings would be imprinted there, something to drive you on when you felt maybe you had done enough for one day or one match. 'Bobby,' he would say, 'in all my time in football I never saw a player suffer a heart-attack because he worked too hard.' In those days I wished fervently I had a pound, even five bob, for every time he said that to me when he suspected I might be reluctant to carry on with a session that had left me weary.

Jimmy was going to treat me, for all my boyish belief that I could play the game, as a work in progress and one that in his mind could never be finished because there was always something new to learn, some fresh adjustment to make.

His voice was untouched by all the years he had spent away from his native Rhondda Valley as a tough half back for West Bromwich Albion and Wales, and then as an army instructor whose ability to draw the attention of a group of soldiers in a wartime camp in Naples persuaded Matt Busby that he would make a most valuable number two. For me this voice would always have an hypnotic effect.

Also, Jimmy was sometimes going to be the most demanding companion for a young footballer who from time to time might agonise over the choice between an early bedtime and maybe a cup of cocoa, or going out into the drinking culture and nightlife that in those days seemed to raise hardly an eyebrow in the hierarchy of even the biggest clubs. He would spare no rage if one of his protégés surrendered the ball too easily in the tackle, or passed it stupidly, but he could also get upset if you turned him down when he invited you for a drink in a pub after special training on Sunday morning, or in his hotel room or a bar on an away trip. Always the conversation would be football, but you couldn't be so sure about the type or the quality of the drink. Jimmy liked a pint of bitter, but he was also partial to sherry and, most disconcertingly if you didn't have a sweet tooth, the Portuguese wine Mateus Rosé.

My exposure to this pitfall waiting for anyone who was picked out by Jimmy as worthy of his special attention would only emerge some time later. One of the reasons was that I was still short of my sixteenth birthday. The other was that at the time when he first met me at the station his entire football universe seemed to be filled by Big Duncan—Duncan Edwards. On that journey, Jimmy had said with shining eyes, 'Bobby, I've got a player you will find hard to believe, he is so good. He has everything. He is tall and powerful, but he also has a wonderful touch. Right foot, left foot, it doesn't matter. I'm going to make him such a player. Just look at him— and then remember I haven't knocked the rough edges off him yet.' I had bitten my tongue on the first thought that came into my head, which was, 'Well, nobody can be that good.'

Instead of challenging Jimmy's assessment I had thought it would be wise to try to change the subject, however difficult it might prove. I asked him about Old Trafford, where it was in the city and how far it was from my digs. The question brought on another burst of enthusiam. 'It's in Trafford Park, and you're going to love playing there,' he said.

Though I had passed quite close to the ground on the day that I had had the Schoolboys trial a few miles across the city at Maine Road, Jimmy's reference to Trafford Park was reassuring after the shock of first seeing my new surroundings, the big, dirty, alien city. 'Trafford Park' had a nice comforting ring, a suggestion of open spaces and clean air, a new Hirst Park. Later, I would boast in many corners of the world about the power and the energy of Europe's largest industrial estate, but at that moment I preferred a vision of trees and grass and a little bit of tranquillity. 'Thank goodness for that,' I thought. 'It can't be so bad.'

The big Victorian house where Jimmy had left me promised roomy accommodation, but I quickly discovered there were plenty of demands on its space, from salesmen passing through as they sold their products to Trafford Park—and from half the team who would soon be known throughout football as the Busby Babes.

One by one my new club-mates introduced themselves, the great Duncan, Jackie Blanchflower, Mark Jones, Tommy Taylor, David Pegg, 'Billy' Whelan, Alan Rhodes—a full back on the youth team—and two goalkeepers, Gordon Clayton and Tony Hawksworth. With the introductions came an astounding discovery—that the new kid, so wide-eyed when he arrived in this strange and intimidating world, had automatic membership of the gang. If they went to the pictures, he could go too. If they went for a walk, he could join them. All our time would be spent together, and this extended to the hours of sleep. At Birch Avenue we slept two-to-a-bed, which

57

in those days, for a working-class lad like me, was maybe the least of the surprises of my new life. My bed-mate was Alan Rhodes. He would not play for the first team, but at that time he shared all our hopes.

In those first days it seemed that I had, after all, been given access to my idea of paradise. I had the friendship of great young footballers who were ready to accept me and so clearly shared my passion to play the game that had always been an inspiration. The days stretched ahead so excitingly that, some years later, I could only nod in agreement with the football correspondent of *The Times*, Geoffrey Green, a great character who wore a long leather coat that was reputed to have once been the property of a colonel of the KGB. (There are several versions of how it came into Geoffrey's possession on a long night in Moscow, but perhaps I should just say that the ones I've heard all suggest a man with a tremendous appetite for life.) He said to me, 'Bobby, when you are doing something you love in the company of people you love, well, every day is Christmas Day.'

Soon enough, though, I learned there were complications in the life of even the most starry-eyed of young footballers. Mine came from my mother's insistence that I must have something to fall back on. It would not be good enough for me to spin out a year or so as a groundstaff boy before I could sign professional and join my new friends as round-the-clock footballers. I had to continue my education even as I tried to learn the game.

My mother had talked with United and I was told that I had been enrolled in Stretford Grammar School, which was next to Old Trafford cricket ground and, like the football stadium, just a short walk from my digs. This was convenient enough, but right from the start I could see the plan wasn't feasible. The class work I was given was completely different from that at Bedlington and I struggled to keep up. It didn't help that I yearned to be with the United lads, living all of every day in football. Looking back, I see that I was still very much a boy who just wanted to play the game and for whom all else was secondary. I lasted three weeks at Stretford Grammar.

The early breaking point came after a football lesson in Longford Park, where the school played its games and where I used to go on Sunday mornings with the lads to watch the local teams. It was the most enjoyable, and important, lesson I would have at the school. They hadn't seen me play before, and maybe because I was so pleased to be out of the classroom I played with even more than my usual enjoyment. I scored eight or nine goals.

The games master came to me as I was changing and said, 'You're in the school team from now on.' I asked him when we would be playing and was shocked when he said Saturday mornings. I told him I was sorry but I couldn't do it. I hadn't come to Manchester to play for Stretford Grammar School; I played for Manchester United on Saturday mornings. 'Well, you can't any more,' he snapped. 'Your first duty is to your school. You're in the team for the rest of the year.' I was terribly dejected. As I fastened the knot in my school tie, I had probably never felt more depressed.

I didn't speak to Jimmy Murphy or anyone at the club. Instead, I made a phone call to Mum. I imagine it is what most fifteen-year-olds who believe their world has just come crashing down would do. I just said to her, 'I have a problem.' She must have heard the desperation in my voice because when I had explained what the games master had said, she asked me, 'What do you want to do?' I told her that in my perfect world I would do what I came down to Manchester to do, and only that. I would leave school and play football. There was a short pause and then she said, 'Yes, OK, Bobby, if that's what you want.' I couldn't remember ever being so happy. A great weight had been lifted off my shoulders. I told the headmaster of the family decision, that if I couldn't play for United at the weekend I might as well have stayed up in the North East. He nodded and said, 'I quite understand,'—and as he did so I got the impression that somebody had told him that, while I was unlikely to become a professor of science or a captain of industry, I was capable of scoring eight goals without any great strain.

Now my life would be without any distraction from football; it would all be wonderfully straightforward. I would spend my days at the football ground, cleaning the terraces, the dressing rooms, the boots, breathing in the atmosphere, and in just over a year I would be a fully fledged professional. I said to my mother, 'What could be better?'—and of course she told me. She didn't like the idea of my cleaning toilets and terraces. It wasn't her idea of preparation for a working life if the football went wrong. She had accepted the need for me to play football seriously, and for the club I had agreed to join, but that was the extent of her concession. There had to be a compromise, she said, and she would talk to the club.

The result was that within a few days I was clocking on at Switchgear and Cowans, an electrical firm a few miles from the digs. The idea, at least in theory, was that I would train as an electrical engineer. There would not be the bonus of the free passes that I would have received as a cub reporter for the *Newcastle Evening Chronicle*, but my feeling was that I would try to keep everybody happy for a year, then get on with the real business of my life.

In practice the job meant that I would spend most of my days filing off the rough edges which are left when hot metal is cut. I was put in the charge of a foreman named Bert Jones, who was one of the contacts of United who helped young players whose parents demanded that they learn at least the rudiments of a trade. Bert understood the reality of my situation. He allowed me to clock off an hour early on Tuesdays and Thursdays, when I trained at The Cliff ground in Salford, and if United had an away youth team match he would give me the time to travel. What he or anyone else could not do was persuade me that I wasn't wasting time. So much of it seemed to be spent on buses travelling to the factory in Broadheath, near Altrincham, and then in the opposite direction to Salford. The bus ride to Broadheath took forty-five minutes, with stops every two hundred yards or so, and it took nearly as long to get to The Cliff.

One of my problems was that I didn't have a watch, which several times meant that I clocked on late at the factory. When this happened your wages were docked, which seemed to me harsh on someone who was earning only £2 a week. The problem was that in the dark mornings I just couldn't guess the time and on one occasion I woke up Alan Rhodes to ask him. He was not pleased.

For a while the only solution was to get out of bed when I first woke up, walk down the corridor to the communal bathroom, stand on the toilet and look out of the window. From there I could just see the blue

61

clock on Stretford Town Hall. It is still there and I always have a chuckle when I pass it. Sometimes it would be as early as half past two. Then I would go back to bed and hope that I didn't oversleep. More often than not there was no danger of that as I lay awake and thought about the future, and anticipated the day when I would be released from the rickety old factory building.

It came, on cue, on my seventeenth birthday in October 1954: Bert Jones thought he was making a news announcement when he said, 'I've got something important to tell you, Bobby. Tomorrow you're going to be signed by Manchester United.' Of course, I already knew, but Bert had read it in a newspaper and I didn't want to spoil his moment. 'You don't have to come in tomorrow,' he added. When he said that, I couldn't help blurting out, 'Oh boy!', but then I was quick to thank him for the way he had looked after me; he knew my dreams had nothing to do with being an electrical engineer and I think he understood my impatience.

When I left the factory in Atlantic Street for the last time I did it with the lightest of steps, but it would be wrong to say that the time I spent there was entirely wasted. It was not where I wanted to be, but Bert and the lads I worked with had always been kind and they also taught me something about real life, about how, if you are not lucky enough to be doing something you love, you cope with the tedium of life in a factory. You try to do it, they seemed to me to be saying, with as much humour as you can and always with a little time for your work-mates.

Later, when Matt Busby talked of the duty of professional footballers to provide a little spark, a little colour, for the men and women who come to

Old Trafford at the end of a working week, I thought of those factory days. Busby said the people didn't want more of the humdrum grind of their working lives. They wanted something to carry them through the drab days of winter. They wanted excitement, and it was a professional footballer's duty to always produce as much of that as he possibly could.

I also learned a little about trade unions, and the need for them when management wanted to impose new conditions unfairly, on their own terms. There would be echoes of that when I came to know Cliff Lloyd, the secretary of the Professional Footballers' Association, who worked so hard and brilliantly to lift the maximum wage limit on players as gifted as my old hero Stanley Matthews. On several occasions there had been talk of strikes at the factory, and I listened to the fierce debates at the union meetings. That made me think of my father and the miners back home, and when one of the lads spoke up with anger and passion in his voice I felt like giving him a cheer. It also reminded me of how fortunate I was to have the chance of a working life beyond the boundaries of any factory or shipyard or mine.

Soon enough, that feeling would be all the more intense when my football education became full time, when I travelled across the country and abroad and the start of my working shift was signalled by the referee's first whistle. Then life was filled to the brim with pleasure—and not least in Switzerland, where United played in an annual youth tournament. There, in Zurich, I stood outside a shop window for a long, long time, trying to decide on the present I would buy myself to celebrate my new status. Then, proudly, I walked inside to buy my first watch.

# CHAPTER 5

# LEARNING TO BE A PROFESSIONAL

On one of the higher slopes, beneath the peak occupied by Duncan Edwards, I found Eddie Colman. He was a boy/man whose every stride and shimmy announced self-belief—but it was also clear to me that he would never be in danger of running away with himself.

He welcomed me so warmly into his family—in Archie Street in Salford, a road which would become the model for *Coronation Street*—that the breaking up of the Birch Avenue football gang after a year was quickly made to seem like just another milestone in days that were now beginning to race by at a sometimes breathtaking pace.

I was moved to this smaller house in Gorse Hill, which also had Old Trafford in sight, when the club decided that the smooth working of the former digs had been irreparably damaged. The problem was that the owner of the Birch Avenue house, Albert Watson, had been surprised and alarmed when his wife walked into their bedroom. He was supposed to be taking a siesta, and Mrs Watson was not pleased to see that he had been joined by one of the maids.

However, any sense of dislocation I might have felt, when the fall-out from the incident persuaded United that their boys should be moved on, was soon dissipated by the hospitality of Eddie Colman's family, and also that of the parents of another youth team colleague, Wilf McGuinness.

Eddie would always ask me to spend Christmas

Eve at Archie Street, which was wonderful, but quite hazardous once I had made the reserve team and we both had to play on Christmas Day, especially as the kick off was 11 a.m. We protested that we had to go to bed early, but it wasn't so easy when Eddie's Uncle Billy, who was a fine singer, arrived in full voice. Christmas, we argued weakly, could not be celebrated by dedicated young professionals, but it was very hard to avoid that drinking culture which was so much a part of the life of many professionals—and even of my mentor Jimmy Murphy. 'You can't go to bed,' the Colmans cried. 'Uncle Billy wants to sing for you—and he's the best singer in the world.' To fuel the celebrations, at short intervals someone went to the off-licence on the corner of the street, with a white enamel bucket to be filled with beer.

Eddie's grandfather, who had a bushy moustache, was also a short man. He had served in the First World War in one of the bantam battalions, formed by men who stood less than five feet, and at a certain point in the evening he would tell of the day he marched past Lord Kitchener as he took the salute outside Manchester Town Hall. 'I swear,' he said, 'that I heard him turn to the honour party and say, "Well, gentlemen, bigger men I may have seen, but smarter men, never."' Whenever I saw him I asked him about that famous day.

Eddie's first role in my career was not supposed to be such a benevolent one. He had been told by Murphy to rough me up in my first practice match. Eddie was very flamboyant, even cocky, at our first meeting and he said to me, 'Jimmy Murphy's told me about you.' After the practice, he said, 'He told me to give you a kick or two and I tried my best, but I couldn't get close enough.' It was his quick and

65

generous way of telling me I had been accepted, and in the following days he made it clear that he was my friend. He seemed especially concerned that I might get lonely in the new digs and, like Wilf McGuinness, he was eager for me to share in the family life that was so important to him.

Beyond friendship, though, on my side there was also pure admiration. I loved the swaggering way he played. It was especially thrilling to see him perform his 'drag-back', when he completely destroyed his marker with a dummy and then went off in an entirely different direction. I had never seen the move before and I shook my head and said, 'Boy, imagine being able to do that.' The crowd loved his confidence and they seemed to associate with him naturally. He wasn't a great star, he was the cheeky-faced, mischievous boy from next door, but of course there was the great bonus that he could also play like an angel.

It was the first of my great privileges to play in the United youth team for two seasons with Eddie and with Duncan Edwards, and also work alongside, in the first year, Billy Whelan and David Pegg. Billy had brilliant close control and was a natural goalscorer. David was a traditional winger, quick and a great crosser of the ball.

However, Duncan, of course, and Eddie to a lesser but still brilliant extent, had other dimensions. They could lift the game on to another plane and you could hear the effect they had on the terraces, which for youth matches were amazingly well filled with crowds touching 30,000 and sometimes more. That was the hard evidence of the magic Matt Busby was creating in the public mind. Make excitement, create colour, he told his young players and you only had to listen to the noise of the crowd, the expectant buzz when Duncan or Eddie got on the ball and the huge roars when those moments of promise were beautifully fulfilled, to know that his demands were being met quite perfectly. If Busby wanted United to be a work of art, Duncan was supplying the wonderfully bold brush strokes and Eddie was performing a series of inspired squiggles.

Murphy had been right, utterly right, when he first spoke to me of the meaning and the possibilities of Duncan Edwards. Every move the big lad made ridiculed the scepticism I had felt on that taxi ride from the station. He made every other player seem like just another lad on the team. He showed awesome power as he ran through the churning mud of pitches that the modern professional, so used to manicured fields which provide true playing surfaces at almost every time of year, would find hard to believe. His tackling was a series of tank traps, as ferocious as it was perfectly timed; his passing was penetrative and accurate; and, whatever the conditions and however heavy the ball had become, his heading was always immaculate in its strength and direction.

In five years of unbeaten FA Youth Cup football there was scarcely a hint of crisis for the team, even after Duncan left us for exclusive action with the first team—and then England. The only serious problem that I recall from my days in the tournament, when I collected three winning medals, was in a tough semi-final second leg game with Chelsea who, under the old England centre forward Ted Drake, had also assembled a fine squad of young players.

The brief but critical loss of certainty was provoked by Murphy's worry that we were becoming too dependent on Duncan. He said that for once we should try not to make giving the ball to him the only solution to any problem. Maybe the pressure would mount, maybe we would find ourselves closed down, but top players should always find a way out of trouble. 'Try to put more pressure on your own ability,' he told us. 'There may be days when Dunc isn't around. Sometimes you have to solve your own problems.'

Against Chelsea in that second leg we struggled with Jimmy's initiative through the first half. Duncan's usual authority had been completely marginalised, and at half time we faced the prospect of going out, which was something that might just have shaken the foundations of Old Trafford. Jimmy certainly wore a rare frown as he told us in the dressing room, 'Remember I told you not to automatically pass the ball to Duncan? Well, forget what I said. Give him the fucking ball whenever you can.'

When I took a corner in the second half I depended totally on Duncan's ability to rise above the pack. I looked up and just thought, 'There he is,' and I lifted the ball so that it would drop into his path. I stood back to watch the flight of the ball and Duncan charging to meet it, defenders just bouncing off him as they tried to stop his run, and then he soared into the air and headed it into the top corner. I shook my head and thought, 'What more can he do, what more can be said? It's just bloody sensational.'

Not so long ago, while walking along the High Street in Wisbech in Cambridgeshire, I was reminded of another example of Duncan's extraordinary power. It was when we were based in Shrewsbury for our National Service and we were picked for a Western

68

Command team playing the Royal Air Force in Cosford. He was at his most masterful. His play was always filled with confidence and authority, but on this day he was particularly dominant. Jimmy Murphy had told him that he should always demand the ball as a right, and that he should do it loudly. 'Maybe there is a big crowd and a team-mate might not hear you,' Murphy said, 'so make it clear that you want it.' Against the RAF Duncan's desire for possession was insatiable. The move that I will never forget started when he shouted for the goalkeeper to give him the ball. Naturally, the goalkeeper complied. Then Duncan passed to the full back, who promptly delivered it back after receiving the firmest order. I was next in the chain. I received the ball and duly returned it to sender. By now the RAF was in full retreat. The last act involved the centre forward. He held the ball for a moment, then rolled it into Duncan's path. At this point he was running into the box. He shot immediately, straight at the head of the goalkeeper. The goalkeeper made no attempt to save. Instead, he ducked as the ball rocketed into the back of the net.

So, forty-odd years later I was walking down Wisbech High Street and was stopped by somebody who asked, 'Aren't you Bobby Charlton?' When I confirmed it, he said, 'I once played against you when you were in the army. I was playing for the RAF against Western Command.' I said I remembered the match very well, and for a special reason, and then I asked him what position he played. He told me that he was in goal and—I swear this is a true story—that it was the proudest day of his life. I said, 'But you were the only goalkeeper I ever saw who ducked a shot that was going straight at him.'

'Maybe so,' he replied, 'but it was still the proudest day of my life.' While I found this a little difficult to understand, given the circumstances, I supposed it was still another strand of the Edwards legend. One certainty is that of all the questions I have ever been asked about football, even to today, Duncan's name has been attached to an amazingly high percentage of them. How good was Duncan Edwards? Perhaps you can say no more than that he was, at least in potential, the best who ever played.

Down the years there would be so many giants standing across my path, from Alfredo di Stefano and Pelé to Franz Beckenbauer, but there were times when I believed that after Duncan Edwards no one could have been more intimidating in his authority than Dave Mackay. Jimmy Scoular was famous for his ruthlessness and when, in a notorious incident, he yanked me back by my jersey when I was running clear on Newcastle's goal in a match which, because of my background, had a special pressure, I came as close as I ever would to hitting somebody on the field—but Scoular was nearing the end of his career then and he never, despite that flashpoint, had the same impact on me as Mackay did.

Dave Mackay talked a lot on the field but, unlike many who did this, he never left you any in any doubt that he would back up his words. He was a hard man who also had brilliant natural gifts. Once, in the 1965–66 season, we were being thrashed by Spurs, and Mackay was in both overwhelming and overbearing form. Jimmy Greaves had scored an astonishing goal, dribbling around the goalkeeper, and we were feeling increasingly frustrated. We had no hope of getting back into the game, but of course you try to put on a good face against such a defeat and certainly I wasn't prepared to surrender.

Mackay was trying to jockey me into a corner and when I pushed the ball to my left he said, a little derisively, 'Go on then, shoot.' I did so and the ball flew into the top corner of the net. We lost 5–1, but at least I had something at the end of a tough afternoon. Jimmy Murphy took a little comfort from this, too, because one of the things he hated most was to see any of his players giving even a hint that they were in danger of being overwhelmed by the opposition.

Such overpowering self-confidence, no doubt, was the aspect of Duncan's play in which Jimmy gloried the most. As he proved when he came to face the cream of European football in Real Madrid, he was simply beyond intimidation. Victory was not a challenge but a right. There was no point in holding him back. The old arguments about carefully nurturing talent, and thus avoiding the risk of burn-out, didn't apply in his extraordinary case. Those huge crowds came to see United's youth footballers because they were fascinated by gauging their progress, seeing them growing stronger and more mature as their experience increased, but Duncan was plainly already a finished article. It was impossible to see what advantage might be gained by sending him down the usual route. So he was allowed to skip the A team and went straight in with the old, hard pros of the first team, doing it so naturally he might have been the veteran of a dozen campaigns.

His confidence, as I saw it, never touched on arrogance; he was who he was, which meant that he was a lovely, genuine lad. When he was gone, so suddenly, the void he left behind was so huge that those who remained, from Matt Busby to a young groundstaff boy like Nobby Stiles, were bound to ask

how anyone else could begin to fill it. That feeling I
had in the Youth Cup tie against Chelsea, when I
came to take the corner kick, summed up the impact he
had on all around him whenever he played. 'Save me,
save us,' was the silent prayer I made when I floated in
the kick and, yet again, he did exactly that.

There was something miraculous about Duncan's
soaring progress into the first team. Mine, I would
learn in the months that stretched into several years,
would proceed rather closer to the ground. Matt Busby
didn't work much with the kids; he occasionally took us
to one side and gave us a word of encouragement
when he walked out to the training field—once he
pointed out to me that I was physically strong enough to
put a little more into my tackling—but he was happy to
leave us in the hands of Jimmy Murphy and, to a much
lesser extent, one of the trainers, Bert Whalley.

Jimmy, as had been so clear from our first meeting,
was the man. He was ever present on the training
field in his track suit top and shorts, his pot-belly
protruding with the evidence of how much he liked a
pint. He was on me all the time, standing close to me
as a practice match unfolded, chiding me, irritating
me. I suppose he was testing my patience when
things were not going right, as when he stepped into
my path and tripped me when I was in full flight.

It was two years before he told me that he had
completed the first part of his job, which had been,
quite simply, to turn me from an amateur into a
professional.

The first of my amateurish beliefs he stripped
away was that the best, most talented footballers
always win. 'They don't, you know, Bobby,' he said.
'They don't when they fail to understand that there are
two sides to the game—and only one of them is about

how well you play. Just as important is how you stop the other fellow playing to his own strengths.

'You can stop people playing if you mark them well enough—and it doesn't matter who they are. So you have to learn two basics: you have to learn to mark someone, and avoid being marked yourself. You have to know how to steal a vital yard with a little dummy and shimmy and hit the ball quickly and on target. You have to shout so that you can help a team-mate get out of trouble—you always have to be available to receive the ball, and that is only valuable when you let your team-mates know where you are.' All this was new to me. He said it was easy enough to sum up. It was teamwork.

Another lesson from Jimmy was that bad players hide away in a match, exerting no influence while just waiting for the ball to bounce favourably, hoping to exploit any talent they have been given—but this, he said, wasn't enough if you wanted to be a real professional. 'If you want to be on the field but you don't want to play, really play, you stand next to the man who is marking you. Better still, you go behind him. You will never get a kick. If you *do* want a kick, if you want to *truly* influence a game and show people you're a serious professional and not someone just playing at it, you've got to find yourself space. You've got to work your balls off.'

His greatest challenge—and it was one which eventually he had to accept was a lost cause—was to get me to tackle. Jimmy carefully explained the technique which had always been a huge factor in his own fine playing career. I understood the theory well enough, but out on the practice field, even with him yelling in my ear, I couldn't get it to work.

Yes, I knew it was right to put all your weight into

the tackle, that it was the best way to avoid injury—and that the opposite was true when you went in half-heartedly and, most dangerous of all, hung your leg out. But then a match would start, and I couldn't get it out of my head that my main job was to avoid players rather than collide with them. No matter how many times Jimmy pointed out how strong I was, and even when his argument was supported by Busby, I couldn't budge the idea that my purpose was not to charge into tackles but to await their outcome, then receive the ball and use it in the most creative way.

It wasn't that I ever refused to make a tackle—I never consciously ducked out of that responsibility—it was just that whenever I did it I was almost invariably pathetic. Each time I failed, I thought to myself, 'There must be easier ways of getting the ball.' This happened to be true when you played a bad team. They would give it to you as a matter of course, but, as Jimmy kept saying with some force, my job was to learn how to compete at the highest level.

Jimmy was nearing the end of his football career when finally, if very briefly, I got it right, and quite perfectly so, while playing for England in the 1970 World Cup in Mexico. It happened in a group game against Romania. We were leading 1–0 and they were coming at us with some considerable force right at the end of the game. A Romanian was carrying the ball towards our goal area and you could sniff the danger as he moved into shooting range. I knew it was a menacing situation, and on this occasion I was also aware that there was no question of shelving the responsibility. It was me who had to make the tackle—or it was nobody. I put my foot in hard—and then something astonishing happened. The Romanian fell over and I carried the ball away.

Later I was told that, as I came out of the tackle with the ball, Emlyn Hughes, a squad member who was sitting in the stand, jumped to his feet and shouted, 'Fantastic . . . Bobby Charlton's won a tackle . . . it's got to be England.' It was a memorable moment for me, and a long-delayed achievement for Wales.

Jimmy did, however, see more immediate results in other aspects of my game. He made me a professional, opening up all the many hidden areas of the game for someone who had once thought he knew it all.

Week by week, Jimmy smoothed away the rough edges of my game as I moved through the Altrincham Junior League—where, with a team of new boys and trialists, we could win by as many as twenty-odd goals—and then in the Manchester Amateur League, which had teams of older men. They came from the factories, sometimes shedding boiler suits before they played, determined to shake up these fancy kids, and didn't worry about being overheard saying things like, 'They're only fucking Manchester United, let's get stuck into the little bastards.' I was given a quick passage through that kind of warfare, and also the Manchester League, where the A team performed.

One strong memory is of an Amateur League match in North Manchester. Les Olive, who I'd seen in goal for United at Newcastle when I was a boy, was playing as a centre half now. He was on the secretarial staff at the club, and after Munich he would rise to become club secretary. He was a good and versatile player, but this day he was taking some terrible abuse from the touchline. I wasn't playing because I was needed for an FA Youth tie the following day, but in this league both teams were expected to provide a linesman, so that was my job, for the only time in my life.

I thought, very briefly, of defending Les against his critics, but then I also thought it would probably be a reckless thing to do. So, to my shame, I kept quiet and, even more disgracefully, I put the flag down quickly after signalling an offside. I did this because a very large man in a flat hat boomed in my ear, 'You're bloody wrong there, son.'

After that, whenever I was asked to run the line I suggested someone else would be better equipped for the job. It was, however, an insight into how seriously football can affect people, and not always for the better. I viewed it as another part of my preparation for the time when I would play the game at the highest level. We turned out in the middle of the week, in all weather, on all pitches and often with the most rudimentary changing facilities. It was part of what Jimmy Murphy—graduate of the Rhondda, tough professional dressing rooms and the wartime army—believed was an essential process in toughening up.

Soon, with my success in the FA Youth Cup, I was understudying the Busby Babes in the reserve team in the Central League. For Jimmy it was the time for fine tuning towards the moment when he would be able to say to Matt Busby, 'Now the boy is ready.' He had to be satisfied that I was gaining strength from my experiences and that I had good understanding of what lay before me if I did graduate to the first team.

As I moved through the ranks, Jimmy's personal tuition grew more intense and more specialised. If he couldn't teach me how to tackle, he could tell me how to avoid the close attention of players schooled in the destructive arts, how to take up the right positions to receive the ball and in the process lose a marker—

and, so vitally for the profile of my future career, he could also teach me more about how to score goals.

Jimmy was particularly relentless about the need for me to shoot and his philosophy on the subject was best embodied in one of his favourite dictums: 'You strike the ball well and you hit it hard, but you always have to remember one thing—the public will forgive you if you shoot and miss, they will not forgive you if you have the chance to shoot and you don't. If you are running into range and you have decided to shoot, don't look up, just hit it low and as hard as you can in the general direction—if *you* don't know where it is going, nor does the goalkeeper.'

It is advice I've always passed on to young players, though of course, you have to be controlled in your shooting. You have to get over the ball and keep your balance and let the power flow through your body.

When I consider most of the goals I've scored, I see that I was following Murphy's basic idea. 'Keep the ball, keep it under the pressure and then shoot,' he would say. When a shot goes wide, and another player says, 'Why didn't you pass the bloody ball?' there is no point in questioning your decision. You have to remember the times you *have* scored by delivering the unexpected, all those occasions when you haven't aimed for the top of the net but seen it finish up there. The basic requirement is to hit through the top of the ball so that it keeps low—and know roughly where the goal is. For me it was the most natural thing in the world.

Jimmy said that you just couldn't get in enough practice and it is something I recall when I read about the demands that England's record-breaking rugby kicker Jonny Wilkinson makes on himself. The

77

results confirm the wisdom of every minute he spends in a perfect kicking groove.

One day, Jimmy took me round to the back of Old Trafford and pointed out a big red-brick wall with plenty of empty space in front of it. He said that when no one was around, I should spend all the time I could kicking the ball at it, with my right foot and then my left, and with as much power as I could find. Then, when I felt I was getting better, I should move further back and repeat the whole process. Often I used to go to the ground an hour early, pick up a ball and go round to the wall.

'Teams will make closing down a player like you one of their main priorities. If you know precisely what you are doing, if you can shoot from various distances with either foot, you will always be able to exploit any chance that comes. Remember, against a good team you might get just one, but you will be equipped to take it—and win the game,' he said.

Once, before a game against Manchester City, Jimmy talked about the special ability of their goalkeeper Bert Trautmann. 'He's brilliant at anticipating what you're going to try to do. It seems that he reads it in your body language. The only chance you've got is if you don't look and don't give him any idea which part of the goal the ball is going towards.' As was so often the case, Jimmy was right. During the match I drove through a crowd of players, but I'd looked to the left before shooting and Trautmann punched the ball away.

One of the great strengths of the teaching was that it was done in the fashion of only the most expensive of schools, it was the ultimate teacher–pupil ratio: one-on-one. Jimmy didn't spread his wisdom across the group at any one time. He could have said, 'Come on lads, let's do a little shooting practice.' Instead he always wanted to pull you to one side. There was also a harshness to his tuition. Frequently he would stop a practice session and berate you for doing something he considered stupid, an over-ambitious pass or some showy dwelling on the ball which surrendered possession.

He could be quite cruel in the dressing room after a game, a fact which was recently recalled by Johnny Giles, who was reduced to tears after missing a penalty in a reserve game at Huddersfield. Johnny was eighteen at the time, one of the most tough-minded young professionals you would ever see. But then he also remembers that at the first opportunity Jimmy balanced the criticism with praise for something well done.

A persistent source of complaint, from Jimmy and some of my defensive team-mates, was my eagerness to attempt the big cross-field pass which eventually became one of my trademarks. Whenever I saw a chance, I launched the long ball, often with a good result, but he was merciless when an attempt failed. As a practice game flowed around us, Jimmy would lay down one of his most fiercely upheld laws. 'If that kind of ball is picked off, you put all your defenders in trouble. The only time you can do it is when you are one hundred per cent certain it will get to where it is intended, and how many times can you be sure of that?'

Sometimes, though, it was impossible to resist the temptation as you looked up and saw a team-mate racing down the wing, but then, if the full back read it and intercepted, your heart sank as you anticipated Jimmy's reaction. If it happened during a match, you usually didn't have to wait that long. Once, in a

79

reserve game, I gave up the ball with a long pass and Mark Jones, normally so amiable and supportive, raced up to me and yelled, 'What the bloody hell do you think you're doing?'

Sunday morning was Jimmy's favourite time for the most intense of our one-on-ones. As I was leaving the ground on a Saturday he would say, 'Bobby, come down tomorrow morning, and we'll do some work.' Often my instinct was to say, 'But I've just played, can't I get a little rest?' Invariably, though, I would nod my agreement because, when I thought of it, Sunday morning in the digs held no great appeal. Soon enough, I knew I would be looking for something to do.

As the groundsmen were cleaning up the pitch after the previous day's game, Jimmy and I would change and go out on the field. Very quickly, he would have me gasping for breath. 'At the top level you have to lose you breath, and you have to keep playing,'he would say. 'Every time it happens, it makes you a little stronger.' After a while, he would set me a few exercises, usually some shooting practice, and then he would go to shower—and prepare to take me to the pub.

This was yet another branch of my education. I quickly learned that when I was with Jimmy in a pub or a bar or a hotel room, the trick was to talk about football so much that it might create a distraction and cause a pause in the drinking. Jimmy loved to compare players, their techniques and their different effects, and sometimes he became so animated that a glass of whisky or sherry or beer or, best of all, the dreaded Mateus Rosé—whose appeal could only have been the shape of the bottle—lay untouched for a little while. If Jimmy was in his best drinking form, however, this was only a precious respite. You could find yourself spending hours in the smoky atmosphere of the Throstle's Nest in Stretford or at his home, or, when you were on the road, in some little bar around the corner from the hotel.

There was always a bonus in the company of Jimmy Murphy, though; always a feeling of excitement about the game—and the fact that you had been picked out for so much of his attention. It is the reason why among my most treasured possessions is a little beer mug from a small bar across the street from the Stoller Hotel in Zurich. It was Jimmy's unofficial headquarters each year when we played the youth tournament. If anyone needed Jimmy, he knew where to find him—but in my case, if a game wasn't imminent, I would probably be in his company anyway. Even today, I pour beer into the mug and raise it to the memory of the man who taught me everything he knew.

Whenever I see Sepp Blatter, the president of football's governing body Fifa, he reminds me of the day he played against us for Zurich in that Swiss tournament, and if he introduces me to someone he invariably says, 'This is Bobby Charlton—we played against each other you know.' I played in the tournament five successive years and, looking back, I see how important those trips were to my dawning awareness of how a football career could fulfil all those yearnings to travel I had had in those days in the North East when I waited, breathlessly, to see where the England Schools tournament would take us.

Some time ago I had to be in Zurich for a meeting of Fifa's football committee, and after it was over I said to Norma, 'Let's go down to the Stoller for old times' sake.' We were having ice-cream sundaes on the hotel terrace when a car suddenly stopped and a man whose face I knew came rushing up to our table. It was Werner, one of the organisers of the youth tournament, and he seemed overjoyed to see us. He said, 'Every time I drive past this hotel, I wonder if I will ever see a Manchester United player. I do it every day, and always I look across to this terrace. Now today, here you are.'

In five years we seemed to cover every corner of Switzerland, and I often thought that the only place I knew more about was England. We played games against little town teams in the Cantons. The most memorable occasion was when we played in 1954—the year of Switzerland's World Cup. The rumour was that the Brazilians were coming to watch us play, but they didn't appear at the kick off, which we thought was just as well because the Swiss lads jumped into the lead. However, they were not a strong team, and as the Brazilians arrived in their yellow track suits and filed into the stand we began to take hold of the game. Inspired, we won 9–1 and Billy Whelan made a fantastic dribble to score. I scored a couple of goals and apparently the Brazilians were impressed, particularly with Billy. We heard that they wanted to take him back to South America, but there was no doubt Matt Busby would have resisted strongly if they had pressed the idea.

Switzerland was the icing on my football cake, or maybe the cream on my apple strudel. It was the greatest adventure of the year. We rarely ventured beyond the Cantons after playing the tournament in Zurich, but on one occasion we went into the American zone of Germany to play FC Augsburg. We were much better, winning 8–1, but there was this tough little kid who seemed ready to play us on his own. He never dropped his head, he kept battling away, and he had the look of a serious performer. Many years later, there was no reason to doubt the strength of that feeling when Helmut Haller scored Germany's first goal against England in the World Cup final. Long after that youth game in Germany, I said to Helmut, 'Do you remember when we played against each other the first time?' He replied with a question of his own, 'Do you think I am likely to forget?'

The Swiss summer was a time when I was open to so many new experiences, and one of them was going to a Catholic Mass with Arthur Powell, who was one of Jimmy's assistants working with the youth team. He was standing outside the hotel one day, and when I asked him what he was doing he said he was waiting for someone before going to church. Though I wasn't a Catholic I asked him if I could go along. He said, 'Bobby, of course you can, anyone can come.'

So I went with Arthur and knelt down and said my prayers, something for which I hadn't had a lot of practice. Mostly they were selfish prayers. I prayed hardest that we would win the tournament—that would please Jimmy Murphy, and maybe he would give me a little peace—but there was also a prayer of thanks, for so many memories that I knew would never die.

# CHAPTER 6

## THE FULFILMENT OF A DREAM

Saturday, 6 October 1956: it was five days before my nineteenth birthday, and six months into my National Service, and I had a date with my dreams. It was my first game in the First Division, the first time I ran out in the shirt of Manchester United, a day when it seemed that Beswick Prize Band, standing in their lumpy overcoats, were playing only for me.

I had no concern that for almost everyone else on the field and in the 41,439 crowd it was not one of the early peaks of the season; they were attending a routine football match with only one likely result—but I had arrived at the centre of my universe. For so long the prospect had come to seem like a mirage; so bright, so tangible one day that I thought I could reach out and touch it, and the next it had disappeared. Now the water and the trees were real.

Once I had run into a classroom with a miner's helmet for a ball. Now the ball, along with everything else, was perfect. Looking back I suppose my graduation was inevitable, but it did not seem so at the time. It didn't matter how much praise I received, how often I was told just to be a little patient, I needed to play that first game. It would calm me down, confirm my status as a first teamer in waiting. The trouble was, there was so much talent stockpiled at Old Trafford. Then, just as I was beginning to feel a touch of despair, the summons came.

Though four United players, Ray Wood, Roger Byrne, Duncan Edwards and Tommy Taylor were away with England, our unbeaten record and top position in the league did not appear to be threatened at the time my name was first written on the team sheet. Charlton Athletic had well-known South African-bred players like John Hewie, who played for Scotland because of his ancestry, and centre forward, Stuart Leary, who was also a fine cricketer for Kent, but they were having a terrible time, so bad that their veteran manager Jimmy Seed had just been replaced by the England trainer, Jimmy Trotter. They were dead last and apparently doomed.

But what did that matter to me? The band sounded no less glorious and the picture I saw when I emerged from the tunnel and into the light was as thrilling as I could ever have imagined on all the days I had fretted about when, if ever, I would get the call.

Compared to today's Old Trafford, the pitch that welcomed me was in the middle of a football shanty town. The Stretford and City ends were uncovered and the stand across from the main one would have looked to the modern eye flimsy and ramshackle. An advertising hoarding perched on the roof announced the sponsors: Woods Contractors. Yet as far as I was concerned it might all have been lit up by the most beautiful neon. 'Bobby, lad,' I said to myself, 'there are no two ways around it. You are now in paradise.' I believed that would have the scene fixed in my mind for ever—and so it has proved.

It is not surprising. My whole life had pointed me to this place—and this time—and before the kick off it was inevitable that I had a jumble of thoughts in my head. It really felt as if my life flashed before my eyes. I thought of all my people and I remembered the occasions which helped create such a huge load of anticipation: the trips to Newcastle and Sunderland with Jack, the sight of Wor Jackie on the run or Len Shackleton applying his sorcery, and the times when Uncle George, using his pro's free pass from Chesterfield, took me into the paddocks at Hillsborough in Sheffield and the Baseball Ground in Derby. There had been a huge crowd at the Hillsborough game: 56,000 people who took my breath away when they filled the bowl in the Pennines with their roars—but it was the Derby game which lingered most strongly now.

Derby County versus Wolves was a legitimate peak of any season. The great Peter Doherty had left the Baseball Ground by then, but there were still unforgettable characters on the field: Jackie Stamps, Billy Steel and Raich Carter for Derby, Billy Wright and Johnny Hancocks for Wolves. It was the first time I'd seen Carter, fair-haired and handsome and full of craft and confidence. As I walked with Uncle George after the game, away from the ground down the narrow streets separating the little houses, I had thought, 'Is this really the way it is going to be? If it is, well, it will be magic.'

The exhilaration I felt as the teams lined up at Old Trafford, and I took my place alongside Billy Whelan and Dennis Viollet in the absence of my admired friend Tommy Taylor, was heightened by the fact that I had been forced to wait so long. There was also more than a flicker of apprehension. I was playing the most important game of my life while carrying an injury.

Although during the week I was fully engaged with my army duties, as was common with many footballers I received time off at weekends to play. I had been scoring freely in the reserves, building a reputation through the match reports in the *Manchester*

*Evening News* and the *Evening Chronicle*. My hard work under the whip of Jimmy Murphy, everyone said, was becoming increasingly evident. Wherever I turned, someone was telling me, 'You'll get your chance soon, Bobby. Keep scoring goals and it will be only a matter of time.' However, when there was a first-team injury or a call from England, it was always somebody else getting the nod. Johnny Doherty, who was a very talented ball-player and seen by many as a key element in the development of the Busby Babes, Eddie Lewis and Billy Whelan were ahead of me in the queue. It made it difficult to check the rise of anxiety. From time to time I would give myself a reassuring little pep talk, something like, 'There's nothing to worry about, keep playing as you can, keep believing in yourself, and one of these days Jimmy Murphy is going to say to Matt Busby, "Boss, it's time to play the boy."'

Most of the time, though, it was hard to suppress the fear that the conversation might not happen anywhere but in my own mind. At the worst of times, I thought, 'Well, maybe you're not as good as you think you are.' Every little incident in a match or in training, every little comment from Jimmy Murphy or occasionally the great man Busby, would be measured for its significance. Something I would learn down the years was that playing football was never guaranteed to make a man feel secure, but the more you established yourself the easier it was to come to terms with the demands on your confidence—and the uncertainties. That's not to say anything could ever be taken for granted but, of course, when you are young and you still have to prove yourself in any significant way, every disappointment is exaggerated, every single setback is multiplied.

There was another concern, one I had discounted so firmly when I first arrived in Manchester and my mother was insisting I carry on with my education or learn a trade. For the first time I had seen, with my own eyes, how precarious the football life could prove. It was when my rival John Doherty was wrecked by serious injury, and it made me wonder why I should think I was different from him. After all, he had outstanding ability and, like me, he had had more than enough encouragement to believe that football would be his life.

He had been troubled by his knees for some time, but one day I saw him in the dressing room when he was particularly depressed. He was showing someone the evidence of a recent operation. 'This is what they did,' he said, pointing to a knee which had a huge circular cut around the top. A potential cornerstone of Matt Busby's empire, someone who had been showered with praise, was explaining why his great chance in the game might already have come and gone. He had had to submit to that primitive surgery, have his cartilage removed and the debris sluiced away, along with most of his football ambitions. A career filled with promise, in which he won a championship medal in the first wave of the new team in the 1955–56 season, was all but over almost before it had begun.

I had always said that injury was never going to happen to me, it was the disaster facing other players, but then it did—just at the time I was beginning to get more than a little desperate about winning a place in the first team.

I was undone by the weakness of my tackling while playing against Manchester City reserves. City's big blond centre half Keith Marsden challenged me in a 50–50 situation and we both made contact with the ball at the same time. As Murphy might have feared as he saw the build-up to the collision, Marsden had prepared himself for the tackle rather better than me. My foot was hanging out and he hit it so hard I knew, instantly, that I was in trouble. My ankle swelled up immediately and there could be no doubt this was the worst injury of my career. The treatment for ankle injuries proved no more sophisticated than the cartilage operations. Ted Dalton, the club physiotherapist, slapped on a burning kaolin poultice and told me that I had to let nature take its course.

Nature allowed me to resume training after three weeks, and though the ankle still wasn't quite right it was something I wasn't going to admit. I had to push on hard now because enough time had slipped by. When I could get away with it I applied pressure on my foot only gingerly, and when I kicked the ball hard it felt as though I was taking something of a gamble, but when one of the trainers tapped me on the shoulder and said that Matt Busby wanted to see me in his office there was no possibility that I would tell him that the injury was nagging on.

The summons came on Friday morning, every pro's appointment with destiny. It was not a time of the week devoted to philosophical discussions. It was when you were either dropped and 'bollocked'—or put into the first team.

When I went up to Busby's office he told me to sit down and, in almost the same breath, he asked, 'How's your ankle?' Later, I learned that he had spoken to Dalton and been told that while I wasn't perfectly fit, there was little risk that I would do any further damage if I played the following day. I told him, 'My ankle has never felt better. In fact it's feeling great.' He paused, gave a small smile, and said, 'OK, son, I'm playing you tomorrow.'

As I went down the stairs I had two thoughts. One was that at last I was a proper footballer. The other was: will I sleep tonight?

I didn't. Not a wink. As the night wore on, and I lay in bed wide-eyed, I played the Charlton game in my head, over and over again; I visualised every possibility between glory and shame. I wondered whether (in those days before substitutes) my right foot would stand up to ninety minutes at full stretch, even though Dalton had been reassuring after Busby told me I was playing. 'You'll be all right, it won't get any worse. You may feel a bit of pain, but you'll get through that.'

When at last I saw through a gap in the curtains streaks of light in the dawn sky, I told myself that this was how it must have been for all the others. Perhaps even Duncan Edwards, who was two years younger than me when he was given a first-team shirt, had had moments of self-doubt. But then, when I thought about the possibility, I found myself shaking my head. Dunc was different. Dunc was beyond doubt. However, as light began to fill the room, I began to feel better. I told myself that this was indeed going to be a great day. I was a young lad, fit and healthy and had devoted everything I had to meeting the challenge that faced me in a few hours' time. I could afford to miss one night's sleep.

I suppose it was partly adrenaline that carried me through the rest of the day; that, and the sheer wonder of being part of the pre-game ritual.

I walked to the ground, resisting the temptation to tell everyone I passed that soon I would be playing for

Manchester United, and every so often testing my injured foot. At 11.30 the team bus took us to Davyhulme Golf Club for lunch at midday: poached eggs and steak. Then I walked out on to the course and watched the golfers, but only with half an eye. Frequently I looked at my Swiss watch. I was counting not the hours but the minutes until the bus took us back to Old Trafford.

It had been at that golf club that Allenby Chilton, the defensive bulwark of Busby's great '48 team, had passed on to me a trade secret that I would hoard well into my twenties.

Chilton was a man of great authority, hard and fearless in the way of the top centre halves. Before he slipped out of the first team, when Busby—who as a young manager had treated him with much deference—announced that it was time to move forward into a new phase of his regime, Chilton was one of the commanding figures of the dressing room. Once, I was told, he had stood up in the middle of a team meeting and told Busby, who was concerned about a run of poor form, that the senior pros would sort things out: Busby was new to the job and the old guys knew what had to be done.

I had learned about the hard side of Allenby Chilton quite painfully, for a sensitive young lad, when I had burst into the first-team dressing room to tell Tommy Taylor, who I knew from sharing digs, that a boy from his part of Barnsley had joined the club. I was unable to get out more than a few words before Chilton rose from the bench and roared, 'Get out!' I knew better than to offer any more than a muttered apology and leave even more quickly than I had arrived. I had broken one of the strictest rules of Old Trafford, and Chilton, whose aura came partly from the fact that he had survived serious wounds while fighting in Normandy in the Second World War, had jumped on me with great force.

He was, however, a more mellow figure by the time he was out of the first team and playing a few games with the reserves. Before one of them, after lunch at the golf club, I saw him swig back a drink. He told me it was a sherry and he took one before every game he played. 'You see, son, at the end of a hard game, when you're gasping for breath, it comes to your rescue.' A few years later I too was spotted downing a pre-match sherry. I was not apologetic when I was quizzed by team-mates. I explained it was something I had picked up from one of United's great players. It was an extremely pleasant trick of the trade. They were unimpressed.

Sherry was the least of my needs when I boarded the bus for the Charlton game. I wanted to be calm. I wanted to remember all that I had been taught by Tanner and Jimmy Murphy and apply it to a game which I knew, even after allowing for the problems of the opposition, would be faster and harder than anything I had experienced before. Most of all, I wanted to score—and last the full ninety minutes.

In fact I should have scored a hat-trick after we recovered, in just a minute, from the shock of Charlton going into the lead midway through the first half. Johnny Berry equalised and then I scored twice, in the thirty-second and thirty-seventh minutes. It was as though I'd never heard such cheers. The first came when I got the ball on my right foot, turned inside and, following Murphy's maxim, battered it in the general direction of the goal. It flew in, and though my foot hurt a little it was a modest price to pay for the sweetest of moments.

I felt a predictable twinge of pain when I hit the second, but there had been no doubt in my mind when I approached the ball. It cried out for the volley and it was simply not a day when such an option could be declined. In the second half I missed an easy chance, but by then I knew that the fears that had come to me in the night had been without real foundation. I could play in the First Division, I could score—and I could feel at home.

More than anything, I suppose, I felt relief. I had come in, I had scored two goals—which was then the measure of my impact because I was seen as a strike player—and the great divide which had existed between me and men I had got to know well, friends like Eddie Colman, Duncan Edwards and David Pegg, was suddenly crossed. I had moved into the inner circle; I had played for the first team.

That was the overriding feeling I had as I headed for the dressing room and the shower. I acknowledged some applause, but really I was overwhelmed by my own thoughts—and especially one: 'You've played for Manchester United, you've done what you were there to do, you've scored goals—no one can ever take that away.'

The Old Man—I would never be able to call him Matt, even, many years later, after he had made a point of telling me I should do so—confirmed the meaning of the day as soon as I arrived in the dressing room. He told me a taxi was waiting to take me into the BBC studios in the city centre. I was pleased, but also a little overawed and maybe Busby saw that in my face. He said, 'Bobby, lad, these are things you will now have to do. It is what happens when you're a football star.' It was another way of saying, I suppose, that I had taken my first steps to fame.

When the headmaster of my primary school had sent me into the classroom in the crimson shirt he had hummed the theme tune of *Sports Report*. Now I was part of the real thing and it was all a little scary. The interviewer asked me how it felt to play in the first team, and to have scored two goals. On the taxi ride into town I had tried a few rehearsals of this moment, but each time they were swept away as I replayed the game. Now I sat nervously in front of the big microphone. What could I say? How could I show that I was ready to be famous? I blurted out the truth. 'Well,' I told the nation, 'it's just unbelievable.'

# CHAPTER 7

# NO INSTANT CORONATION

When I took my first hero's salute and then walked on air into that primitive BBC studio, I tried not to forget one fact of Manchester United life—that they did not stage instant coronations at Old Trafford, not unless you happened to be Duncan Edwards. My high had been on the field and the *Sports Report* airwaves; I came back to earth the moment I reminded myself of the resources at Matt Busby's disposal. I knew I had to see my performance against Charlton as a statement about the future rather than some overwhelming claim on the rest of the season.

I had to be satisfied with making a mark—and be determined to repeat it at every opportunity. I did that well enough. In the FA Cup semi-final at Hillsborough I scored a quite spectacular goal against Birmingham City, the hard-tackling team who had lost to Don Revie's Manchester City at Wembley in the previous spring. 'Charlton Special Sees Reds Through' declared one headline that may have helped to ensure I kept my place against Aston Villa in the final at Wembley. Most significantly of all, I was catapulted into the second leg of the European Cup semi-final with Real Madrid at Old Trafford. When the issue was already decided against us, I scored a late goal, but what mattered to me more was that I had been trusted to go on the field in the presence of men like Alfredo di Stefano and Raymond Kopa.

Though it would be a year after my debut before I could contemplate a first-team place by right, and my fight for recognition had entered its most demanding stage, there was no doubt that now it had a foundation, a conviction rather than a hope that I would be able to meet the challenge. Instead of the old frustration, there was a steady supply of encouragement. Out of the thirty-one remaining league games, I played in another thirteen, and as a result received a championship medal in the spring. In those fourteen matches I scored ten goals, including a hat-trick in the return game against Charlton at The Valley.

Another sign of growing confidence was that I was no longer bashful about wearing the club blazer presented to you when you sign professional. There had been a time when its most regular airing was in front of the mirror back in the digs, but now I wore it in the street proudly—especially when, after training, I waited to see my new girlfriend, Norma Ball, as she left her office in Lever Street, which was the centre of Manchester's rag trade.

Mike Yarwood, who was still to make his mark as the star TV impressionist of his time, worked nearby, and many years later he reported, 'When you started to play regularly for United and then England, I remember thinking, "That's the lad I used to see standing in the street in his blazer, looking like a top toff—and quite pleased with himself."'

I had no right to look so pleased yet. I would have to fight off fresh waves of impatience before I could claim my own peg in the first-team dressing room, that holy of holies which had been guarded so ferociously by an old pro like Allenby Chilton. I was still the kid who stepped in for the big men, Tommy Taylor, Dennis Viollet and Billy Whelan; when they went down, I went in, and when they came back I stepped down. However, because big injuries were inevitable, a player in my situation was guaranteed plenty of work. The more I played, the more I realised the validity of that pressure from home to guard against the worst of fate.

Broken legs were the greatest fear, and one that would be horribly realised by my friend Wilf McGuinness, a tremendous force as he moved through the ranks and into the England team before being cruelly cut down in his twenties. Ligament injuries were also commonplace. A twisted knee for Tommy Taylor, for instance, was another chance for Bobby Charlton.

Despite the hazards, though, none of my boyhood dreaming had been seriously touched. Yes, I understood now a lot more about the professional game. I grasped, finally, that behind the joy there was also cruelty and pain. For everyone who succeeded, there would be a John Doherty or a Wilf McGuinness, intelligent and, in their different ways, hugely talented players who had failed only in the department of good luck. At Old Trafford, too, there was the additional pressure of expectations which had been primed by the first decade of Busby's insistence that the club could have players only of the highest quality.

Naturally, I studied intently the special contributions of the players whose level of performance I had to try to reproduce when the call came for me to fill in somewhere along that glittering forward line.

Dennis Viollet was slim and deadly quick. My feeling was that he was so prone to injury because he was so thin. His bones seemed too close to the surface, and this was maybe the root of my theory that it is the people who are without a little bit of fat who are most likely to go down hurt. As an inside forward, he was expected to be creative and he rarely disappointed in this respect, but it was in the penalty box where he was often unplayable. Just ten days before I made my debut against Charlton, he had left me in a state of awe when he scored four goals against Anderlecht in the famous 10–0 thrashing of the Belgian champions in the first round of the European Cup. At a rain-lashed Maine Road—Old Trafford was still awaiting floodlights—it was dazzling to see such tigerish finishing. Later there was a rare comment from the man in black, Welsh referee Mervyn Griffiths, who was as stunned as everyone else: 'You couldn't pick an England team to beat this United,' he declared.

Viollet was the cutting edge, the wielder of the rapier. Matching the effect of Billy Whelan, the man so admired by the Brazilians, was a different but no less demanding challenge for me. The Dubliner was tall and nothing like as quick as Viollet. His forte was to scheme, to shape possibilities with his skill and excellent vision. Yet Whelan scored so many goals from midfield he would be a wonder of today's game. In 1956–57 he finished with a stunning twenty-six, three more than the club's top scorer the following season, Viollet. Wherever I looked there was competition of a daunting kind.

In those days there was a basic requirement for a centre forward. He had to be good in the air. Tommy Taylor was wonderful, but he was also superb on the ground. He was so quick, and had such good control, he could go through half a team. He was a beautiful athlete, but one who had terrible knees. For him, he admitted to me on several occasions, a professional football career meant living on a knife edge. Sometimes he would show me how his knees worked—and sometimes didn't. The joints would go off in directions far from normal. He would shake his head, and say, 'Well, Bobby, I just have to play.' In his circumstances, he did it with extraordinary courage, but when he couldn't it would be another call-up for me.

Injury was one of the aspects of the game on which you just couldn't afford to dwell. Another was that, even though your career could be cut off at any moment, the most you could expect as long as you stayed healthy was a rise of £2 a week, despite being a member of arguably the most attractive team in the English game and playing in front of vast audiences. And even this would come only when the Professional Footballers' Association applied pressure, drumming up publicity and even making the dark suggestion that one day it might come to a strike to bring about the abolition of the maximum wage for footballers.

However, all this was not a burning issue for me as I waited on Lever Street to see my girl, no more than it was for most young footballers. Most of us, I suppose, belonged to a breed of dreamers, working-class boys who, because of a certain ability, had been able to join a world isolated from so many everyday cares. No, we couldn't, like the young stars of today, give ourselves financial security for life when we signed a single contract, but we could do what we loved and tell ourselves that we had been given well-paid jobs, certainly receiving more than our fathers who worked in factories and mines.

The fact that seems so odd, in these days when every player seems to have an agent agitating aggressively for better terms, is that the issue was so low on the everyday agenda of the dressing room. When in time a young player acquired a wife and had children, and had a mortgage to pay, perhaps his thoughts turned more to money, but it happened so slowly, and with such little force, that someone like Cliff Lloyd, a former player and a brilliant secretary of the Professional Footballers' Association, must sometimes have despaired of ever generating the kind of commitment and passion for the union cause which would eventually break the £20-a-week maximum wage.

Though in time I became interested in the PFA, and worked with Cliff, I was certainly not in the forefront of protest—unlike my young club-mate John Giles, who, before building his reputation at Leeds United, had the nerve to challenge Matt Busby over wages. I might have warmed to those impassioned speeches by the lads back at the electrical factory in Broadheath, but in my own life I was like so many of my co-workers. I took what was offered. Someone like John Giles, who I know cared passionately about the game and was deeply dedicated to improving his skill and his knowledge, would no doubt say that I had not so much bought the football dream as inhaled it, but for me it was always the privilege of playing football that was uppermost in my mind. I had that, and—certainly as I saw it then—I had good money for anyone of my age and my background.

It was only later, when I had my responsibilities as a family man and realised, for the first time maybe, how hard it was to put money on one side for the future, that I too began to ask the question that was being posed increasingly in activist PFA circles: where is all the money going—and where did it go in those incredible boom years after the war, when every ground seemed to be filled to the rafters and yet a great player like Wilf Mannion returned from

England duty at Hampden Park, after being watched by 120,000, sitting on his cardboard case in a third-class rail carriage?

The money certainly wasn't all used in players' wages. Also, how much was being spent on the grounds? Of course that question was still being asked when the Taylor Report was published in the wake of the Hillsborough tragedy in 1989.

I would never be militant. I would never issue ultimatums. It simply wasn't my style. But then, perhaps inevitably, I did come to consider the differences between football and, say, show business. Mike Yarwood's vision of me as a toff certainly had more to do with appearances than any financial reality. When he saw me on Lever Street I was on £16 a week in the winter, £14 in the summer. The rises came at the rate of £2 per union negotiation, but when the maximum reached £20 the PFA suddenly raised the stakes in a way that shocked the bosses of the Football League. The demand was for a £4 rise and the response was indignant. 'This is ridiculous,' said the League.

It was at this sticking point that the pressure for a strike began to build at a greater rate, and created the atmosphere at a PFA meeting in Manchester that, looking back, I grew to believe may have been the moment that changed the whole of football.

There were a few anti-strike speeches, and one of them was notably articulate: the argument that a strike would be ruinous to the game, and to the prospects of the players, was hammered home. It was a strong speech, but its effect was counter-productive. It brought the fierce Bolton Wanderers full back Tommy Banks to his feet. He said that while it was true we did not have to clock on at a factory or go down a mine, we did entertain thousands of people, and however hard a lad worked down the mine he didn't have to take on Stanley Matthews. 'Am I worth a rise?' asked Banks. 'Yes, I am. I was never paid enough for the number of times I was ridiculed by Mr Matthews.' He sat down to deafening applause.

When the £20 maximum wage limit was finally abolished in 1962, when Johnny Haynes became the first £100 a week footballer, my wages were raised to £35. By then I was an established England player.

In my eyes it was a dramatic pay rise, but Jimmy Murphy told me how the figure had been reached. He and Matt Busby had been running through the squad list, discussing the progress of individual players and what might be their proper reward now that the maximum wage limit was being dismantled. Apparently, when they reached my name they agreed that I would probably accept whatever they offered, whether it was £20 or even £18.

But then, according to Jimmy, Busby said, 'No, this is not right. He has to have a proper wage.'

Now, when I recall that Haynes, though he was a player I always admired deeply for his wonderful passing skill and his vision, was on more than three times my salary while playing for Fulham, a club famous for being charming and friendly but no great claimant for the highest honours, I see that my attitude to such a basic matter as my wage packet was maybe a little too passive.

Comparisons with today are certainly laughable. My generation played at a time when the Football League and its member clubs saw players as workers to pamper in their travel and even their recreation, but not to be granted the employee rights that were common in other walks of life. It was like saying that football operated in a cocoon, both unique and frozen in time.

This couldn't go on, of course, and as I began to move away from adolescence, still believing football would be at or near the centre of my life, I came to recognise another world was going on outside its borders. It was something I had to acknowledge sooner rather than later if I was to offer Norma a good life, after rebuilding a relationship with her that, maybe because of the distractions of football, and a touch of celebrity, I had allowed to drift from what it could and should have been.

However, in all the highs and lows and complications of the life I was making, and briefly unmaking, there was one constant, a character which revealed itself a little more each day: the dark but vital sprawl of Manchester. Its power and its energy pressed against Old Trafford, reminding me always of that purpose of football to bring a little light to those who worked in the soot and the clanging noise. There were two huge black warehouses next to the ground and two enormous chimneys, one off-white and the other dark coloured. It was one of the great advantages of playing at home, the familiarity of it and the fact that whenever you looked up you saw one of the great chimneys and you knew precisely where you were. For visiting players it was, I always thought, another part of the intimidation of the place.

Because The Cliff was needed for junior matches, the pitch wasn't really good enough for the first team to work on, so sometimes we trained on a field set in the middle of the rugged, man-made landscape, beside the big Ship Canal—and when that was not available we had another works pitch next to a smaller canal. The sounds of the factories were all

103

around us, and at the approach of lunch-time we knew what was on the canteen menu at the massive MetroVics plant—you could smell the spotted dick or the rice pudding.

When it was snowing or frosty we worked wherever we could around the ground, beneath the part cover of the stands at the back of the stadium and the nearby greyhound track, and wherever you looked there was steam and smoke and industry. Part of our working background was formed by Glovers, a factory which produced huge coils of cable which were carried across the canal on a pulley and then lowered into the ships which would take them to all parts of the world, where they would go under the sea. It was exciting to see the power at work that generated the city's wealth, and deep down I felt great pride that I was representing such a place on the football fields of England and, maybe soon, Europe.

Some years later I saw a picture by my friend Harold Riley, the fine Salford painter who learned his art as a protégé of the great L.S. Lowry, which moved me so much that I bought it for a friend. It rekindled all the emotion which came to me when I looked at that great scene of industry, with the prows of the ships poking into a dark and gritty sky framed by cranes and chimneys and warehouses. The art of Lowry and Riley is very important to me now because I believe it is interwoven with the roots of so much of my life. When I first saw Lowry's depiction of fans walking down to the Bolton Wanderers' ground it took my breath away; it seemed to capture all that I had seen and felt as a boy, and then as a youth at the Broadheath factory; it described the lives of the workers and the lure of that patch of green at the football stadium. I was always reminded of that

104

Lowry pitch when going to the ground. So many people walked to see a game, often straight from the factory after clocking off on Saturday lunch-time. It was so uplifting to see them striding out, laughing and talking and, it seemed to me, in a way coming alive.

In this, my everyday life at Old Trafford kept strong my attachment to the North East. Up there were the mines and the shipyards, here was a massive workplace, the home of the industrial revolution, smelly but also glorious. Down the years I made extraordinary discoveries. The atom was split in Manchester University, and they also developed the first computer there. It was apparently as big as a room. Manchester had the first railway station, a hub for the nation's industry, and the great plant of MetroVics, employing 25,000, sending out trains and viaducts into every corner of the world. When, years later, I came to act as an ambassador for the city, in an Olympic or Commonwealth Games bid, or in speaking for industry and business, I would never feel I was performing a chore, and I'm sure this was rooted in those days when I felt myself being drawn into something wider than merely a new job in a new place. Manchester set me on my way.

# CHAPTER 8

## UNDER THE SPELL OF EUROPE

During my National Service, when a plane flew over the camp I would look up longingly in the belief that maybe it was the boys flying off again into the new world of European football that had suddenly become the most glamorous place in the world. I imagined them joking and playing cards, and all of them filled with that zest for life you feel so strongly when you are doing something new and exciting. Those were my down days in khaki. Big Dunc, who had been such a great companion, almost a guardian, had already done his time and was at the front of the European campaign, and some days I would mutter to myself, 'The army is really useless for me.'

My salvation, in the absence of Duncan, was Company Sergeant Major White, known to me only as Chalky. He was a great football fan, had a car and was eager to make a deal. 'You get the tickets, Bobby, and I'll get you the leave passes and drive you up to Manchester whenever United have a home game in the European Cup.' Chalky, like so many who played or just followed football, felt that Europe was a new dimension to the game, a place of excitement beyond the old trenches of league and cup warfare.

Stan Cullis, the hard man of Wolves, the manager who became legendary for the demands he made on his players, was always seen as a dour figure in the game, but he commanded the greatest of respect from Matt Busby, not least for his understanding of the potential of European competition. The floodlit friendly games Wolves played against Spartak of Moscow were like electric currents running through English football and the rapturous reaction of the fans who filled the Molineux ground convinced Busby that this was part of the future. However, Alan Hardaker, the secretary of the Football League, notoriously, did not agree, and when the reigning champions Chelsea applied for permission to compete in the new European Cup he persuaded the league chairmen to turn them down flat. Busby was incensed at such narrow thinking and when United succeeded Chelsea as champions he made it clear that he would not tolerate such a restriction on his and his club's ambitions.

Hardaker argued there was already enough competition, and that the European Cup would be an unnecessary distraction from the league and the FA Cup, but United were the flagship of English football and Busby had a vision which could not be obscured. It was inevitable that in the end he would win the battle. In the aftermath, Hardaker almost immediately pushed through a new competition, the League Cup. It made a nonsense of his resistance to Europe, and soon enough he must have felt like the little Dutch boy with his finger in the hole in the dyke as European football came in on a flood of anticipation.

Chalky duly drove me to Manchester to watch United's first home game in the European Cup, that 10–0 dismantling of Anderlecht, and there were times when we looked at each other, shook our heads and murmured, 'Unbelievable.' It was a wet and dreary night and the Maine Road floodlights had feeble candlepower, but my club-mates created a glow of their own. Dennis Viollet could not be contained as he scored his four goals and David Pegg simply ravaged the right side of the Belgian champions' defence.

Before leaving camp in Shrewsbury, I had run the usual gauntlet of NAAFI canteen debate. In the army you live with so many different kinds of people—and so many varieties of football support. The fans of Liverpool and Manchester City, Arsenal, Celtic and Rangers were all questioning United's prospects in the new arena of Europe. 'You may be the champions of England,' they said, 'but this is going to be much more difficult. This is Europe.'

Even though I said, 'Well, why don't we wait and see,' I had my own concerns. For this game, United had a 2–0 lead from the first leg in Brussels, but Belgium was one of the weaker European nations. Reports and flashes of film were showing that leading clubs like Real Madrid and Barcelona in Spain and Juventus, Milan and Internazionale in Italy were operating at a much higher level than most of the opposition they were facing from other parts of Europe.

Much of this worry melted away in the rain of Maine Road, however. I knew that Duncan Edwards, Tommy Taylor, Dennis Viollet, Eddie Colman, Roger Byrne and Johnny Berry were excellent players, but this was probably the time I realised quite how good they truly were. As Chalky drove me back to the army along empty roads—there were so few cars in those days you never had to worry about traffic jams, even after the biggest games—my head was filled with the future. United had produced more than a spree of goals. They had played with a power and a majesty which was quite stunning, especially when you considered the age of the team. The 'veteran' captain, Byrne, was still just twenty-seven, and Duncan, the best player, the one who was already providing evidence that he might soon be the greatest in the world, was still short of his twentieth birthday.

When we returned to the camp in the early hours of the morning, I could hardly wait for breakfast, not just for the bacon and eggs but also the chance to enjoy massive bragging rights. Naturally, the jocks and the scousers, the geordies and the cockneys were keen to rubbish the quality of Anderlecht—'What kind of team gives up ten goals, man? What kind of bloody game was that?' was the reaction of most—but I pointed out, as coolly as I could, that what Chalky and I had seen was something quite special. 'No one could have stood up to that performance,' I claimed.

Yet the hecklers were not without some seeds of truth. The going would get tougher soon enough, and it was no doubt true that the deficiencies of Anderlecht had inadequately represented the depth of the European challenge. Certainly that was the theory of the press after the next game at Old Trafford, one which sent Chalky and me back to Shropshire in a much less exultant mood. Another claim of the press was that United, and not least Duncan, might be getting a little big for their boots. The press box detected a touch of damaging arrogance in the performance against Borussia Dortmund.

Dennis Viollet was again dynamic, scoring twice in the first half, and with David Pegg adding another before half time, United again looked at least one class above the opposition. However, the second half was a completely different matter as the Germans scored twice, and made the away leg in Dortmund a much more formidable challenge than anyone had imagined when the draw was made. It was a huge relief two weeks later when the news reached the camp: United had held out in a goalless but fiercely fought game.

Confirmation that United were indeed performing in a theatre much tougher than it first appeared was swift. It came in the cold of Northern Spain, where Bilbao, the Spanish champions who had qualified alongside the holders Real, confirmed the fierce competitive instinct of the Basques. After the game, there were pictures—disturbingly prophetic, it would turn out—of the United lads clearing snow away from their plane for the return flight to Manchester. No doubt there was an urge to retreat from the scene of defeat as quickly as possible.

The Basques had hit United with three goals in the first half, then came again with two more after Tommy Taylor and Viollet led a comeback early in the second half. At 5–2, the exit door had swung wide open, but then Billy Whelan breathed back some life five minutes from the end. The passionate crowd was stunned by the United resistance, but it didn't take away any of our foreboding.

Chalky again pointed his little car towards Manchester, and for the second leg we were in the stand. Afterwards, I was agog for the detail that lay behind the magnificent recovery, a classically patient performance which, I learned, was partly the result of a typical Busby contribution in the dressing room. At half time United had been still two goals away from their target of a 3–0 win, and no doubt the mountaintop would have seemed even more impossibly far away if Viollet, in the form of his life, creating danger whenever he received the ball in an advanced position, had not scored just two minutes before the break. The Old Man, however, concealed any alarm he might have felt. 'Boys,' he said, just as he would say so many times in my hearing, 'do not panic. Play the game as you know how. Make your passes and do your running, but, above all, keep your patience. If you can do that, we will get there.' He was right, and gloriously so.

There were eighteen minutes left when Tommy Taylor scored the second, and just six when he made the life-giving third for Johnny Berry. There was a great eruption in the ground—part of it being a celebration of value for money by those of the fans who had paid as much as £11—well above the average weekly wage—for tickets with the face value of seven shillings and sixpence. The United players who showed their competitive nerve, who announced that they were indeed ready and equipped to compete at the highest level of European football, were still five years away from the end of the maximum wage. This was something to think about when they heard the news that Bilbao had been on £200 a man to win the chance of deposing their mighty and much hated masters in Madrid. However, the glory of playing for Manchester United—and winning a dramatic match—still outweighed all else.

The effect of the result swept beyond the boundaries of the city. Manchester and so much of the rest of English football had burst into new life. Matt Busby had declared that this was the future of the game and here, in this match, beyond the celebration of the goals orgy against Anderlecht, was the hardest evidence that he was right. United versus Bilbao had produced the best of football, some brilliant skill and a razor edge of competition. Charges that United had got above themselves were promptly withdrawn. You could only guess at the reaction of Alan Hardaker, the man who had tried so hard to slam the door on

Europe—and at the same time wonder why he had been so dead set against pushing back the boundaries of English football.

Some years later, I had what might have been a small glimpse into some of his attitudes when I was on a bus filled with club chairmen who, at least in theory, were supposed to be the league secretary's bosses. Hardaker was the last to get on. When he got to the top of the steps, he looked round and said to no one in particular that he was reminded of some film on TV he had seen the night before. It had shown pigs being taken to market. Most of the chairmen laughed, and one said, 'What a character!' Presumably he had received a similar reaction from his employers when he announced, 'I wouldn't hang a dog on the word of a professional footballer.'

I cannot judge Hardaker or his overall contribution to English football but, in that flash of 'humour' when he boarded the bus, what I saw in his joke to the club chairmen was more than a hint of arrogance. Did a team like Manchester United in Europe somehow lessen his power? It wasn't really my concern, and by then I was able to reflect that the issue was closed: Europe was part of the fabric of English football, and unquestionably the area of greatest challenge and excitement.

That United would go to the heart of it all back in the spring of 1957 and, finally, carry me along, was confirmed by the semi-final draw. Fiorentina of Italy would travel to Belgrade for their first-leg game against Red Star, and we would go into the jaws of Europe's greatest team in Madrid.

At Old Trafford there was a giant collective intake of breath when the news came in. Matt Busby had been to Nice to see the reigning champions cruise into the semi-finals on an aggregate of 6–2, and everyone was impatient for him to be back. In those days you couldn't hop on a plane as though it was a bus. When he did come home, he was besieged by questions: 'Boss, how good are they?' 'Are they really as strong as they say?' 'Is Gento the quickest thing in football?' 'How will we play di Stefano?'

Busby frowned a little and said, 'Boys, I don't want to talk to you about it. You just concentrate on what you have to do: playing the best you have ever played.' We believed we could see between the lines. The Boss had obviously been extremely impressed and now he had the air of a scout in a cowboy film who had gone to the top of the hill and seen more Indians than anyone could imagine.

I was allowed to go to Madrid because of the possibility of one of the regular first teamers going down with a training injury or a bug, and though I would have given so much to play, I knew that just being there was a mark of progress. I expected to be at least a little awestruck and I was not disappointed. The Bernabeu ground was enormous and dramatic with its two famous columns rising against the skyline of the Spanish capital. Under one of the stands there was a chapel with an ornate altar where the Real players would go for their pre-match prayers, as the matadors did before they faced the bulls down the road at the Plaza Monumental. The tension was established the moment we set foot in Madrid. For the first time there were crowds waiting to greet United at an airport and I remember saying to Eddie Colman, 'Well, we've got something in common with Real: their fans are as daft as ours.'

I joined in the training on a beautifully manicured pitch and the roll of the ball was so true anyone

113

would have been aching to play the following night. Instead, I had to make my way to a seat in the stands. What I saw from there was so entrancing that for a little while at least the pain of defeat, by 3–1, and anger at the rough defensive tactics greeting my friend Tommy Taylor particularly, was somehow reduced in importance.

David Pegg played one of his best games for United; brave and elusive, he made the life of the right back Becerril so miserable he would not appear in the second leg at Old Trafford. Real were held for an hour before they scored after the referee waved play on as Gento shook off a foul by Bill Foulkes; then di Stefano, fifteen minutes later, lobbed Ray Wood quite beautifully.

United still had some fight, however. Taylor, having survived various assaults, reduced the lead with eight minutes to go, only to see Mateos restore Real's advantage five minutes from the end. In the beaten dressing room, the wounds from punctured hopes were not exactly soothed by another bonus report: di Stefano and his team-mates, we were told, were on £350 a man to reach the final—for us, more than half a season's wages. However, one thing was beyond any souring. It was an unprejudiced appreciation of di Stefano's extraordinary talent.

I thought, 'Who is this man?' as he made his early impact on the game. 'He takes the ball from the goalkeeper; he tells the full backs what to do; wherever he is on the field he is in position to take the ball; you can see his influence on everything that is happening.' Whenever he got into any kind of decent position in midfield it was the signal for Gento to fly. He would go at a hundred miles an hour, di Stefano would send the ball unerringly into his path, Gento would go bang, and you just heard yourself saying, 'Oh God.' It was pure revelation. I was high in the stands, taking in the sweep of the great stadium and a crowd estimated at more than 130,000, but from the moment my eyes settled on his compelling figure they rarely strayed. Everything seemed to radiate from him.

I had never seen such a complete footballer. The magic of Stanley Matthews would never die, the growth of Duncan Edwards was a wonder, and in later years I would know Pelé as both an international opponent of stunning range and a warm friend, but the impact of di Stefano crossed all boundaries, despite the disappointment that my club's brilliant arrival in Europe was being dealt a heavy blow and, as it would prove two weeks later at Old Trafford, one that did not permit recovery. It was as though he had set up his own command centre at the heart of the game. He was as strong as he was subtle. The combination of qualities was mesmerising.

By the time his playing career was over, di Stefano had had three nationalities, Argentinian, Colombian and Spanish, and that night it was easy enough to understand. What football nation on earth wouldn't want to adopt such a man? At the time I thought that his changes of nationality were too easily accomplished, certainly I couldn't see it happening under the gaze of an Alan Hardaker, but then on the other hand it was suddenly so much easier to understand why the big Spanish and Italian clubs thought nothing of paying huge amounts of money to move players from one side of the world to another.

Pelé, Maradona, Georgie Best, Denis Law, Johan Cruyff . . . they would all make their claims to be the best talent I ever played with, against, or watched, and it is the kind of argument that could go on for ever, but there was something unique, I felt, about di Stefano on 11 April 1957 in the Bernabeu. I was a midfielder still learning my trade under the prompting of Jimmy Murphy and maybe it was a benefit of that education, or simply that di Stefano made the game seem so simple, but I understood everything that he was doing. One point can be made with certainty. Pelé was a more instinctive player, someone who reacted as situations came along, and in this he was beyond comparison, but with di Stefano it was as though he had worked things out beforehand.

And everything di Stefano did carried the announcement, 'I am the best.' He expected to be treated that way. When he wanted the ball it was his, there could be no argument. He was still the same many years later when we played in a testimonial match in Frankfurt. Ferenc Puskas also played, and you could only marvel at the intensity of the two middle-aged men around a football: di Stefano the leader, Puskas, tubby but still lethal when he was anywhere near goal.

In Madrid di Stefano had dominated the game so profoundly that on the run-in to the second leg you just couldn't get him out of your thoughts—and for me this became even more overwhelming when I was told I would be replacing the injured Dennis Viollet. I was thrilled, of course, but along with the pleasure of anticipating such a huge match there was the question that everyone, from Matt Busby down to the newest recruit to European football, struggled to answer. What tactics might neutralise di Stefano and Gento?

I played the game in my head a hundred times. I knew that I had the capabilities to put in a decent performance—I was sure about passing, and if a chance came I would remember all the advice of

116

Jimmy Murphy—but it was when you came to the potential of di Stefano to change the match so suddenly, and Gento's remarkable speed, that you had to wonder if you were just kidding yourself when you imagined how we might win. Though David Pegg had played well at the Bernabeu, he was not Gento, he couldn't leave you for dead in a flash, and I was certainly not di Stefano.

We worked on the offside trap with Gento in mind, but the tactic is always vulnerable to exceptional speed and brilliant passing, so Busby stuck mostly to his usual theme before we walked down the tunnel: remember to enjoy the experience, he said, play your game and don't forget the basics, don't rush anything. This was a team that could punish you cruelly for one misplaced pass, one hurried and faulty tackle.

Though the Old Trafford crowd was only half the size of the one in Madrid, they seemed to be making the same level of noise. As the early going was marked mostly by some hard tackling and a burst of fouls I began to hope that maybe the smaller ground, the closeness of the fans, and our refusal to allow any free space, might just unsettle Real.

Such optimism was destroyed after twenty-four minutes. Di Stefano released Raymond Kopa and the Frenchman stroked home the ball with shattering ease. Eight minutes later, Gento finally erupted, and Ray Wood could only beat the ball down to the feet of a Real forward. Our offside trap was in ruins, we were 5–1 down on aggregate, and I had been weaving a fantasy. Maybe the fans were not so close in places like Barcelona and Seville, but this was not a team who could be easily separated from their style and their scoring instincts.

At least we could tell ourselves that we didn't give up. Tommy Taylor kept probing away and sixteen minutes into the second half he scored. I also did what I was picked to do, I scored another goal, but unfortunately it served only to excite the crowd and, maybe, suggest happier times in the future. It came five minutes from the end, but Duncan seemed to believe that that left enough time to pull off something even more remarkable than the defeat of Bilbao. When a Real player went down and stayed down, Duncan was convinced he was feigning injury, so he picked him up and carted him over the touchline. The Real players went mad. One of them had sufficient English to shout, 'You can't do that!' but of course there were times when the big man thought he could do anything. It was too late, however.

In the dressing room Matt Busby was comforting. He said that we had played well and bravely, and showed what kind of a future we had. That was encouraging but the reality was that on the day we were just not good enough to make up the two goals. When I played back the game I noted that Kopa, who had struck so devastatingly, might easily have scored at least one more goal, and there had always been di Stefano and Gento ready to raise their ambition, and their play, if the need arose.

Yet a point about our potential had certainly been made. We ran out of time, but when the late goals went in we learned something about Real—and ourselves. We had got to a stage, though very late, when we felt we could truly compete with the best team in Europe. We did have cause for a little satisfaction. It was as though we outran our doubts and discovered that if this team from Madrid was hugely gifted, even magical, they were still human. If you cut them, blood would come, and there was no question that when Tommy and I found the net, and the crowd went mad, they became more than a little rattled. This was a tremendous encouragement for future campaigns, and a genuine reward for Busby's half-time speech. He had said, 'Just keep doing what you are doing, you're looking good, keep passing the ball, keep hustling, and get at them whenever you can.'

In that endeavour we were hugely helped by the Stretford End. There were times when we laid pressure on Real's goal, when we had broken down one of their moves and were pouring in on their goal, when I thought to myself, 'How did we get here? Did the Stretford End just suck the ball down to this end?' The crowd had certainly helped to create a surge of tremendous desire to show Real that we could play at their level, and that they were sure to be seeing quite a bit more of us in the years ahead.

As we came out of the shower and began to dress, Eddie Colman was the young philosopher. 'Well, boys, we've had a hell of a ride,' he announced.

It said much about the instant hold Europe had taken on the imagination of the team that we had a strong sense that in some ways the season was over, at least the best of it, despite the fact that in ten days' time United—and this would once more include me—had the chance to land the first league and cup Double of the century.

Five days before the second Real game we had collected a second straight First Division title, with three games to spare, and would finish up six points ahead of Spurs. Now only Aston Villa, a mediocre team who would finish tenth in the league and twenty-one points behind us, could deny us our assignment with history.

119

When I had been picked to play in the semi-final against Birmingham City my friends Tommy Taylor and David Pegg had hammered home a hard lesson. They told me that it was the one game in which, beyond any question, you had to be prepared to run hard right up to the final whistle. 'This is the game no one wants to lose,' Tommy said. 'You have come a long way, and it would be terrible if you failed at the final hurdle before Wembley.'

I had quickly learned the value of their advice. Birmingham didn't have our skills, but they had some formidable players: Gil Merrick in goal, right back Jeff Hall, and Trevor Smith, the big centre half. They had all played for England and their whole team carried the conviction that it was just too late in the day to surrender all that had been achieved on the long, tough road to the cup.

It was the biggest game I had ever played in, and though Birmingham, who had a reputation for kicking, seemed to mellow a little in the spotlight of Hillsborough, they were running quite as hard as my team-mates had predicted. As the game raced along, I thought, 'It's exactly how they described it. There is just no easy way of winning.' You have to concentrate every minute, you have to think and, most of all, you have to run. It was a lesson I would never forget when I prepared for a cup game, even against the least considered of non-league opposition.

The first thing you had to do was make sure you ran every bit as much as they did. If you did this, the fact that you were better players had to be decisive. Against Birmingham, we got into our stride very quickly, and when Johnny Berry wriggled through to open the scoring in the twelfth minute it meant that our opponents had to open up the game, which immediately made them vulnerable to our greater attacking resources.

In another minute we were two ahead when David Pegg reinforced his pre-match theory with fine action. He outstripped the Birmingham cover and delivered a perfect cross for me to increase the lead. This meant there was only one way we could lose, and that would be to assume the match was already over. Birmingham never gave up, not even in the last minutes when it was clear enough to everybody else that they would not be returning to Wembley.

After all this, how could a teenaged footballer—I would not be twenty for another six months—feel that a Wembley cup final might be tinged with anti-climax? No doubt the only reason could be that the spell of Europe, the yearning to be playing instead in the great final that would now see Real triumph over Italy's Fiorentina, was still so powerful. The Villa game, and the possibility of the historic Double that would have reflected the development of the team so perfectly, was maybe no longer the great aim it should have been. One moment we had the whole football world at our feet. The next, that world had been scaled down.

The process was completed when Villa's Northern Irish international left winger Peter McParland crashed into our goalkeeper Ray Wood after just six minutes. This was a regular challenge in those days, but Ray's cheekbone was fractured and Jackie Blanchflower was given the jersey. It wrecked our plans to play composed and flowing football. Instead of dominating the game, on Wembley's strength-sapping surface, we were chasing an extra man, and maybe also were feeling the weight of expectation. Courageously, Ray returned to supply a nuisance value on the wing—the latest of a long list of Wembley's gallant walking wounded in those days before substitutes. Blanchflower performed well in the emergency role—it was one that I managed to avoid throughout my career—but he was powerless when McParland, of all people, scored twice in the second half.

This provoked Matt Busby into one last gamble in an effort to retrieve the Double which would have crowned arguably the most brilliant piece of team building and replenishing in the history of English football. Wood returned to goal and Duncan Edwards, the man for all situations and seasons, was pushed into attack. With Ray back between the posts Villa had lost the numerical advantage they had cleverly exploited with McParland's scoring burst between the 67th and 71st minutes and Tommy Taylor retrieved a goal with seven minutes to go. We roused ourselves to a frenzy of effort, winning a stream of corners, but Villa hung on to their advantage.

Busby's post-game speech was another testament to his style. He thanked the team for its efforts, and noted that no one could question our commitment or our ability. Sometimes football was like life. You didn't always get what you deserved, but the trick was to continue to believe in yourself—and never to forget the need to do the right thing. He was proud of us all. We were young and there was still so much to achieve. It should not be forgotten that we had won our second straight league title and reached the semi-finals of the European Cup. He raised a glass to the future of Manchester United.

CHAPTER 9

# INDESTRUCTIBLE

A few months after the FA Cup final, we beat Aston Villa 4–0 in the Charity Shield. Ray Wood and Peter McParland were captains for the game, which meant that they shook hands and closed, as warmly as possible in the circumstances, a chapter that had caused much bitterness among United fans. I now believe that Villa had been charged up that day, nobody more so than Peter, and I am convinced that what he did came out of determination to steal an edge rather than from any bad intention. However, less than a year after, the sense that we had indeed been victims of some very rough larceny still surfaced strongly if ever the subject was raised. But then football, like life, rolls along and on Saturday, 1 February 1958, at Highbury, we would probably have laughed at the idea that somehow we were a team who might draw more than the occasional wound from unkind fate.

We beat Arsenal in a stupendous game, one that some would tell me later was the best they ever saw. It was also true that no one at that time could have been less susceptible than me to a bout of brooding over the future. The team flowed beautifully and once again I had that boyish feeling that I was indestructible. I may still have been in the dog days of my army life, but as a professional footballer I was touching new levels of confidence in my ability. The dictums of Jimmy Murphy were no longer a set of difficult demands. They formed the code which I knew now could open all the doors.

However, this was only after I had noted that in football more than most places it is a tide which can suddenly change direction. Back in the autumn, for example, it was hard not to view prospects rather more pessimistically. There had been a dip in the team's performance that had brought the worry that the tumultuous events of the previous season might be bringing a reaction. I was also growing a little restive that Billy Whelan and Dennis Viollet had reclaimed their places. Increasing the frustration was the fact that neither in their form nor their fitness were Billy or Dennis offering much hope that I could quickly reclaim some of the attention that had come to me in such a flood the previous spring.

By the start of February 1958, however, the last of the doubts were over—both, it seemed, for me and the team. In the game against Arsenal we were marching again and with the sharpest touch of my career I was able to play a significant part.

We had returned to the basis of all previous success. It is an aspect of football that it is very easy to forget what first made you a force. It is supposed to be a simple game, but lost sometimes is the amount of work and thought necessary to make it so. You win a few games and you assume that winning is a right as much as an achievement. You stop doing the things that made you great—and this is when a great teacher and enforcer like Jimmy Murphy plays his most important role. If he does it well, he becomes part of your conscience.

For me it was a return to the truth that I had discovered just a few weeks after my debut against Charlton the season before, and was then underlined by Tommy Taylor and David Pegg before the semi-final with Birmingham City.

Lesson one had came against the Wolves team which Stan Cullis had built on such solid foundations. In fact at that point, back in November 1956, they were in some ways superior to us, despite Matt Busby's accumulation of outstanding talent. They had worked relentlessly and they were in every sense a team. In that first season with the seniors, I was told constantly how difficult it was going to be, moving up to First Division football. You couldn't afford to make a single mistake in the process of nullifying everything the opposition were bound to throw in your direction. Against a poor Charlton Athletic that message was hardly borne out; against Wolves it was underlined by every minute of the game at Old Trafford—my third in the top flight.

Though Peter Broadbent, an inside forward I admired so much for his craft and his eye for dangerous situations, was missing, Wolves were still formidably strong with England men like Billy Wright, Ron Flowers, Bill Slater, Dennis Wilshaw and Jimmy Mullen. Before the game the consensus was that we would be happy to win by the odd goal. In fact we won 3–0, and long before the end of a match I had expected to be the hardest I had ever played, I was telling myself, 'Well, Jimmy Murphy was right to say if you work hard enough, if you make stopping the other team playing a vital part of your game, you're halfway to victory.' It was a fundamental lesson against a team who had been growing stronger as the season progressed and came to us on a run of six unbeaten matches.

The basic point, I realised, was that everyone who played football for a living had a duty to involve himself in all aspects of a team effort. Winning wasn't guaranteed, I noted against Wolves, even as

Billy Whelan and David Pegg scored early, and Tommy Taylor completed a win which, in the end, was so comfortable that Billy Wright, the England captain, was said to have been rendered speechless. Planning was required and worked. If you knew exactly what you were doing, and who on the opposite side was your particular responsibility, the challenge was quite straightforward. If you ignored the demands made on you by someone like Jimmy, your team would lose—and there would be nowhere to hide.

I had looked across the field, picking out all the big-name players in the famous old-gold shirts and black shorts and had said to myself, 'Some people think this is really the best team in England but we're beating them 3–0. It's really true. The best team doesn't always win.'

Fifteen months later, against Arsenal, football was easy again. It was both a rush of some of our best form and a celebration of the fact that we had grown strong on what had proved a surprisingly tricky road.

Even before the 1957–58 season's first kick off—a comfortable 3–0 victory over newly promoted Leicester City, which saw Billy Whelan score a fine hat-trick that helped shut the door on any hopes I had of a swift return to glory—there had been a couple of unsettling developments. Both of them flowed directly from the splash we had made in the European Cup.

Internazionale of Milan, having seen the impact of John Charles, the great Welsh international, after his transfer from Leeds United to Juventus, began to court Tommy Taylor, much to the fury of Matt Busby. Then the Italian Football Federation, noting the way Busby had developed his team at Old

Trafford, went to the top of the United tree and invited him to become their national coach. The Old Man declared, as he had the previous year when Real Madrid came courting, that he wasn't going anywhere, and nor was Tommy, however much money the Italians put on the table.

Having dismissed such distractions, United went charging into the new season, thrusting their way into the leadership of the First Division for a third straight year. However, momentum flagged in September and we began to lose, three times in four games while slipping to fourth place. Busby was concerned that Ray Wood may have lost some of his nerve after his nightmare at Wembley, and Tommy Taylor, perhaps unsettled by the Italian interest and the fact that he was the latest English player to discover he had no control over his own destiny, was finding goals more elusive than usual. Busby was never prone to panic, but nor was he a manager inclined to sit on his hands in the face of signs that his team were in danger of drifting away from their best standards.

By December we had a new goalkeeper, Harry Gregg, bought at the record price of £25,000 from Doncaster Rovers, and a new forward who was being invited to make himself a permanent part of the team. That was me—and by way of celebration I began scoring almost as a matter of course. Everything that came my way on the field, I went for. I was no longer afraid of shooting at distance. Every time I did I believed I would score a goal, and often I was right to have such confidence.

I had heard about the Taylor situation only at second hand. Tommy, a shrewd Yorkshireman, kept the matter to himself in the dressing room, and in this he may have been recognising the fact that most young United players—and perhaps along with Wilf McGuinness I was a classic case—would no more think of leaving Old Trafford than join the Soviet astronaut programme. At the financial convenience of English clubs, there would over those years be a trickle of players going to Italy—led by John Charles and followed by players like Gerry Hitchens, Jimmy Greaves and my future team-mate Denis Law—but for most of us the idea was unthinkable.

In nearly twenty years as a professional with Manchester United, I wasn't notified of a single approach. Inevitably, there would be the odd rumour and a whisper in my ear, but there wasn't anything even vaguely official. I heard that Glasgow Rangers had made an enquiry about the possibility of signing me, and I was told later that there had indeed been something in it, but I didn't attribute any deviousness to Matt Busby's failure to notify me. I'm sure he just assumed I wouldn't be interested. And of course he was right.

A few years later I had reason to believe that Real Madrid might try to persuade United to let me go. Santiago Bernabeu, the president, was always very friendly whenever I saw him and he sent a present when Norma and I were married in 1961. Given the aura of Real, and all they meant to me as representatives of beautiful football, it was extremely flattering, but Busby knew better than anyone that my vows to United were, in the context of football, as strong as the ones I had made to my wife.

The following year I was involved in the one 'tapping-up' incident of my career. It happened when I went with England to Chile for the 1962 World Cup: a Chilean goalkeeper, who had connections in Argentina, told me that Boca Juniors were anxious to sign me—and make me a very rich man. I said that it was quite out of the question. When he asked me why this was so, I told him that one very good reason was that Norma was pregnant, and I wouldn't want her to have any upheaval at such a time. He tried to brush away my objections. Finally, he said the difficulty of the pregnancy was a problem that could easily be solved. Boca Juniors were an important club and they would have no trouble arranging for Norma to have the baby in the British embassy in Buenos Aires. However, at no stage would such talk ever be more than a fantasy.

This was never more so than when 1957 turned into 1958. At last the club had given me reason to believe that I could bring to an end the phase when I was just the boy who could fill in for established stars like Viollet and Whelan and, looking back, I see that I produced exactly the right response. I scored in three of the four games against Leicester City, Luton Town on Christmas Day and Boxing Day, and Manchester City, but this was no more than a relatively gentle prelude to a break-out against the formidable Bolton Wanderers defence of Tommy Banks, Roy Hartle and John Higgins in mid-January. I scored a hat-trick and had never felt so confident on the ball, a mood I took into the fourth round FA Cup tie with Alf Ramsey's Ipswich Town the following week, scoring both the goals at Old Trafford. One of them was of the spectacular variety with which I was being increasingly linked.

Going into the Highbury game the following week, Busby had a choice between a fully fit Whelan and me, and when he announced the team he was also saying that I had achieved another rite of passage. Nine goals in ten games had earned me the Busby nod in my own right.

As the game unfolded, Arsenal simply couldn't cope with the level of our confidence or our touch. Duncan scored after ten minutes, from twenty-five yards. He bounded across the muddy surface before giving the fine Welsh international goalkeeper Jack Kelsey no chance. As was so often the reaction of opponents when Edwards exerted himself so powerfully in the early going, you could see Arsenal heads drop and this was a particular encouragement to our left winger Albert Scanlon.

Albert was a quirky character, brilliant one day, indifferent the next, but this was one of the performances of his life. Invariably he would concern his marker with his pace, but it could be said that his last ball wasn't always his best. However, this day he touched perfection. I could only feel sympathy for my namesake, Arsenal's right back Stan Charlton. The defender was tortured by Albert's speed and trickery. It was as though the boy from Salford, who spent so many hours watching the latest Hollywood offerings in the city-centre cinemas, had woken up with the conviction that this day he would be in a film of his own. It was classical wing play: quick, functional, and totally committed to the final act of supplying a deadly cross. After thirty-four minutes he laid on the second goal, passing the ball to me after a seventy-yard run down the wing. 'It's easy, Bobby, lad,' he said when I gave him a hug. Then Tommy Taylor scored our third just before half time.

Fifteen minutes into the second half David Herd, who would join United a few years later, smashed a shot past Harry Gregg, and in a few more minutes Jimmy Bloomfield scored twice. Cheers rolled down from the stand as we contemplated the bleak possibility that our run back into the title race—we had reached third place and were just six points behind Wolves, who were due to arrive at Old Trafford the following Saturday—was suddenly in danger of being halted.

It was an excellent test of our nerve. After the game we would be flying to Belgrade for the second leg of our European tie with Red Star of Belgrade. We had heard stories of how ferocious the Serbs were on their own soil, and we had had a taste of their force and skill at Old Trafford, when we'd had to battle to our limits to gain a 2–1 advantage, one of our goals coming from a Scanlon cross which I was able to hook home. Everyone said, from Busby down, that we would have to redouble our efforts if we were to survive. Now, here at Highbury, we were having something of a dress rehearsal. Duncan, as always, took Arsenal's recovery as a personal affront, and from Roger Byrne there was the usual cool leadership. He wasn't a shouter but he had a great presence. It was clear that we faced the kind of examination that we couldn't afford to fail; it might just shape the rest of our season.

Dennis Viollet pushed us back in front from another cross by Scanlon in the sixty-fifth minute, four minutes after Bloomfield's equalising strike, and then, after another seven minutes, Taylor scored his second goal from an angle which Kelsey must have thought impossible. The 5–3 lead seemed like an invitation to cruise home. Arsenal, and their ecstatic fans, had been swiftly subdued. At least it was a pleasant idea for the five minutes it took for the Welsh international inside forward Derek Tapscott to pull his team back into the game.

Nine goals might point a finger towards poor defence, but the quality of play was sustained, and was as thrilling to be involved in as it apparently was to see. We beat back waves of Arsenal attack to keep our lead, and at the final whistle the London fans perfectly reflected those days when a majority of supporters went to the game in the spirit Jack and I had always taken with us on our pilgrimages to Newcastle and Sunderland. They did not march off sourly to the buses and the underground trains. They had come to Highbury, it was plain to see and hear, with two purposes. One was to see Arsenal win. The other was to see good football, something demonstrated no less brilliantly by such as Duncan Edwards, Roger Byrne and Albert Scanlon because they happened to be wearing the colours of another team. They stayed and they cheered.

Recently I read an old account of the game which brought back so many warm memories. *The Times*, no less, reporting under the by-line of 'our football correspondent' in those days when Geoffrey Green was still the anonymous bard of football, could not have been more extravagant in its praise. 'The thermometer was doing a war-dance. There was no breath left in anyone. The players came off arm in arm. They knew they had finally fashioned something of which to be proud.' Then there was the recollection of the Arsenal full back Dennis Evans. He recalled, 'Everyone was cheering. Not because of Arsenal, not because of United, but because of the game itself. No one left until five minutes after the game. They just stood cheering.'

It was something, I suppose, that players of later generations, for all the increase in their financial rewards and their celebrity, would never quite enjoy, not in that force, not in that sense that they had been part of something which went beyond themselves—

and beyond the detail of which team happened to win or lose. Football won that day, hands down.

We could only hope for a similar outcome in Belgrade, though it would hardly be true to say that we were on a mission as ambassadors for the great game. We might pride ourselves on the quality of our play, and we might have won more admiration than ever before with the performance at Highbury, but the game against Red Star, we knew well enough, was unlikely to be about the beautiful game. We were going to win—or at least preserve our advantage from the first leg—and however pretty or dramatic the match, anything less would have to be recognised as a terrible setback.

The truth was that our fascination with the new world of European football had hardened into an extremely strong conviction. It made us itch for another go at the masters from Madrid; we believed we had served our apprenticeship in the game's wider world. The Highbury salute had been wonderful, but it didn't deflect us from an ambition that had so quickly come to outweigh all others. We had grown into the belief that we could win the European Cup. Why not? Maybe we weren't ready for the likes of di Stefano and Kopa and Gento that first year, but we were more serious customers now. We were fresh from a 3–1 aggregate dismissal of Dukla Prague, champions of the most sophisticated of football nations, who had been led by a brilliant Josef Masopust, soon to lead Czechoslovakia to the championship of Europe. If some corners of Europe, including our latest destination, Yugoslavia, were still a mystery, we had plenty of reasons now to think we could resolve any problem with some confidence.

Part of the thrill of Europe was that suddenly all its

rewards seemed to be within our reach. There was also the sense that we were no longer merely representing the city of Manchester. Attempting to win the European title now meant that you carried the hopes of the whole nation, and there was something of that, we felt, in the great send-off we experienced at Highbury. It was the perfect launching pad for Belgrade, the confirmation that we were indeed England's team of destiny. The plane would fly us to the Balkans, with a stop in Munich, and somewhere along the route it seemed entirely possible we might touch the stars.

CHAPTER 10

# BELGRADE

On the Saturday morning of the Arsenal game there had been a kerfuffle in our London hotel when it was discovered that George Whittaker, one of the club directors, had died in his room during the night. There was a conflab of club officials and hotel staff in the lobby. A doctor arrived with his medical bag and an ambulance stood in the street.

Directors always travelled with us, and occasionally we would exchange a few words, but there was no real contact. Generally they came from a different stratum of life and there would be very little conversation beyond those few pleasantries. Directors were men of the world and important business. They dined separately and, we presumed, talked about their professional affairs and investments, and maybe a little bit about football. We, of course, talked mostly football but also music and girls and films and what we might do after the game. Really, we inhabited separate worlds from the likes of Mr Whittaker, and it was only Matt Busby who travelled between them. Still it was sad, we all agreed, that a man should go like that, on the road, away from his home and his loved ones.

However, for the Busby Babes there was not much that could dent our optimistic view of life. It was a known fact that when you got older there was a much greater risk of dying suddenly, but the young were proofed against such a thing; they could go about their business confident that when the sun rose in the morning all their ambitions and their hopes would still be alive. The young were immortal. If you had a degree of ambition and talent and a little courage there was nothing you couldn't do. Already, for us, it was a belief that had been encouraged by great tides of cheers. At Old Trafford, with the rise of the youth team and the march of so many brilliant young players, it had become nothing less than an article of faith.

Events at Highbury had underpinned once again our belief in our prospects, and certainly almost everything that happened in the first half in the big, cold concrete stadium of Red Star served to deepen the confident frame of mind we now seemed to be carrying from match to match as permanent baggage. We played with a freedom that could only be described as sensational.

In our work-out on the day before the game we had been relaxed and that mood had been maintained on the drive to the stadium on match day. The banter was ceaseless—and inevitably led by Eddie Colman. He talked about the latest Sinatra song. Albert Scanlon discussed Marilyn Monroe's latest film. Through the windows of the bus there were so many new things to see: great banners of Tito on the big grey buildings, a unit of tanks clanking over the cobbles, smoke rising from the street stalls where they sold food and roasted nuts, and women in heavy boots working on the road. There was plenty of material for social observers— and the comedians—on the bus.

I was still the young boy among the young men, but my self-belief was growing with each game and I no longer feared so much the kind of rebuke that had once been delivered to me by Allenby Chilton when I spoke out of turn. I had scored a few goals so maybe I could make the odd contribution to the talk.

In the dressing room before we went out Matt Busby was as composed as ever in his big dark overcoat and smartly snapped trilby. 'There are no terrors out there for you boys now,' he said. 'You know this team: they are good but not good enough to beat you. We've beaten them once. Now let's do it again. Enjoy the game, express yourselves. Don't forget your own strengths, always play to them. You should know that you have nothing to fear.'

We started as we had at Highbury, Dennis Viollet scoring after two minutes, with me adding two more in the thirtieth and thirty-second minutes. It was a cold day and there was a light covering of snow. There was frost on the pitch, but not so much that the surface wouldn't take a stud. You could run and you could pass and shoot, and we did enough of all three to subdue the big crowd in their long coats and their woollen hats. Duncan retained the dominant mood he had displayed at Highbury, and for most of the half we seemed to be quicker to the ball and to have plenty of time to play it.

Red Star had fought hard and showed a lot of skill in the first leg at Old Trafford, and our long journey to Belgrade had not been without a touch of apprehension. They had a little midfielder, Dragoslav Sekularac, who was so good, so clever in Manchester, that I found myself asking, 'Why haven't I heard of this fellow before?'

They also had a player, Kostic, who showed us for the first time how it was possible to bend a free kick round a defensive wall. He did it brilliantly after Harry Gregg was caught handling the ball outside his area—and this was after the Yugoslavs had already pulled back two goals. The first of them seemed to be no more than a small alarm call at the time. With the

137

goal advantage from Old Trafford, we were still three goals clear, and in the first half we had simply torn them apart. But Red Star came alive with their strike and when Kostic brought the score on the day to 3–3 with four minutes to go we were under hard pressure. It was another glimpse of the depth of European football and its capacity to spring an ambush the moment you took anything for granted.

Sekularac was a classic example of somebody who, despite being completely unheralded when he first arrived in England, had skills and subtleties which gave a whole new dimension to the game. In my international career I would collide with him again on several occasions, and each time I marvelled at his ability to shape a game with both his skill and speed of thought. Over the years I would get to know him quite well. He was a proud gypsy and told me about his background. Certainly it was not difficult to imagine him performing intricate dance steps beside a camp fire. In 1970, when I was preparing for the World Cup in Mexico, I met him in a little town in the Andes. I said how strange it was to find him in such a remote place, but he explained that there was good money to earn in Colombia if you were able to teach the game. He was surrounded by youngsters who seemed to hang on his every word and gesture.

In Belgrade he had a few lessons for a Manchester United whose belief they could win the European Cup was still on the rise. However, we were quick and confident students and just as we did at Highbury, we avoided the worst consequences of relaxing, however subliminally. The Serbs invaded our goal but Harry Gregg put behind him his earlier mishap, as did Bill Foulkes who had conceded a penalty, and we held firm under the pressure.

The Old Man told us we had passed another test on our way to the semi-final with, as it turned out, the powerful Italian club AC Milan, and this, with local beer and a drop of slivovic, was more than enough fuel for a night of celebration in a club which featured the usual array of East European cabaret acts, including jugglers and dancers, and later on at the home of a British embassy official. It was all part of the great adventure that stretched before us so dazzlingly. The toast, as it always was then, was to the future.

There were a few thick heads in the morning, but no serious casualties. In those days it was not frowned upon if a player took a drink, even if it was more than one or two, and smoking was quite commonplace. It seems bizarre now, but a player was put in charge of himself in such matters, and it was quite a few years later before a combination of my wife and my daughters persuaded me that smoking was not a good idea.

Back then there was a strong feeling that if you did your training, and performed well on the field, you were entitled to live a relatively normal life. There were certain rules of course. If you represented a club like Manchester United you had responsibilities that could never be put down. It was unthinkable to go drinking before a game. If you did that you were letting down your club and your team-mates and, not least, yourself. However, a few drinks and some music were your due after a good performance. If you strived hard enough to win, you were free to celebrate, within reason of course and with prearranged time limits. So there was little remorse among those who had had a drink or two before setting off to Belgrade airport; only the exhilaration that came with the conviction that once again we had put ourselves in a position to claim the greatest prize in Europe.

You looked around the bus and saw one strength piled upon another. If we didn't have di Stefano or Gento, we had virtuosos of our own: Duncan was touching new levels of authority, Dennis Viollet was playing with tremendous bite and was just irrepressible around the box, and Eddie Colman was producing a little more swagger and a little more confidence with every game. Harry Gregg had brought a lot to the team with his fierce protection of the goal and his fighting spirit.

On top of all this was the extraordinary leadership of Roger Byrne. I was never close to the captain, not as I was with almost every other member of the team, but he always had my immense respect. I saw him as an aloof master in all that he did. I didn't have the nerve to speak to him freely because he seemed to be operating on another level of life to the rest of us. He seemed so well educated, so cosmopolitan in my eyes, and I marvelled at the fact that he spent most of his free time away from the club working in a hospital, where he was training to be a physiotherapist. I was told that when patients and staff talked to him about football, he was reluctant to get involved. He said that football was just part of his life, and when he was at the hospital he expected to be treated like everybody else. For a lad like me, who had viewed education as a necessity to be suffered before the real business of playing football, it seemed almost unbelievable that someone just a few years older could do so much with his life and make so little fuss along the way.

He didn't hang around with the lads because he had his own life in Manchester, and was married and not in need of boyish company. It was no surprise to learn that one of his best friends was Brian Statham, the great Lancashire and England fast bowler—no more than it was that he was an accomplished cricketer and rugby player. Indeed, I thought it was typical of him when I heard that, when Statham was selected before him for the National Service RAF football team, he made no complaint, no angry protests about his status in the game with Manchester United, preferring instead to immediately offer his services to the rugby coach. He promptly became the team's star performer. That seemed to be the essence of Roger Byrne: natural confidence and a fierce independence.

On the field Roger would shout his instructions firmly enough, let you know who was in charge of affairs, but generally he was quiet off the field. He had the aura of a true captain. If you did well, scored a good goal, say, you would not expect more than a cursory pat on the back, yet from him it was a gesture you would prize very highly indeed.

Those who saw him as an untouchable force at Old Trafford included the Old Man. After Byrne's first game for United, when he had joined such giants as Jack Rowley, Johnny Carey and Charlie Mitten, Busby had declared, 'It is hard to imagine a young player could make a more mature debut. Within a few matches, I think you will see this boy make his case to play for England, and when he gets in the team I think it will be impossible to get him out.' I was told that Busby had once angered him by leaving him out of the team after a bad defeat. Roger had the feeling that he had been made a scapegoat and his frustration welled up during a training session, when Busby shouted an instruction. Byrne's response was dismissive and his language was quite rough, and the manager retired to his office with something of a dilemma. Could he accept this challenge to his authority—or did he have to impose some discipline? His decision, before it was quickly revoked, was sensational. He put Roger on the transfer list. But not for long, when he pondered how much the team would miss his style and leadership, which had already made him a fixture in the England team, and how much interest was beating against his door.

Busby had that famous saying, 'That's not United,' when a player's behaviour was deemed to have fallen below expected standards, and this no doubt was such an occasion—but for Byrne a compromise could be made. Busby knew that he had a rare leader who would be a vital factor in any conquest of Europe.

One key to a successful team is a balance of respect, an understanding of the strength of individual players but also the wider sense of dependency on each other. The captain had no separate lists in the matter of criticism if there were mistakes on the field. Whoever you were, you could be exposed to the force of his leadership. It didn't matter if Duncan Edwards did something amazing if other members of the team let themselves down. Nor was Duncan shielded from criticism when he had Roger Byrne's critical eye on him. Sometimes even the big man felt a shaft of the captain's displeasure.

There were no challenges to the captain's rule. He led by example game in, game out. He was never flustered, never panicky. He had that little bit more experience than the rest of us. He was the founder member of the Busby Babes, the second oldest member of the team, and though he was still two days short of his twenty-ninth birthday when he led us on to the plane in Belgrade, he had the bearing of a general who knew that he had just led his young army to yet another striking achievement.

It was only later that I would learn that Roger Byrne was subject to terrible superstition and some dark fears. Behind the front of confidence there were, it turned out, some of the doubts that we all shared in the small hours of the night in some distant hotel room. Once, his room-mate John Doherty reported, Byrne woke up at 3 a.m. to report that he had had a terrible dream. He never told John the detail of the nightmare, merely conveying the sense of an awful premonition. It was a haunting episode for Doherty because it happened on the eve of a routine cup tie against Bristol Rovers, and, in a season which saw United take the title by eleven points, the cup performance was a disaster. United lost 4–0. No one could remember such an incoherent performance from the team that down the years had become known as the Red Devils.

According to John, there was another strange incident later in that 1955–56 season. Again Byrne woke up in the small hours complaining of a nightmare. This time he had dreamed of missing a penalty in a vital game, and he declared that if a penalty was awarded in the coming game with Blackpool—one that could settle the title—there was no way he would take it. Predictably in the circumstances, United were given a penalty and Roger asked Johnny Berry to take the kick, but Johnny said, 'I don't mind—you take it.' Byrne's face clouded over, he yelled, 'You take the penalty,' and then he turned his back. To everyone's great relief, Berry scored, and Byrne promptly reverted to a mask of absolute authority.

Something else not widely known about our captain that February morning in Belgrade was that in the two previous Februarys he had had life-threatening experiences.

In 1956 he had driven his car into a lamp-post and broken his collarbone. In the following year, he had crashed near the Busby home in the Manchester suburb of Charlton-cum-Hardy, and the Old Man had rushed the short distance to the scene of the accident. He was immensely relieved to see that on this occasion Roger had escaped serious injury. This did not stop him delivering a fierce lecture on the need for safe driving. At the time the captain was the only member of the team who owned a car, and Bill Foulkes later reported that on one occasion he and Ray Wood had been passengers on a white-knuckle ride with Byrne at the wheel. Wood swore that he would never travel with the captain again.

Any superstitious dread was hidden when Roger Byrne strode on to the chartered British European Airways Elizabethan—call sign G-ALZU AS 57—at Marshall Tito airport on the morning of 6 February 1958. His face was impassive and, like all of us who marched up the steps, two by two, he was extremely sure of himself and, of course, indestructible.

# CHAPTER 11

## MUNICH

It was a wonderful state of mind we took on to the plane and in its last few hours of life it had maybe never been more intense. In the cabin there was a buzz of conversation and bursts of laughter and the card players were aggressively at work. We were heading home for yet another red carpet welcome, another return of conquering heroes.

I spent much of the flight to Munich, where we would put down for refuelling, discussing with Dennis Viollet how it was that we had so suddenly fallen away from our complete mastery of Red Star in the first half. It was true that we had come through the crisis well, but it was one we should really have avoided. We had been forced to survive in a match we had seemed at one point to control completely. Maybe, we speculated, it had something to do with the after-effects of the Highbury thriller, which had received rapturous press accounts. Perhaps also there was a little concern that we had to hold back something for Saturday's challenge against Stan Cullis's league-leading Wolves. This match, certainly, was clearly on the mind of the Old Man, who, having been denied an historic Double of league title and FA Cup the previous spring, had set his heart on three straight titles to match the achievement of Herbert Chapman's Arsenal back in the thirties. If we were to stay in the race, we had to take two points off Wolves; we had to show that what happened against Arsenal, and against Red Star in the first half, was part of an established pattern and not some flash of fleeting brilliance.

Ushering us through the airport in Belgrade, Busby had no doubt been concerned by the need for a prompt departure and swift completion of our trip. The requirement to rush home to Manchester through the snow-filled skies of Europe had been spelled out by the Football League, which had been so emphatic in its refusal to give a blessing to our Continental mission. Under new league regulations, any team competing in Europe had to be back in England a full twenty-four hours before they were due to play a championship game. League secretary Hardaker no doubt argued that he was protecting the 'integrity' of the Football League, preventing important matches being squeezed into the programme in the shadow of European action. Another interpretation was that he was making it as difficult as possible for the man who had defied him with his insistence that United would fight on this new frontier of football.

The Old Man had placed an extra burden on his team, and himself, but Dennis and I agreed that if any type of football team was equipped to take on the challenge of a long domestic season and the new demands of European competition it was surely one bred in England. Though we had so much work to do at home, there were good reasons to believe that we could cope with the physical pressure of another European semi-final and the possibility of an appearance in the final on top of commitments in the league and FA Cup. Certainly it had not been any crisis of stamina that had caused our downfall against Real Madrid the previous season. Indeed, the Old Trafford crowd, and some of us in the dressing room, had decided that if the second leg had stretched on for a few more minutes there would have been a very good chance of us getting the goals which would have earned a replay and ultimately a final against Fiorentina, a team we would have strongly fancied ourselves to beat.

Pushing ourselves to our physical limit, Dennis and I agreed, was simply part of the job. It was something which we trained for intensively in the pre-season, and which was built into us by the work we had to do on often heavy pitches and under the demands of crowds who never made any secret of the fact that as long as we were on the field we were obliged to give maximum effort.

Many years later the great Dutch player Johan Cruyff would say that in club football the English player was always hugely respected for his willingness—and ability—to fight until the last kick of the game. He said that the great fear of even the top European teams, heavy with skill and tactical nous, was that an English team would never know when it was time to quit.

The victory against Bilbao the previous season had been a classic of resolution and pressure evenly distributed over a game which required a 3–0 victory, and against Real Madrid we had absorbed the barbs of di Stefano, Kopa and Gento and finished the game, having clawed two goals back, pressing into the howling expectations of the Stretford End. Such recollections brought Dennis and me to another point of agreement: we were as keen as mustard to get back to England and carry on the battle.

When we landed in Munich the weather was as bad as I had ever seen it on my football travels; beneath the low clouds the sky was filled with snowflakes, and when we landed we saw there were six or seven inches of slush on the runway. However, we were assured that we would be on our way soon enough. While we had coffee in the terminal, the plane would be routinely refuelled along with everything else that needed to be done, both to the aircraft and the runway. It was nothing to do with us; our job was to play football, not debate the value of de-icing procedures or safe levels of runway slush.

The mood of the team was still happy, even bubbly, as we returned to the plane. If we had any fears they had only to do with the possibilities of delay and missing the Hardaker deadline. The airline had a job to do, they had to get us home. We had done our work for the time being.

Travelling was not pleasant in those days before the jet engine. Everything seemed to take so long, and sometimes it seemed as though you might be in the sky forever. It was also true, as I mentioned earlier, that I never enjoyed the Elizabethan aircraft. It always felt as if it was too heavy for its own good, an impression heightened by the fact that it seemed to take far too long to climb into its flight path. However, for me, and I think most of the party, there was no point of concern until after the second aborted take-off. Then the mood dipped, not in any dramatic way but quite perceptibly; certainly conversation became less chirpy and the card players were less absorbed by their game. Frank Swift, the former Manchester City and England goalkeeper, who was now a football reporter for the *News of the World*, demanded to know what was going on, and was told that there was a small technical problem that was being sorted out. I just assumed that there was a shortage of power, and that it was something they were working on and were determined to get perfectly right before we took off.

After a brief second coffee break in the terminal, we returned to the plane hurriedly and to assurances that everything was now fine; our home journey to Manchester would proceed without any further interruption. The issue of de-icing and clearing away the slush from the runway would later be key elements of the inquiry into what had gone wrong, along with captain James Thain's attempts to prove that he had behaved in a perfectly professional way. For most of us in the passenger seats, however, it was still a simple matter beyond our control: the airline and airport people would make sure everything was safe.

In opening this account of my life I felt there was no alternative but to go straight to the tragedy of Munich, and so already I have touched on the salient points of the disaster, and the unshakeable emotional impact they had for me on all that would follow, down to this day—but perhaps what I haven't so far conveyed is my sense of separation from the sickening events that unfolded so starkly. In so many ways I was part of the horror, but I was also, in the strangest way, detached; it was almost as if I was disembodied, a silent, traumatised participant in a terrible dream I could neither act in, nor escape from.

When I was first aware that there really was a problem, when the Elizabethan, even by its own standards seemed to have been roaring down the runaway for an eternity, I was conscious of the quiet in the plane and that neither Dennis Viollet nor I had uttered a word since we had started on the take-off. As we went through a fence and collided with a house, I didn't hear the semblance of a scream. There had been just a vast and empty silence in the plane. I suppose we were in shock; overwhelmed with disbelief, certainly. What could we do? We were strapped in our seats and everything was happening out of our control. The pilot was in charge. What I did was something that I suppose came instinctively: I bent my head down and braced myself for the impact. The last thing I remember, before coming round away from the plane, was the terrible rending noise of metal on metal.

Why had it happened? Was it an engine fault? It seemed to me that the slush had neutralised the power of the plane. Random thoughts and questions came in and out of my head. The pilot had been so determined to get us into the air, and in the end he couldn't do it. Why was it so important to go off into that blizzard? Because Matt Busby had to fulfil a deadline set by the Football League?

The Old Man, we know, suffered the most terrible regrets, blaming himself for what happened, and only came back to the game, wounded, almost broken, after the fierce persuasion of his wife and all those who were closest to him. We all knew that Manchester United had become his life, and who among that group of cheery, indestructible young men who had a few hours earlier boarded the plane in Belgrade, would have questioned his instinct to take us all on the great adventure. Certainly not me as I took off my overcoat and laid it across him as he groaned in pain on the wet tarmac.

Though I had not seen the condition of my dearest friends on the team, Duncan, Eddie and David Pegg, I knew by now that there had been terrible losses. In the snow I saw one team-mate who was obviously dead, and someone told me that Roger Byrne had gone. He was said to have joked, thinly, when the plane had made its third take-off attempt. 'It's now or never,' he had muttered, but if he had one of his terrible premonitions it had apparently not shown on his face.

There was smoke and grit in the cold air and a blare of sirens, and sitting beside me, having been pulled out of the seat in which, like me, he had been thrown away from the plane, Dennis Viollet was drifting in and out of consciousness. My team-mates Harry Gregg and Bill Foulkes, however, stayed conscious from start to finish, and maybe this is why, when you look at the picture of them after they played their first match after the tragedy, their eyes are far away and they are so distant from their new team-mates in a victory that had been drenched with the deepest feelings it was a possible for a football side and their fans to share.

Later, Harry Gregg said that I had been unconscious for about ten minutes, which explained why I was unaware of how I had got away from the burning wreckage, and the parts Harry and Bill had played in those first minutes following the crash. I was still dazed when Harry helped me into the minibus which rushed us through the Munich streets to the hospital. The rest of the night was pain and anger and disbelief, and that emotional eruption of mine when I thought the hospital orderly was treating so lightly the fact that our entire world had come tumbling down in a few catastrophic seconds. The injection that put me to sleep merely took me that much closer to the moment of terrible realisation that the horror would never go away.

When I awoke, the German boy reading from the newspaper, listing the dead, brought back the pounding questions that I would never be able to answer properly, the ones that asked, 'How could I survive that? How could anyone survive? Why did *I* survive?'

I had a sudden desire to get in touch with home, let everybody know that I was still alive, even though that fact had been reported in every morning newspaper. I sent a message through the British embassy, saying that not only was I alive, I was without serious injuries.

Harry Gregg and Bill Foulkes came to my bedside before leaving for Manchester, and when they went away I shrank from thinking about what they faced: the funerals, the mourning, the feeling that a great city had stopped dead, and then the need to train and prepare for their next game whenever it came. I wasn't ready for any of that, and this was confirmed when Jimmy Murphy arrived at the hospital with a full report. The newspapers had been kept away from us, but you can keep reality at bay only for so long. I found myself staring into a mirror and asking the question which would become so familiar down the days and the weeks and the years, 'How the hell is it possible to come through all that with just a bang on the head and a small cut?'

There was never an instinct to try to put Munich out of mind, to say that it was something terribly sad but had to be relegated to the past because how else you could you deal with the present and the future? Munich was just too big, too overpowering, to permit that kind of reaction. It was something that you knew, right from the start, you had to learn to live with. It was a reality that was reinforced with every account of a funeral, every description by Jimmy Murphy of how it was at Old Trafford with the people milling around the ground.

Jimmy, typically, was the strongest presence in those days when the Old Man was surviving only with the help of an oxygen tent. He said that we had to fight for our existence—and the memory of the team-mates we had lost. He had been through a war when men had to live with the loss of so many comrades, had to fight on through the suffering and live with what was left to them. It was the same now at Manchester United, Jimmy insisted. But then later I heard that it was just a front that Jimmy put on. One day he was discovered in a back corridor of the hospital, sobbing his heart out in pain at the loss of so many young players he had adored for their talent and who he loved like sons.

Very soon it was clear that Jimmy Murphy, and everyone else at the club, needed one thing to happen more than anything. They needed another match, some sense of continuity, some belief that, however haltingly, the club was moving forward from the worst of the grief. For several days I had pushed away the idea of returning to Manchester, of picking up again the challenge of playing football, but now I felt a few stirrings, partly inspired by the courage of Harry Gregg and Bill Foulkes, partly by the fact that before I left the hospital I was able to walk up the stairs and see both Duncan and the Old Man. Both of them were so ill that it was obvious we were in danger of losing them. To lose one would be the most terrible blow; to lose both, unthinkable. Something had to be done. Their work could not be allowed just to slide away—though saying that seemed a lot easier than dredging up the effort and the will to begin the job.

When my mother and Jack collected me at the docks in Harwich, I certainly felt a sense of relief that they were taking me not to Manchester but to the North East, where I could have respite, however brief, from the challenge of facing all the new realities of United's life and my own. Once home, I saw friends, I took some walks, and one day a photographer caught me kicking a ball in the street with some of the local kids. The worst moment was when my mother came into my room and said, 'Duncan Edwards died, son.'

I could hardly bear it. When I'd first arrived in Manchester I'd been helped so much by my fellow players. Two of them, Eddie Colman and David Pegg, were now gone, but it had been Duncan, everyone's great young hero, who had made a point of looking after me. In the army he had made that effort to find me a comfortable mattress, and that was just the opening statement of his friendship. One day he gave me one of his shirts, saying it fitted him a little tightly, but I suspect he had noted what passed for my wardrobe. Most important of all for a young lad who in many ways off the field wasn't as sure of himself as he tried to pretend, he gave me his attention.

He was fantastic and I loved him.

At the time of the accident he was just beginning to think of settling down with his girlfriend, Molly Leech. There was talk of marriage and I'm sure it would have happened quite quickly.

I went to see Duncan's mother Sarah a few years ago, shortly before she died. She was a fine, tough lady. She had known tragedy before she lost Duncan: a baby daughter had died at fourteen weeks. There was a report that she had suffered a burglary at her house in Dudley, in Worcestershire, and when I drove down there I was amazed to see how strong she was. She told me how she had found a strange man in her house and was so incensed that she wanted to fight him. I could see Duncan in her as her eyes blazed with anger as she told me the story. Years earlier I had stood with her when they unveiled a statue to Duncan in Dudley, and the local vicar declared, 'Talent and genius we will see again, but there will only ever be one Duncan Edwards.' I could only murmur, 'Amen.'

I took it so hard when my mother broke the news that he had died because, even though he was in terrible pain in Munich, and the doctors were not optimistic, I had had a sense that he might just make it. All the sadness flooded back when, many years after the accident, a surgeon told me that with modern technology, coupled with his fighting heart, there was no doubt that his life would have been saved.

Down the years I have tried to keep in touch with the relatives of those I was closest to at the time of the crash, particularly Sarah Edwards and the mothers of David Pegg and Eddie Colman. I also talked with Roger Byrne's wife Joy, a very strong woman who seemed so well matched with the man I admired so much from that certain distance. I went to the Colman house in Archie Street, and in that place where I had spent so many happy hours I was overwhelmed by sadness. Eddie's father Dick was suffering terribly and he told me that at the heart of all the pain was the fact that in Munich there had initially been some confusion in the identification of bodies. This was distressing, but here at least there was some reassurance when Eddie's body finally came home. His pet dog had waited each day on the corner of the street, but when the coffin finally arrived he immediately ran to sit beside it.

In the North East I was shielded from the emotion that was being publicly expressed in every street and pub and corner shop in Manchester, but of course there was no protection against my own memories. I was trying to heal my feelings, and get some grasp on what happened, among my own people. I made several visits to our local doctor and I did talk with him about how I felt, but there was no truth in a report, attributed to him, that I had said I would never play football again.

The most crucial development in my recovery to the point where I felt I could play again, run out in the red shirt of Manchester United, came when the club was required to play its first game after the accident, an FA Cup fourth round tie against Sheffield Wednesday at Old Trafford. I was in a local pub with my father and a few of the lads when I realised I had to be at the match. I asked my uncle Tommy Skinner, the only member of our family to own a car, if he would drive me down. He agreed straight away. In those days, in that part of the world, you shared everything with your family—a pig, vegetables from the allotment, a car. It was a long drive down to Manchester on those old roads and I don't suppose I was the best conversationalist, but I didn't have to make excuses to Uncle Tommy.

The confusion before the game about who would play against Wednesday was so deep that the match programme was printed with a blank page where the United team should have been. The club had been granted special dispensation to make emergency signings, and Jimmy Murphy had invested in two of the elements he considered most vital to a successful team . . . some craft and some iron in defence. The craft was supplied by little Ernie Taylor, the Blackpool and England inside forward who had acted as such a brilliant manservant to Stanley Matthews in the 1953 cup final. For the hard-tackling, Jimmy opted for the extremely tough Stan Crowther, a member of the

Aston Villa defence who had torn away our chance of the Double.

The emotion in and around Old Trafford was so extraordinary that, among all your other reactions, you had to feel a little sympathy for the Wednesday players. They were suddenly the team almost everyone in football wanted to see beaten.

I went into the dressing room before the game and the scene that greeted me was overwhelming. Harry Gregg and Bill Foulkes were there and, with the exception of Shay Brennan and the new recruits, they were surrounded by kids from not only the reserves but also the third team—boys like Bobby Harrop, Reg Hunter and Reg Holland who had been bumped up into the squad, although they didn't actually play in the match. None of them would go on to have famous careers, but they had this one incredible moment in football history, and I could see on their faces as I gave each of them a hug that they were utterly committed to proving that they had every right to be at this famous club.

Shay, who was a wing half at the time, played forward and scored two goals. When they went in you wondered if Old Trafford might be split apart by the great tide of cheers. As the night wore on, as the emotion kept hitting new levels, I said to Uncle Tommy, 'Well, this is ridiculous, me going back to the North East from here.' For a moment, I thought, 'No, I'll not go back, I will not budge from Manchester,' but then I thought it would be better if I did return home for a couple of days. I did have some things to do there: I had to collect some clothes and I had to thank my family and all my people for the support they had given me at such a terrible time.

After the game I told Jimmy Murphy, 'I have to

come back—I'll be here in a couple of days.' Jimmy said the timing was up to me, but he gave me a hug and he gave me the impression he was very pleased. For me it was as though at least some of the pressure had lifted from my shoulders, and that perhaps the worst of the pain had lessened, at least to a small degree. I knew what I had to do; I had to start playing at the first possible opportunity now. I was also lucky that I could join in a crusade that took on even greater significance, given the unlikelihood that our reduced strength would enable a realistic pursuit of a third straight league title: we could make a run at the FA Cup.

The media attention was a help. It put football back into the equation. It said, in effect, that victory over Sheffield Wednesday could indeed be the starting point of recovery. Nothing then in English football was so romantic as the FA Cup; you could play quite peerlessly from August to the end of April, but if you slipped up in the old tournament you were denied a place in the last drama of the season; like the rest of the nation you had to watch the final on those small, grey television screens.

There was one great relief for me as I returned to the challenge of football. It was that I had missed the funerals of all my friends. I say this, and it is something I have thought about many times, because I just don't think I could have coped with my feelings in a public setting. Maybe it was my youth, maybe my nature, but I have never, not one day since the tragedy happened, lost my respect for what Harry Gregg and Bill Foulkes managed to achieve in the minutes and the days and then the weeks and the months that came after.

The fact that I went directly from Germany to the

North East had nothing to do with my medical situation, at least my physical condition. I had a cut on my head, but the stitches could have been removed anywhere. What I was suffering, I know now, was a great weight of grief. For a little while, I just couldn't get out of my head the enormity of what happened. Looking back at myself in those days, I see that everything had changed for me profoundly. Before the accident I was always advised by players who I respected so deeply. I was the kid asking the questions, and then, suddenly, it was different: I was supposed to be the experienced hand. I'd played against Real Madrid, I had played in a cup final and people were talking about me as a future star of England, but if everyone thought I was experienced, that I had grown quickly into the role of an elder statesman, the truth was that inside there was no difference. So much more might now be expected of me, on and off the field, but, when I looked at myself, on the inside I was still just an ordinary lad. I wasn't a captain, I was a young player still learning my trade.

All that had happened to me was that from the moment I sat beside Uncle Tommy in the stand at Old Trafford I was obsessed with the idea that this football club would indeed get back on the road to progress; it would grow strong again. I couldn't advise Jimmy Murphy on his next move into the transfer market; I couldn't come up with some tactical masterplan, but I could respond to suggestions I heard that the club might go under, that the effect of Munich would not in the long run be a point of defiance, an inspiration, but the start of a relentless decline. I could play better than I had ever done before. I could carry with me the memory of Duncan and Eddie, Roger and Mark, David and

Tommy, and Billy and Geoff every time I went on the field. I could help us avoid relegation, which would have been the first terrible suggestion that we might be on some irreversible decline. I could help drive us towards Wembley—and the chance to bring some joy back to the United fans who had seen a team that had grown so huge in their lives die before their eyes.

I could help to prove that there was indeed life left in Manchester United. I felt that belief course back through my body and my heart.

CHAPTER 12

# RESURRECTION

There was never a morning when I woke up with a great conviction that my destiny was to be a vital figure in the resurrection of Manchester United—it was just that I knew I could play a part, and that I had this tremendous belief that the job could be done.

It was inevitable, I worked out, that those of us who had survived the crash would be looked up to in a certain way, as though our escape in itself had given us a certain aura. That didn't have to weigh us down. It just meant that we had to play at the peak of our ability every time we went out on to the field—and also be grateful that our survival in the FA Cup had given us such a clear focus for our effort to get some life back into the club.

Above all, the situation was a reminder of something that I had learned very early as a young pro. Football allows you to detach yourself from everything that is going on in other parts of your life. You have a job to do, a position to fill, and in those weeks after Munich there surely could not have been a finer therapy. In trying to record your life as accurately as possible there is maybe a temptation to compartmentalise all of your experiences: Munich was rock bottom; the march to Wembley in the wake of that experience was uplifting and liberating, a new dawn.

Well, of course, life isn't parcelled up so neatly. Munich hadn't made a mature philosopher of me overnight. I was still just a kid who had had a bloody

161

awful experience. However, there was no doubt about the value of the therapy that came with our involvement in the cup. It was as good for the players as it was for the fans. We had something to play for, and they could go back to their old places in the stand and start making new dreams for a new team. Looking back, I see that this feeling of renewal, the idea that something could still be made out of the future, did more than anything to get me over the worst of the memories.

Inevitably, there were days when, without the adrenaline accompanying a big cup game, I would find myself back in some of the old confusion. Who could really explain what happened? Not a priest, not a psychologist, not Harry Gregg, who lived through all of it with maybe the most open of eyes. I was lucky, compared to Harry and Bill Foulkes—I saw only flashes of the horror. I was cosseted away from the worst of Munich. God knows what they witnessed, terrible, terrible things I have no doubt, but even they couldn't answer that nagging question that wouldn't go away: how could I be fifty yards away from the plane, alive, still attached to one of those big seats that were, when the house was hit, presumably just flung out from the middle of the plane where Dennis Viollet and I were sitting? I don't know and I'll never know. I can only go back to that amazement I know I will always feel about the fact that Harry and Bill were able to help people. This will always underpin my memories of that time when I seemed to have awakened to a kind of hell, with the Old Man groaning in pain and one team-mate lying near me, unmarked but plainly dead, whose identity, for reasons I'm now not completely sure of, will always be my secret, locked away very deeply.

Perhaps in other circumstances such a trauma would lose some of its rawness, because in the end I suppose time cures almost everything as it adds new layers of experience down the years, but with Munich this could never be so. It was a public matter, and the old who remember it want to talk about it as much as the young who have only read about it in books or seen it on old, grainy film. There is also another truth that cannot be denied. Munich changed not only those who were involved in it but also the club and the fans. United was no longer just a great football club: it embodied that experience, it was a dream that needed to be reawakened.

I think it helped me that I was always aware of my good fortune. It wasn't something I ever had to work on, and it helped me to survive—as the club survived—because I felt a responsibility that went beyond my own concerns. It was not, anyway, as if I lacked any examples in the matter of fighting on through the worst of situations. Ultimately, there was the example and the resolution of the Old Man.

When he came back to Old Trafford his face was deathly pale and you could see all the pain etched so deeply into it. He had seen so much of his football revolution and, much more importantly, so much of his life disappear in the flames of Munich. He looked around the dressing room and you could see in his eyes how hard it was for him to note all the missing faces. Perhaps inevitably, tears came. He said that for the moment Jimmy Murphy was in charge, but he was always thinking of us and the job we were tackling so well. I think beyond everything, he felt guilt that it was on the business of his great football dream that his boys had died. He had thrown them into big-time football years ahead of their time, and

163

they had not let him down. His eyes played across the faces of his new team, but they didn't seem to engage in real contact. It was as though he was looking for a point of recognition, something to reassure him that really the horror hadn't happened.

He left us with his favourite saying: 'Enjoy your football, boys, express yourselves. Let your talent out.' It was the classic belief that he would take to his grave nearly forty years later: a feeling about the way football should be played, the point of it, and when he returned as the master of Old Trafford, after convalescence in Switzerland, it would once again be at the centre of all he tried to achieve.

In the meantime, there was the job of winning the FA Cup, the league having slipped, predictably, out of our grasp with a string of defeats. It was a task Jimmy Murphy tackled with all his usual ferocity.

The tie against Sheffield Wednesday had been won on the greatest tide of emotion I would ever be part of in a football stadium, but it was a little different in the sixth round at West Bromwich. They were a strong and polished side, determined not to be caught up in the national wish fulfilment that United would rise up quickly to glory after the terrible events in Munich. In this, Albion were helped by some big-name players who were particularly keen to stick to the agenda of their own ambitions, notably wing half Bobby Robson, right back Don Howe and Derek Kevan, a big, strong centre forward who was in the process of bustling his way into the England team.

Jimmy Murphy's desperate attempt to strengthen our team in the leeway provided by the FA's waiving of the normal transfer regulations, had found a glint of gold in the signing of little Ernie Taylor. He might have been five years down the line from his massive

164

contribution to the 'Matthews Final', but he still retained a wonderful sharpness of thought and skill. He gave us the early lead, then helped to push us back in front when his brilliant shot smacked against the crossbar and rebounded into the path of young Alex Dawson. Albion had been helped by a dubious decision by referee Kevin Howley, who awarded them a goal which Harry Gregg, in his inimitably passionate way, insisted had not crossed the line. We were five minutes away from the semi-final, but then Albion, urged on by the voluble Robson, never a man to comfortably accept defeat, fought hard to earn a replay.

There was no capping the rising passion. Four days later, more than 30,000 fans tried to gatecrash Old Trafford. This second match was really hard, and we were having to stretch ourselves a little now because adrenaline can carry you only so far; in the shortfall, there is a lot of painful running to do, a lot of sucking in breath and telling yourself that you have to find a little more in yourself.

West Brom were over-running us for most the game, but I kept thinking, 'Well, maybe we can hang on, perhaps we can take some half-chance and nick it.' We had to do that because I felt that they would be too strong for us if it went to a third game; most of the time we were hanging on the ropes. With a couple of minutes to go, the ball came to me as I ran into what I thought was a likely position out on the right side, something I had been given the freedom to do in the new set-up. I knocked it past the Albion left back, Stuart Williams, in pursuit of what Jimmy Murphy said was one of an attacker's optimum situations— the ball in your control on the dead-ball line.

'Get on to the dead-ball line,' he would say,

165

'because when you are there the opposition panic. They're going in the wrong direction and you can't be offside.' Ideally, you have time to take a little look, but I was going too fast into a position about ten yards away from the corner flag. I had to be first to the ball because the referee was about to blow the final whistle and this might be the moment we could shape so much. I was able to answer another Murphy demand: 'Catch the defender on his heels, and by the time he's turned you're gone.' I was. When I did look up, I saw a single red shirt amid a clump of blue-and-white ones. God, I drove that ball in, putting into it everything I had left, and as I did so Colin Webster found a patch of space and turned it into the net. The crowd went mad; we all went mad; and when Bobby Robson was moaning after the match, I thought to myself, 'Well, we were brave, we did stick to the job.' Bobby was complaining, 'We got bloody nothing from the referee, we didn't get the bounce of the ball, and then they go and score right at the end.'

Jimmy Murphy was as ecstatic as the crowd because he had received from his players the gift he treasured most in football. His team had played beyond themselves and their physical resources because they knew, when they measured the odds that had piled up against them, that this was an opportunity that would not come again.

For the semi-final at Villa Park we drew a Second Division team, but one with some very special ingredients. Fulham had the magnificent general Johnny Haynes, Jimmy Hill, an eccentric but spectacular winger Tosh Chamberlain, a fine goalkeeper in Tony Macedo, the famous former striker, now converted midfielder Roy Bentley, an England left back Jim Langley, and a young, quick, right back who was taking his first strides towards the 1966 World Cup final—George Cohen.

This was a team with the balance of enough talent and enough experience to exploit the tiredness to which we had become increasingly prone with all the emotion that had gone into our performances in recent weeks—and which was a big factor when, just three days after our replay win, West Brom returned to Old Trafford and thrashed us 4–0 in a league match.

George Cohen recalled many years later that after the first semi-final match, which ended 2–2, I went up to him and said, 'Well done, son,' which I presumably intended as a gesture from a mature old pro to a young contender. I was, after all, a full year older than George. He had played well, but then so had I, scoring two and crashing one against the crossbar. In the replay at Highbury, Fulham had the fate I had feared for United in the quarter-finals against West Brom. They had had their moment, but it passed. Young Dawson, a powerfully built lad who maybe suffered down the road from the level of effort he was required to make through the months after Munich, put us in control of the game with a hat-trick. Then, after Fulham had fought their way back to 4–3, I was able to make the game safe in the ninetieth minute. I ran on to a ball on the right wing and hit it in my stride. It flew into the top corner. Somehow we had made it to Wembley—forty-nine days after the Munich air crash.

It was perhaps our finest moment since the tragedy, and in some ways the greatest achievement of my friend and my teacher Jimmy Murphy. He hated the limelight and as the Old Man recovered in hospital and then at home, he made it clear that he longed for the day 'The Boss' returned. Matt Busby was the leader; Jimmy Murphy was the faithful helper and minder. No manager ever had better cover for his back, no assistant was more selfless in his work for a club, its manager and its players.

Jimmy hated some of the jobs in football. He was happy to work in the rain and the wind, hour after hour, with some young player he thought of as a real prospect, but he could not bear to tell a player that, in the end, he had failed his test as a professional. That, he said, was a manager's job. Jimmy didn't want to hire or fire, he didn't want to impart news that he knew would cast a shadow over a young person's life. He was a teacher, a passionate and sometimes unscrupulous motivator, but if you wanted somebody to do the nitty and the gritty and the dirty of the manager's job you had to look elsewhere. The problem, though, was that United couldn't do that when Matt Busby lingered between life and death. Murphy was Busby's right arm and now that limb had to come into play. It did so magnificently. The background enforcer stepped into the harshest of light.

One of his shrewdest decisions, and a big reason why we were able to make our run on Wembley, was to more or less withdraw his young team from the post-Munich cauldron of Manchester. He realised that there was nowhere a young player could go in the city without feeling the great build-up of emotion and expectation. So much of it was meant kindly, but in the end pressure is pressure and Murphy rightly concluded that somehow it had to be dispelled.

His solution was to take us on frequent trips to Blackpool and the familiar, and relaxing, environment of the Norbreck Hotel. There we trained, walked by the sea, and had saunas which seemed sometimes to be doing more than drawing out sweat and impurities: you could sit in there and look at the wooden walls and feel cut off, utterly, from a world that at times seemed to be too close, too demanding. It was as though United had become too popular, too much a piece of public property.

This was still the feeling when we travelled down to London for the final. Every newspaper headline, every broadcast named us as the nation's team—everywhere, that was, except Bolton. Five years earlier Bolton Wanderers had battled against such country-wide partisanship when they came close to wrecking the romance of the 'Matthews Final'. This time they went a step further. They beat us 2–0.

Bolton had played hard but also well, and we had no bitter complaints. The Old Man was frail and grey on that spring day, and you could see on his face what an effort of will it had required from him to come to the famous ground and re-immerse himself in the passions of a big football match. He thanked us again for our performances and our willingness to give everything we had to the club. His words touched my belief that in a way the result of the cup final had been irrelevant. The important thing had been to get to Wembley. In the rush of games that followed the suspension of our season, and which we mostly lost, slipping to a final position of ninth in the league, the idea of getting to the final was the spark, the link with the past, and the inspiration.

The European Cup also went the way of the league. I flew off with England on their summer tour, while my United team-mates travelled by train to Milan to defend their 2–1 first leg advantage against such brilliant individuals as Juan Schiaffino of Uruguay and Nils Liedholm of Sweden. The Old

169

Man stayed at home to continue his recovery and hear, with a sigh, that his survivors, his new boys and his veteran stop-gap signings, had gone down 4–0.

So we had to settle for the Wembley experience which, as symbolism went, was potent enough. When the sirens blared on the field in Munich, Harry Gregg, Bill Foulkes, Dennis Viollet and I had been confronted with a future that made no sense and gave no encouragement. We grieved for our team-mates and we feared for what might lie in our own futures. Not one of us could have believed that in three months' time we would be playing in an FA Cup final. It told us, and the rest of the football world, that Manchester United were not a club who would go down easily. At the time the Old Man was asked how long it would take for his team to be a power again. Uncannily now when you look back, he said it would be five years.

CHAPTER 13

# FAMILY MATTERS

Five years is a long way down the road of a football club—and a man's life. Everything can change in that time and for both Manchester United and me it did.

United signed Denis Law from Torino and I married Norma Ball. Both United and I were huge beneficiaries. Law invigorated United with his astonishing competitive personality and wonderful talent. Norma bowled me over in a way that no girl had ever done before and would never do again for the rest of my days. She made my life, gave it a dimension and a depth that was beyond my grasp right up to the day I met her.

This conviction was confirmed in the deepest way by our marriage at St Gabriel's Church in Middleton, North Manchester and then by the arrivals of our daughters Suzanne and Andrea.

Because I am who I am, because there is something in me which has always made me uncomfortable with the celebrity side of football, I was a little disconcerted when some United fans showed up at the wedding in their red scarves, noisily offering their best wishes by wielding their rattles, but I was sure they meant well. I also suspected that nothing less than a full-scale earthquake could have detached me from the view that this was the happiest, most significant day of my life.

Certainly in the ensuing forty-six years there would never be a single moment when I had cause to doubt that youthful verdict.

In all that time I have had just one regret, one that I have never publicly addressed before. I have always hated the fact that the woman who brought so much to my life, who became the most important person in it, was put at the centre of a dispute I had with my family, and most controversially by my brother Jack.

Jack told the world—and confirmed it in his autobiography—that he believed it was Norma who drove a wedge between my mother Cissie and me; he said that my wife had airs and graces, indeed that she was 'hoity-toity', and it was because of her that I became estranged from the person who had given me so much from the moment I was born. For the record, I reject that now in public as I have always done in private.

Somehow, Norma was portrayed as the person who, rather than enriching my life and supporting me in every possible way in everything I tried to achieve, stood between me and my ability to keep close links with all that I held dear as a boy growing up in the North East. My mother is dead and I would never breathe a word that would dishonour her, or take away the love a son has for his mother, but I have to say that it is a travesty of the truth. Of course it is a great sadness that, as my married life progressed, as Suzanne and Andrea grew up, the links with Ashington became frayed and strained, but I have talked with people across a broad spectrum of life, and I am always amazed by the fact that so many have had similar experiences.

The truth is that when Norma first accompanied me to the North East, I know she went with every intention of getting on with my mother and all the family. In the latter ambition, in most cases, she succeeded easily, receiving a warm reception from so many of my relatives. However, things were never comfortable with my mother, and I can only speculate how many sons have had the same problem when they have gone home and introduced their girlfriends and future wives.

Why there should be friction was never a mystery to either Norma or me. My mother, perhaps because of her background, was always a strong character; always felt that she had to set the agenda for her family. Norma has rarely spoken of the decline of her relationship with my mother, and certainly not publicly, but I think I can speak for her in one very basic way. When my mother suggested something, and on occasions that is perhaps a mild way of putting it, Norma did not necessarily readily submit; she had her own way of doing things, her own perspective on the world, and I suppose that was one of the reasons why I had been so drawn to her.

Yet Norma's independence was never wrapped in any conscious effort to be defiant. She was more than ready to meet my mother at least halfway in order to facilitate compromise. Unfortunately, my mother wasn't always open to such overtures, from Norma or from others. This needs to be said in defence of my wife because of the impression that has been created publicly that she was the only member of my family to ever be at odds with my mother.

I had no fears about Norma's approach to the business of meeting and getting to know my family when we first travelled back to my roots. However, it quickly became apparent that my mother, such a strong woman who had become famous for her passionate interest in my football career and that of my brother Jack, would never freely embrace the girl with whom I intended to spend the rest of my life.

When I look back now, it seems unbelievable to me that it can happen that a son does not get on with his mother. Friends have told me, 'Oh, Bobby, it happens in so many families.' Perhaps so, but it does not make it any less painful, and this is especially so when you read about your own problems in the newspapers. The press interest made a major difference in the trials of the Charlton family; our situation inevitably became more high profile when Jack and I began to play for the England team, and our mother, for the reason that she was indeed a great character, seemed at times to become as famous as her sons.

When I trace back the difficulties that came to the surface down the years, and received publicity which I have always found very distressing, I see that perhaps part of the pattern was shaped by the fact that I mostly had to do things on my own. It's true my father often used to take me to the mine when he collected his wages, but quite a bit of my boyhood was spent away from home and maybe it helped to make me a little independent from my mother. I never doubted that she wanted the best for me, but sometimes her way of doing things, her style, was so different from mine. I had a tendency to hold back, almost to seek the shadows. That was not my mother's way. Once, when I was a kid, someone asked me for my autograph and I shrank back, but my mother insisted I sign. I suppose I'll never forget the embarrassment that overcame me at that moment.

I'm not suggesting that this was the reason why my mother and Norma did not get on, or why, for such a long time, I became much less close to my family, but maybe it was a contribution to the breakdown in understanding—maybe it was the grit in the corner of your eye that can make you weep.

I have always been hesitant to deal with this subject because I don't think anyone of feeling wants to discuss such problems in public, but now, as I'm trying to give some account of my life, I do not see how I can avoid it. Jack had his say when he wrote his book and I have to be honest: I was deeply offended by the picture he painted of my wife. He suggested that she had never tried to get on with my mother, and that it was because of her that the division in the family became so deep. I therefore feel obliged to defend my wife in a way that neither she nor I believed was necessary when the controversy first arose; we had our own lives and felt no obligation to fuel a fire which we believed would, in the way of all family disputes, either settle or not in the course of time.

The fact is that there has been some repairing down the years, and today, with my mother and father gone, Jack and I have rebuilt our relationship in a way that works for both of us. Maybe we are quite different characters, but a brother is a brother. We have the same blood and have made similar journeys in life. I'm proud of what he has achieved, both as a player and a manager, and I know that he has always been generous about my ability and my dedication as a player. We shared something when England won the World Cup that few families could ever dream of, but then if brothers are brothers, families are families; blood, no doubt, is thicker than water, but sometimes it does not flow so easily.

Now, in this my own story, the priority for me is that, with regard to Norma, the record is put straight, because of her character and the love that she has always given to my daughters and me. She has been a wonderful partner and mother, and I cannot shake the view that for some time she was badly treated by some members of my family.

If I reach for a word to describe her it is invariably the same one as all those years ago. The word is 'sensational'. She has travelled with me all around the world—and always I have been proud to have her at my side. If she comes with me to a match or some public occasion and we get separated, whenever I look for her I find her surrounded by people, this still young person—young to me—and I get a flush of never-changing pride that so many people agree with me, that she is so bright and lovely and so interesting.

There has never been an edge to Norma. She has also been very strong at times when I have had to make difficult decisions. She has always been at the forefront of such conversations; never dominating any discussions, but always making her points, always presenting a full picture of our needs as a family. She can be very tough. She doesn't mess around if she disagrees with me—or anyone else. She says what she thinks, but not in any abrasive way, and certainly she puts me in my place if she suspects, almost invariably correctly, that I'm getting a bit carried away with myself. One of the criticisms of Norma that Jack aired publicly, and I found most hurtful, was that she put herself up above other people. It has never been so in my experience—and certainly not when she found herself caught up in the company of characters like Jimmy Murphy and Bill Shankly.

When Jimmy was keen on having one of his sessions, Norma would be invited with me to join him for a few drinks, and she would listen attentively to all his theories about football. Once I remember her saying, 'Now, Mr Murphy, what do you think of the 4–3–3 formation?' and of course the old football man was charmed. That, too, made me proud; for Jimmy, football was the centre of the world, and no question could have been more guaranteed to take any awkwardness out of the situation of a young woman being drawn into the alien world of football talk fuelled by beer and whisky or, if you were unlucky, Mateus Rosé.

Once, when we were newly married, my mother-in-law Nora, who lived with us after Norma's father Tommy died soon after the wedding, reported early one morning that a strange man was lurking in the garden. Did we have a stalker? We were living in the Cheshire village of Lymm, where a lot of football teams, including the Brazilians of the 1966 World Cup, stayed at a nearby hotel when they were playing in Manchester. On this occasion it was Liverpool, and the man in the garden was Bill Shankly. He had been told I lived in the village and, as always, he was restless on the day of a big game. He had come to seek me out for some football talk, so I said to Norma, 'I'm sorry, love, but I think you'll have to put the kettle on.'

Norma was such a perfect hostess, talking about football with Shankly in a way that I found a little stunning, that I became a mere extra in the scene and soon enough I made my excuses and prepared to leave for the game. They were deep in conversation when I left. When I returned Norma explained that the Liverpool team bus had eventually pulled up outside our house, summoning the manager with a toot of the horn.

I do not wish to make any unfair and, still less, any unflattering comparisons between my wife and my mother, but plainly they were different people, different characters, and my hurt was that right from the start it was clear they would not get on. Any son will tell you how important it is for his wife and his mother to have an easy relationship; anything less than that, and there is an immediate problem, a pain and a stress in his life that in almost every case is unwanted and, in its way, shocking.

My mother was strong in a different way from Norma, but there was no question about her love for Jack and me or ours for her. Of course she had to be strong. You had to be resilient to come through a war and bring up four lads in the North East on such low wages, when every day was a battle to put some decent food on the table. I have never forgotten that. But however close you are to someone, and who could be closer than a mother and a son, it is still difficult if one has a certain nature and the other's is not really compatible.

There is no doubt that in many ways I was more like my father; he sometimes complained that he was fed up with football, the need to talk about it all the time, and there was quite a bit of that in me when my mother told me that time to sign an autograph for some stranger and I was just a kid of thirteen or fourteen and was embarrassed by the whole business. My mother didn't recognise that; for her, life was a matter of going and getting what you could and not being too shy in celebrating your success, because if you didn't, who would?

What was most difficult for me was my mother's pride in my football ability. She would talk openly about it in front of people I didn't know well, and that would make me cringe. It made me want to run for the shadows. My mother couldn't understand those feelings. At times like that I think I rather bewildered her. She was a Milburn and it was the most natural thing to be good at football. I suspect, deep down, it was something of a regret for her that she wasn't born to play the game herself. Certainly her career would not have suffered from any lack of confidence. She had enough for herself—and her sons.

As soon as I met Norma, I knew straight away that she was what I wanted, what I needed, and it wasn't just that she was beautiful. I felt good around her; it felt so natural to be in her company. I was a little slow to make that feeling clear to her, though, and we stopped seeing each other for a while. She fell out with me because she felt I had taken her for granted; perhaps she thought that as a young star of Manchester United I had an idea I could just snap my fingers and the pretty girls would come running. In fact, it wasn't quite like that at all, and after our relationship was back on and set up properly, most of my friends and team-mates said that she had had a scarcely believable effect on me. I paid more attention to my appearance, my smart club blazer came to the fore, my shoes were cleaned more regularly—but before that, she had been required to give me a rather serious dressing down because of my sometimes negligent approach to our relationship. That was why we'd split up.

Then, one day, I was having lunch with a couple of pals in a little place called Snack Time, just across the road from the Queen's Hotel, when she walked by. The effect on me was instant and overwhelming. Wordlessly, I left my lunch—it was probably my usual pie and chips—and my friends, and said to myself, 'You've made a pig's ear of this once, don't do it twice.' As I followed her down the street, moving smartly now, I kept repeating, 'You know this is it, it has to be it.'

179

It was indeed—but in all the pleasure and the joy of being together again, there was the sticking point of my mother's resistance.

She didn't like Norma and, I have to say, in the course of the relationship, that feeling was reciprocated. At first, when I suggested I take her up to the North East, to introduce her to old friends and family, and of course to show her off, Norma was willing enough, but increasingly she became reluctant. She got on well with so many people in my world, especially my dad, but there was no meeting point, no common ground with my mother. It was very painful and I couldn't get it out of my head that my mother was being very unfair both to Norma and me. This, after all, was the woman I loved and wanted to be with.

It made me think about the past and my relationship with my mother, and maybe it brought back some old and half-buried resentments. I honour my mother's commitment to my career and my potential and to the influence of her father, the great Tanner, but in the drive to fulfil my own dream, and perhaps my mother's, maybe something was lost along the way.

She never forced me into anything I didn't want to do, but I suppose that at certain times I felt she was pushing me a little too hard, when sometimes I didn't want to be pushed.

I have already touched on one of the great myths of my life in football—that my mother taught me how to play, how to kick a ball. It made a nice newspaper story, and sometimes it was even accompanied by pictures, but in fact I had made my own decisions about my future, even at the earliest age. I was totally focused, secure in the belief that I would make it in the game. My mother's great gift to me was that she always supported me—right up, that is, to the matter in which I couldn't be pushed: the choice of my wife. Unless you are a very odd sort of person you do not go to ask your mother if you may marry someone.

It started badly, and I'm afraid the frost never thawed. I hoped that the years would soften things, and that when the girls came along it would help the mother and the grandmother to draw a little closer, but it never happened. The relationship refused to get better. At first, when I returned to the North East, on some football business perhaps, I would make a point of going to Ashington, and I would reclaim my old room for a day or two. But it was difficult and as time went on I saw very little of my mother. My life was going on, my kids were growing up, and Norma and I had to make our own way. If it was hurtful in a way that I have rarely expressed, it wasn't so difficult in the sense that I believed I had to make a choice: it was never a case of split loyalties. I had made a contract with my wife, I had my own family, and I could hardly tell the most influential women in my life that they had to do something that was clearly beyond them. I couldn't make them like each other.

You might ask if Norma tried hard enough, but I would not accept the validity of the question. Norma is a strong-willed woman—it has made her such a strength to me over the years—but in one respect she is probably no different from most people: she wants to be liked, she doesn't want to feel that in someone's eyes everything she does or says is bound to be wrong. There was a clash of personalities, right from the start, and I realised early on that, even if Norma could make friends easily in my old world, even if many members of my family could embrace her, there was no doubt that she was involved in a losing battle with my mother.

The added difficulty was that Jack not only took my mother's side, which was of course his right in the privacy of family life, but he also went public with criticism of my wife. I found this quite unacceptable, and I told him so. I said that often life was a lot more complicated than he made out, and the fact that our mother and Norma did not get on was something that was not uncommon in families. It was a sadness, no doubt, but it was not a matter for handing out easy blame.

There were times, certainly, when Norma could not go along with my mother; it was her right, and however sad I felt about the way things had gone, I always stood by my wife. She was the woman I loved, the mother of my children, and if I had been so lucky in so many things, it was my misfortune that this wonderful woman could not be accepted by my mother. Of course I loved my mother, and of course I respected her, but over the question of Norma I could not say anything other than that she had been unfair. There are occasions in life when it is necessary to be clear in your mind about such a matter.

At the end, when we went to my mother's funeral with great sadness over the futility of any effort to heal the wounds, I accepted that what had been said and done had to be over. Now, when we meet at England reunions, Norma and Jack's wife Pat speak and talk about our families, and it is the same with Jack and me. When he is in the Manchester area, he pops into our house and sometimes it is easy, sometimes less so. We are brothers and we have shared so much, and I'm grateful that we are still able to be together, and that it is natural for us to see each other. There were moments, especially after Norma was criticised in public, when I might have exploded, and if that had happened I think everything would have been over for ever. However, life goes on and if I have learned anything it is that it is necessary to accept the need for a little bit of give and take.

Jack has a good heart, I know, and there is no question that along the way he too has been hurt, but my point to him—as it was when I was critical of him publicly when, while we were still players, he announced on television that he had a little black book which listed the names of opponents he intended to get even with on the field—was that occasionally he can be too impetuous, too eager to speak, and to lash out, before thinking through a problem.

I'm pleased to be able to report that Jack is now more receptive to Norma, seems to accept a little more that she has no feelings of regret about her relationship with my mother because she went into it hoping for the best and doing all that she thought she could without losing any pride in herself.

For myself there will always be the sadness that after the great day Jack and I shared at Wembley after winning the World Cup in 1966, when we embraced and agreed that no two football brothers from the North East could have shared such a moment of fulfilment, when maybe our bloodline could not have been more perfectly expressed in the colours of our country, the joy of our experience was somehow clouded by what followed. But then this was only to a certain extent, because, after all, we were our mother's sons, and there is no question that, whatever came after, she had that supreme moment of pride we shared with her.

Would we have got there without her? Maybe,

maybe not, but of course on one huge detail there could be no question. She gave us life and she brought us up the best way she could; she did it with a great passion of her own and in a style that was quite inimitable. She enlisted the help of all her football clan, assuming that they would be as enthusiastic as she was about the prospect that her sons would add to the legends of the family. She fought for us and she made sacrifices for us, and I will never stop loving her for that. The tragedy, for me, was that in the end she could not give me what I wanted most. She couldn't love my wife. I just wish that she could have understood how much I love Norma, and how important it was for me to have her accepted for what she has always been: the shining light of my life.

CHAPTER 14

# REBUILDING

The genius of Matt Busby reappeared in those years of
renewal after Denis Law made his dramatic entrance
and Manchester United once again became a team of
colour and excitement, but there had been a great
weariness on his face when he calculated that it
would take five years for the team to be truly
recognisable again.

Law was signed for £115,000 in the summer of
1962, before we returned to Wembley to win the FA
Cup against Leicester City after the long, bitter
winter of 1962–63. I had seen him play many times for
Manchester City before his move to Italy, and you
could not but be impressed by his speed and his
intelligence and that mysterious ability of all great
players to suddenly appear in the right place at the
right moment.

I was delighted the Old Man had made a signing of
such quality—it worked against the idea that the club
would never again touch the levels of consistent
brilliance and excitement that were achieved in the
years before Munich. I told Denis this when he
arrived for his first training session. I said, 'It's very
good to have you around,' and he gave me that
sidelong, slightly quizzical smile that would become so
familiar to me down the years. It was as though a lot of
the magic and the aura of the old United had been
conjured up at a single stroke.

Matt Busby had also picked up Paddy Crerand
from Celtic. He passed the ball quite beautifully, and,

with Johnny Giles having an impressive game on the right wing, there was real quality in the performance which brought the club the FA Cup, its first trophy since the tragedy. Spring was turning into summer, after an unprecedented fixture pile-up, and there was real warmth and expression in our play. On this day we were no longer grinding out results, patching up our weaknesses. We looked like Manchester United again. We passed, we ran, we scored, easing up with the race well won at 3–1. For United, who had a young Irishman called George Best limbering up in the youth team, the promise was of the best of times.

However, before the arrival of Law and the eventual eruption of Best, sometimes it had to be admitted that even the five-year plan seemed to be an optimistic forecast. The reasons for this could not be avoided; you couldn't have a great young side torn literally from the sky and expect to proceed with just a few missed heartbeats. This was especially so if the architect of not just a team but an idea, a unique philosophy, carried so much hurt and sadness in his eyes. The fact was that to be close to Matt Busby in that first year or so after the crash was to fear something that was very hard to admit; something that struck at the very heart of the drive for resurrection. It was that even if the Old Man managed to fight back with all the nerve and judgement at his disposal, and know great success again, the chances were he would never be quite the same as he was boarding that plane in Munich. He would never stop drawing the line between good players and great ones; he would never lose his vision of what football should be—and in the end he got to where his deepest ambition lay—but there were times when the struggle was desperate and you knew that he was suffering doubts he had never known before.

It wasn't just a question of physical pain and the matter of whether he could any longer take the strain of the football life—his wife Jean, and so many admirers, led by Jimmy Murphy, persuaded him that he could do that in the days after we had fought our way to the 1958 FA Cup final. What became apparent was that his body could recover to some large extent, but his old conviction, his amazing ability to transmit confidence and composure, was beyond any complete healing.

During his recuperation in Switzerland in the summer, Jean Busby conquered her husband's terrible doubts about the wisdom of his carrying on— and his belief that he had let down all those parents who had entrusted their sons to his care and his great European adventure. But down the years, one by one, the secrets of his torment became visible in a sigh, in a distant look in his eyes and—in the last crisis of his career, when so many blamed him for refusing to let new managers like Wilf McGuinness and then Frank O'Farrell have their heads—in a word or two to someone like me that he had reached a point when he no longer had the heart or the energy for the battle.

In the first months after Munich he doubted himself, his calling as the messiah of a great football club and, he confessed later, he even doubted the deep faith in God that had carried him through so many difficult days since, as a young boy, he lost his father in the First World War trenches of France.

All this made it remarkable that United should emerge under his guidance for a third time with a third team of great brilliance, but in some ways, I know, he became almost the reluctant leader.

People told him, 'You're still the only one who can do the job' and he accepted the burden. He felt he had to because if Jimmy Murphy was a superb lieutenant, and the most courageous stand-in when his beloved boss lay in a hospital in Germany, he was not, by his own admission, a natural leader of a great football club. That was Matt Busby's renewed destiny—but as the years wore on you could see clearly the cost to him.

What happened in the long run after Munich was a kind of miracle, no doubt, and the Old Man never ceased to be an inspiration and a force—but sometimes, towards the end of his reign, he confided to me that a combination of weariness and pain had taken an unshakeable hold. He yearned for someone to take up the burden, so that he could withdraw into the margins—but be sure that the club that had become his life would be secure.

It would take a quarter of a century for that man to present himself in the form of Alex Ferguson, but of course in the meantime, the job had to be done and a football empire preserved.

The first part of the campaign was survival, and on the opening day of the 1958–59 season that objective seemed to be attainable to an extent beyond anyone's dreams, not least my own. I scored three goals in a 5–2 defeat of a Chelsea who could not build on a piece of brilliant individualism by their new young scoring sensation, Jimmy Greaves—and if you listened to the sound of the 52,000 Old Trafford crowd you might have believed that suddenly mere survival was the least of our challenges. There had been serious fears that our Wembley appearance against Bolton a few months earlier had been a step away from reality, and that the patching up done on the team in the days after Munich would break apart soon enough.

But wasn't there magic in the air again? We prayed

so hard that it was so, and three days later, at the City ground, Nottingham Forest were put to the sword as mercilessly as Chelsea. In just over twenty minutes we were three up and untouchable. I scored two more and Albert Scanlon seemed healed and was brilliant again. He had undermined the Chelsea defence with his speed and his crossing and he was no less sharp against Forest, scoring our second goal. Here, surely, was a powerful symbol of the team's resurrection. Before we flew to Belgrade, Albert had been rampant in that unforgettable game at Highbury, and now he had regained his pace and his confidence—at least it was convenient and uplifting to think so.

There were gaps in our side, both physically and mentally—deep down we knew that, I think—but in football there is always the element of hope and potential and this was, by any standards, a remarkable start to a season which had been greeted with such apprehension. Not only did little Ernie Taylor appear to be comfortably maintaining his ability to create rhythm with his precise and clever passing, but my friend Wilf McGuinness was producing performances of such power and confidence that within weeks he had made a stunning arrival in the England team. No young player had ever faced a more daunting challenge; he had to run in the footsteps of Duncan Edwards in both the shirt of Manchester United and England, but if this created any doubts in his mind, he concealed them magnificently. His running and tackling created great surges of conviction through the team. Looking back, it is so easy, and with hindsight so distressing, to remember how passionately Wilf embraced the vision of United as the team who would not, could not, be snuffed out by the cruelty of Munich.

He was a great friend and a great competitor, and it was one of the quirks of life then that when I was getting married, and nominated him as my best man, the ruling wisdom of the day was that it would be wrong for him, a Catholic boy like so many of my closest friends at United, to take those duties in a Protestant church. Maurice Setters, who was made of similar tough material and came to us from West Bromwich as a man to give us some force and steel, took over Wilf's duties in the church—and in the team. Maurice was signed soon after Wilf broke his leg in a reserve match, a personal tragedy that was fought against with courage right up to the moment medical advice came crashing in on the spirit of a player cut down so early, so harshly.

Wilf's disaster came a year after his extraordinary efforts to repair the damage that had been inflicted on the club. For everyone in the dressing room it was another terrible reminder that in football danger can lurk at moments of the greatest certainty. Wilf McGuinness was surely set for a great career, but then so had been Duncan Edwards and John Doherty. Duncan had gone in the great tragedy; John and now Wilf had suffered the kind of random blow that football can deliver at any moment. It gave me another jab of anxiety.

On reflection, it was as though the sad fate of Wilf confirmed one apprehension at Old Trafford—that maybe our present run into second place in the league was more than anything a mirage, an illusion that took us away from certain truths. The fact was that, despite a run of victories, an impressive revival after some drastically sliding form before Christmas, we were never going to catch Wolves, the eventual champions in the 1958–59 season.

Under Cullis, Wolves had kept their strength and their standards and while we fell away from contention the following season, they failed to keep their title, against the challenge of an impressive Burnley team, by just one point. Tottenham were also back in the race now, fortified by David Mackay alongside Danny Blanchflower, and with Cliff Jones producing remarkable form on the left wing, and were about to achieve the Double—the milestone that the Old Man had held so high in his ambitions before Munich. Underlining our discomfort was the fact that the quality of the Tottenham football, particularly, could not fail to remind us of the levels United had achieved before the crash.

It was around this time, I suppose, that I acquired a certain reputation for being a little aloof, and perhaps somewhat reluctant to accept the arrival of players I didn't know and had not grown up with in the way I had the Busby Babes.

I believe the truth was that I felt I had enough to do just playing my game; I didn't feel equipped to do anyone else's job and, for example, I was a little uncomfortable when the Old Man came to me and asked my opinion of Maurice Setters in the wake of Wilf's injury. What did I think of him? Maurice became a good friend, but I didn't really know him at that point. All I could say was that he was an extremely strong presence when he played for West Bromwich; you knew you had a serious opponent on the field when he showed up so obviously full of determination and ready to tackle anyone. But would he fit in, was he a United player? I just didn't know. I was, I reckoned, still too much of a kid to pass such judgements.

As it turned out, Maurice played with great

commitment for the club before he finally lost his place to Nobby Stiles after suffering a knee injury; he had a good spirit and good humour, and I always recall with a smile the time we played together at Liverpool in an especially hard-fought game. We were pushing to get back into the match and were about to take a throw-in. Maurice bustled over to the touchline to collect the ball but a young lad kept hold of it. Before joining United, Maurice had had talks with Liverpool, but he was still amazed when the boy, with the ball still tightly gripped in his hands, said, 'Maurice, why didn't you come to us? Were the clubhouses not good enough for you?'

This was a period when my perspective was that things had been happening to me very quickly, and then suddenly people were coming to me for views and opinions that I didn't really feel ready to give. This included other players who had problems, and there were times, if I am honest, when I wondered how long some of the new players would last at the club. It was not a question, at least in my own mind, of my passing negative verdicts on any of those who had come into the void left by Munich, and if my demeanour was a little cool maybe it was because, despite the goals and the upward profile of my career, I too was in the position of just feeling my way forward.

Certainly I could see the point of Ernie Taylor's craft and the tackling power of Stan Crowther—and the skills of Albert Quixall, who joined us from Sheffield Wednesday in 1958 for a record fee then of £45,000. Albert played a significant role in my rush of goals—when I broke through an offside trap often it was to get on to the end of one of his perfectly placed passes. However, it was also true that Albert, behind

192

the image of a new blond star of English football, had his own difficulties in settling down in a club which expected so much from everyone, and not least from a record signing.

It would be wrong now to ignore my sense that in the club's hope and determination to rebuild there was not also a touch of panic. You couldn't have the old seamless growth in the new situation in which we found ourselves; inevitably there was a need to speculate and take chances.

In the meantime, we had to battle as best as we could towards a point of breakthrough. That came, I believe, with the signing of Denis Law. Before that Matt Busby and Jimmy Murphy had had to probe the market with limited funds, and therefore had to look for the best in home-grown young players like Alex Dawson and Mark Pearson. At the time it didn't create in me an overwhelming feeling that our future success was in any way guaranteed. The boys were rushed into action and they did well for a time, but there was an immense pressure on them and I imagined there would be a point when the club would ask: how much are they improving, are they going to emerge with the amount of quality we need?

Alex Dawson was not the most rounded footballer, but he had been physically awesome as a youth and was someone who fitted perfectly the stereotype of the big, strong striker. In those days, when so many managers picked a team they wondered, 'Who is going to knock around defenders and score the goals? Who is going to dominate in the air?' For a while, before he was transferred to Preston North End, big Alex was able to supply the answer.

There were some bleak days indeed and after one game at Burnley, a team of champions brilliantly orchestrated by the great Northern Ireland inside forward Jimmy McIlroy, the ever controversial Bob Lord made a bitter attack on the new United. He said that we had turned into a team of 'thugs'. The Burnley chairman was no doubt a remarkable character, and unquestionably his club were doing a lot of things right, but his attack after a rough game seemed to many to be below the belt. Maybe it was a settling of some old scores, from old battles when the balance of power was somewhat different, but it did represent a low point in our efforts to rebuild both our team and our image.

My own reaction was to shrug my shoulders because it seemed that a day didn't pass without some lesson being handed down from the Burnley mountaintop. However, I recall an incident some time later, when I happened to be sitting next to Bob Lord at a testimonial dinner. It was when the issue of players' wages was boiling to the surface and, during the course of a wider conversation on the subject, I couldn't believe that such a man was involved in negotiations that would affect the prospects and the livings of so many people: young men who loved to play football but also had families to think about. Eventually, I made my contribution to the debate and said, 'But surely these are matters which have to be discussed in this day and age? We are talking about the rights of men in a free society, and these are issues which are not going to go away. Directors are just a part of football—they don't own it.' He turned to me with what seemed to be heavy contempt and said, 'Come back and see me in five years' time, sonny.'

Nearly half a century later, I can only speculate on what he might have had to say on the day that Cristiano Ronaldo signed his new contract with

United. Neither of us could have anticipated that a twenty-two-year-old, even one possessing the most startling gifts, would be guaranteed around £6 million a year for five years, but no doubt the effect on Mr Lord would have been rather more dramatic than it was on me. Yes, the scale of the rewards being handed to Cristiano were coming from a new world, a new dimension, but if so much money is pouring into football, if the market can stand it, who better to profit than a young player giving so much excitement and pleasure to the people who sit in the stands, or turn on the televisions, and make football so strong? Back at the turn into the sixties Bob Lord just couldn't believe that footballers would one day have the right to negotiate out of their own value and their own strength.

The signing of Noel Cantwell from West Ham United in November 1960 was one of the club's more positive and successful moves. He gave us, maybe especially in the light of the kind of charges made by Bob Lord, something that we sorely needed— authority and a deep sense of self-belief, the kind that Roger Byrne had carried so easily.

Noel was a big, handsome man, a natural sportsman who had for some time been the captain of the Republic of Ireland. He filled a gap that maybe we had not clearly realised had existed as we scrambled to recover from the effects of Munich. He came from the West Ham hothouse of tactics and new training ideas which over the years would produce a stream of managers and coaches like Malcolm Allison, Frank O'Farrell, John Bond and Malcolm Musgrove—and would eventually be commanded by Ron Greenwood, one of the game's most influential figures after his work in cultivating the great World

Cup triumvirate of Bobby Moore, Martin Peters and Geoff Hurst.

Noel was impatient with the training methods that existed generally in the game—and at times he made it clear that he thought a club of United's status should have made greater strides in this area. Yet, however strong his views and however freely he expressed them, he had a knack of getting his points across without causing any lasting offence. Maybe he wasn't a diplomat in the way of the Old Man, but he certainly had great style. He talked about the game constantly and with much eloquence, and later it was no surprise when his name was mentioned as a future manager of United. That possibility receded when it became clear that Matt Busby had recast the side soundly and had made it competitive again, along with conquering many of his own post-Munich doubts and demons. Cantwell's career later became somewhat becalmed at Coventry City, but it said a lot for his impact at such a difficult time of transition that so many saw him as a potential leader of the club.

As someone who always tried to keep his nose out of such issues until they sought me out, my appreciation of Noel Cantwell was much more straightforward. I liked him as a man and, if there was such a thing, I thought he was a United type. I also admired him as a player. He suffered from injuries, and eventually the challenge of Tony Dunne, and sometimes the quality of his playing ability was overlooked, but he was a defender of considerable class, strong on the left side and with a very nice touch. When he led us out for the 1963 cup final, I thought, 'This is good—we have a real captain.'

At that point, when I was in my mid-twenties, I

had no ambitions for the armband. I still felt, and to be honest deep down the thought never left me, I had enough to do supervising my own performances. Still, I felt a sense of great pride when, a year or so after Cantwell's departure, I was taken aside by the Old Man and told it was time for me to take up the leadership of the team. After Munich the role had gone briefly to Dennis Viollet and Bill Foulkes, and then, when their hard-driving successor Maurice Setters lost his place through injury and the rise of Nobby Stiles, Denis Law had a spell of captaincy. Maybe in the end it was decided I had accumulated the right amount of experience, and perhaps that I had a certain evenness of temperament for the job. I said I was honoured and that I would always try to lead the only way I could, which was by example.

After Cantwell, Matt Busby and Jimmy Murphy were thwarted when they made what they thought would be an equally crucial move for another top-class defender—Blackburn Rovers' imposing Welsh international centre half Mike England. A £100,000 bid was put in to Blackburn, but it was rejected. For many years Jimmy went on about the scale of the miss, saying, 'We could have had one of the best centre halves around if we'd forked out another £7,000.' Even today, I think of Murphy's fury when I see clubs haggling over the cost of a player a manager has identified as a potentially vital recruit. So much of United's buying in those transition years was aimed at strengthening weaknesses rather than shaping a team for the future, and that was probably inevitable in our circumstances. Stan Crowther had supplied some muscle and strength in the first months after Munich, but you never really felt he was going to become part of the building. Perhaps understandably,

I remember him most for the fact that in all my years in the game he was the one opponent, after he moved to Chelsea, to leave a permanent mark on me—a small scar on my left leg.

Ernie Taylor, like Crowther, had been parachuted into the emergency, and in their different ways they confirmed Jimmy Murphy's ability to recognise valuable qualities across the whole range of football talent, but they were both gone by the halfway point of the 1958–59 season, Taylor returning to his North East roots when he signed for Sunderland.

Taylor and Crowther missed our charge up the league in the New Year, but it was a feat which was made to look merely cosmetic soon enough as we entered what might be classed as the years of struggle. Ironically, we reached our lowest point, a nineteenth place in the First Division, during the run-up to the 1963 cup final which would prove as much a deliverance as a triumph.

One reason for our losing momentum was that it became clear soon enough, after that rush of goals and second place in the league in the first post-Munich season, that the pace and cleverness along the wings that had been a United staple since the days of Jimmy Delaney and Charlie Mitten had run low with the loss of David Pegg and Johnny Berry.

For a while there had been some reason for a more optimistic view. Warren Bradley had done well for us after being drafted in from the top amateur club Bishop Auckland. He didn't have the wiles of Berry, but he was quick and brave and he knew how to cross the ball. His initial impact was good enough to win him a few appearances with England, but in the long haul it was clear the Old Man wanted more. Warren, who would go on to a fine career as a headmaster, was sold to Bury.

Also, Albert Scanlon had at first promised a full recovery in the 1958–59 season, scampering down the left wing and putting in a stream of crosses, many of which I benefited from as I scored twenty-nine goals, missing Jack Rowley's club record by just one. But behind Albert's appearance back in the limelight was a sad fact which became more and more apparent down the weeks and the months. He was not the same man. He was not the winger who performed so brilliantly at Highbury a few days before Munich. The reality could be pushed back only for so long. His career was ebbing and he too was sold the following season, to Newcastle United. On Tyneside he made just a few appearances before slipping down into the lower division—another survivor of Munich who found the years hard and painful after the first relief of coming through it with his life, and after a brave fight against his injuries.

Another contender was the Ulsterman Sammy McMillan, a game player but one who, for all his effort, failed to provide the bite and the spark on the flank that Matt Busby and Jimmy Murphy now believed was vital if the team was to get back its old rhythm and balance.

At that time a lack of width, and thus no regular stream of crosses, was still seen as a basic deficiency, even though new trends working against the orthodox brilliance of wingers like Stanley Matthews and Tom Finney were on the horizon. The old convention that a full back alone would tackle a quick and talented winger was running towards the end of its shelf life, and at Manchester City Don Revie had been given the deep-lying role pioneered by the great Hungarian Nandor Hidegkuti. However, even though there were breezes of change in football, if not a full blowing wind, the prevailing fashion was still to have a big centre forward feeding on crosses, and doing it quite ruthlessly with pushes and shoves and plenty of use of his elbows.

At Old Trafford a decision was made. We needed a new winger. It was late in the 1959–60 season, when the problem had become very apparent, that the Old Man spoke to me after a training session. He said, 'You can use your left foot and your right. We're struggling a bit on the left side. What about playing left wing?' It was typical of the Old Man that an order would be couched in terms that suggested you might have a choice. It was bit of a shock because I had grown to love playing in midfield; I liked the freedom of action, the ability to roam wherever I wanted in pursuit of a chance to move on goal. But I did see the problem. We had wingers, but we didn't have one creating danger—or winning the confidence of his team-mates as they launched themselves into runs on goal. For one reason or another they were not delivering, and the scoring opportunities for Dennis Viollet, Quixall and me—which had been so plentiful the previous season—were dwindling at a critical rate. It was a surprise to be asked at that point in my career to play an entirely different role, but I thought, 'Well, I'm quick enough, I can cross the ball, why should I be worried? I can play left wing.'

It was frustrating in the first training sessions that followed the move. When the cries kept swirling in from Jimmy Murphy, 'Stay on your line,' my first reaction was, 'Oh, maybe I'm not sure about this.' But even though I missed my freedom so acutely, I did tell myself, 'Well, I'll adapt, the important thing is that I'm playing, I'm not harmed by injury.' Though it was jarring to be placed in what felt a bit like a straitjacket, I did meet some early success. In my first game on the wing I supplied the cross for the opening goal from Alex Dawson in a 3–1 defeat of Nottingham Forest, then scored the other two. On the right side Johnny Giles, who like me thought of himself as a midfielder, also had a lively game.

When I really thought about it, it was not so hard to see the point of the decision. I was sharp over twenty yards and I could use my left foot. I scored three more in the next three games and for a little while I was quite mollified. 'Well,' I thought, 'it's not as though I'm out of balance and I can't use my left foot. I'm playing well, and anyway, I probably won't be out here for too long.'

It was three years before I returned to what I would always regard as my natural hunting ground, the wide stretches across the middle of the field. Some of the time was made quite hellish by Jimmy Murphy's voice in my ear. I was so close to him out there on the wing and he was relentless. 'Stay there, don't move!' he would yell, and my frustration often came close to breaking point. Once, at Nottingham Forest, I swore I didn't touch the ball for twenty-five minutes. It provoked the saying at Old Trafford that you could die of cold out on the left wing waiting for a pass.

However, I never reached the point of complaining officially, despite the prompting from Jackie Milburn, who thought I had graduated to the point where I could make my own demands. Trouble was, I couldn't have made the argument to Jimmy or the Old Man that I wasn't playing well. They could have said, 'Look, you're helping the team, you're scoring goals and you're playing so well you have even been recalled by England.'

In fact I was enjoying the benefit of both my own

natural speed and that early education by Jimmy, who spent so many hours teaching me how to 'throw a shoulder' and strike when my marker was on the back foot. 'Just do it straight away,' he urged me. 'Throw that shoulder as if you're going inside and you'll catch them on their heels and be gone.'

On my way back into the England team I played for the Football League against the Scottish League. They had a little right back called Bobby Shearer, a typical little red-haired Scottish full back of the type that was beginning to go out of fashion. He was a good, hard-tackling pro, but after the game I said to myself that I hoped I would be playing against him when Scotland came to Wembley in a few weeks' time. He played, we won 9–3 and I lost count of the times I was able to follow the Murphy formula and knock the ball past him. I didn't score, but did have a very effective game.

Overall, the conclusion had to be that despite the irritation—and sometimes I made it clear to the bench and my team-mates it was more than that—of not seeing enough of the ball, I was still able to make an impact at regular intervals, and a good contribution to the team. However, there were difficult days. For instance, playing against my future World Cup team-mate George Cohen was never an easy challenge. He was at the forefront of the new full backs, quick and hard and unwilling to give a winger an easy yard. Once, during an England game in Peru, I was made angry in a way that summed up so much of the frustration that I carried in my years on the wing. The Peruvian right back just grabbed me whenever I went by him. Each time the referee waved play on. Later, at a reception, I said to the official, who spoke very good English, 'I don't want this to sound like sour grapes, but isn't there a rule somewhere that when a full back is beaten he is not entitled to wrap his arms around the player who has gone by him.' Straight faced, the referee said, 'Yes, you're quite right, but we don't follow that rule here.'

In a new era of defensive play, with the development of quick and often highly ruthless defenders, it seemed inevitable that my professional life could only get harder. Then a miracle came along and the Old Man and Jimmy Murphy decided that I had served my time on the wing and I could return to the wide and welcoming terrain of midfield. The miracle had a name. It was called George Best.

# CHAPTER 15

## TEAM OF STARS

On the field, if not always off it, I understood immediately the meaning of the arrival of first Denis Law, then George Best. In the past I had wondered whether my ideal of the Manchester United player had been lost forever. Now that doubt vanished.

Though we were never close in a day-by-day, personal way, and our lives rarely intertwined beyond the affairs of the football club, we knew how each of us contributed to the rise of the team, and I know, when everything else was set aside, we gloried in our ability to make exciting and, quite often, beautiful football. That was our pride. Our good luck was to be thrown together, and this was the mark of Matt Busby's genius in grasping the chemistry of the game: how different characters and types of talent could meld so well that, at the very best of times, they became one. Denis would always be a loner to quite a sharp degree, the maverick Scot making his own sense of all that he found before him, and George, of course, went his own way so often when the training was done—with or without his involvement—in the later stages of his time at Old Trafford. It is the way things are, I imagine, in any dressing room or company of men when great deeds are achieved: individual strengths and weaknesses are absorbed, and compensated for, in the growth of a winning team.

I will always be proud to have been part of the Big Three, to have my name linked forever with George and Denis, and that was the overwhelming feeling I know Denis and I shared when we all came together one last time in the hospital room in London shortly before George died at the end of 2005.

But before the Big Three attracted so much of the attention and the glory in the third coming of Busby's United, there was the Big Four—the rather ironic title Shay Brennan, David Herd, Nobby Stiles and I applied to our dressing-room alliance in those formative years of a new and all-conquering team. At the start there were just the three of us: Shay, always amiable and mischievous and carefree; David, the new signing from Arsenal; and me. We drifted together quite naturally, played cards, went to the pictures and for a while I used to go to the dogs at Belle Vue with Shay.

I was never really interested in the dog racing itself, but I enjoyed Shay's company, you could have a good meal at the track, and I found it remarkable that it didn't seem to matter to him whether he won or lost. He was drawn to the excitement and the uncertainty, and when he lost he simply shrugged his shoulders. I remember being in the dressing room one morning when someone said that Shay had taken a big loss at the dogs—it was when my attendance had fallen, partly because of failing interest and, probably more importantly, because it cut across the demands of my new married life. The word was that Shay had lost £200—or roughly a month's wages. I was both concerned and fascinated to see how he would be. In fact he was exactly the same as always. He made a few jokes as he changed for training. He was happy-go-lucky, at least on the surface, in a way that I could never be. In earlier times I would arrange to meet him in town after a match on Saturday. The meeting place was the public library in the centre of town, near to a little cinema we used to go to after a beer or two. Sometimes, though, he would be an hour late and I would be fuming. 'Where the hell do you think you've been?' I would ask him. 'I've been standing here for an hour, wasting my life away.' He would just make a joke of it and say, 'Bobby, why get yourself worked up?' Sometimes, usually after he had made me laugh, I would say, 'Well, I wish I could be like you.'

Nobby Stiles was a late entry into the Big Four. He was very close to John Giles, whose sister Kay he would marry, and when John made his rebellion against Matt Busby, arguing that we were badly treated after our FA Cup win when we received a bonus of just £20, and was promptly sold to Leeds United, Nobby seemed to be a little lost.

We invited him to the pictures and he seemed happy to accept—in fact he stayed with us for ever. We called him Happy because he was always moaning. I soon came to love Nobby, and that feeling has never lost its strength down the years. I make no apology for claiming that he was a great player. He had a reputation for being rough and tough, a kicker, but that assessment only ran along the surface of his ability. Nobby Stiles did things for United, and England, that no one else could have done.

At United, as it would be with England, an entire team was in his debt. He would make his name marking Eusebio on behalf of England, but that was the most visible and obvious point of his brilliance. There was so much else. In the dressing room, on the team bus or in a hotel, he could cause mayhem with his clumsiness, but on the field he saw every threat to our defence.

No doubt he would have made his way in the game

206

anyway, as a midfielder of fierce tackling and aggression and great vision. However, it was more evidence of the brilliance of the Busby–Murphy reading of potential that it included the picture of Stiles the terrier and big Bill Foulkes fusing together so well in the centre of the defence that they might have been just one set of defensive reflexes.

Nobby read the game as though he was equipped with radar, and if I will always feel the greatest pride that I played in the company of George and Denis, the same is equally true of Nobby Stiles. He was the often unsung fourth great player and for me it is one of the happiest facts of my career that he and I enjoyed so much success together and, as it happened, shared the achievement of being the only Englishmen to win both the European and World Cups. In many ways he was the forerunner of Roy Keane in that he was always at the heart of danger, sniffing out points of trouble like some relentless tracker dog. He was a dog of war, if you like, snapping and snarling at both his opponents and his team-mates. When we entered the most vital phase of our campaign to win the European Cup, for Busby and for our fallen team-mates, Nobby was a giant in both his will and his understanding of what had to be done. It was a vital point of the story that was beginning to unfold, and when we came to the detail and the execution of it the little man became a giant, unscrupulous at times no doubt, fiercely committed always, but also someone who loved the challenge of the game, and the feeling he got from being in a winning team. No one I would ever know in football was prepared to do so much for his team-mates and when sometimes, so long after the battles have been fought, I call him and he says, 'What's up, Bobby?' in a voice which still comes straight from the streets of Collyhurst, I experience an old and precious tide of feeling.

Where he differed somewhat from Roy Keane was that he didn't so much see himself as someone at the centre of the battle, with a duty to go forward and spread his influence all over the field and into every corner of the team, but more as the trouble-shooter, someone whose job was to clean up the difficulties, make it easier for people like George and Denis and me to operate at the top of our games.

Sometimes your heart would leap into your mouth as the opposition seized on a mistake and then, in a flash, there would be Nobby mopping up danger, passing the ball on with a few choice remarks for the team-mate who had surrendered it. If he didn't shout at you, the expression on his face would be eloquent enough. It would say, 'OK you stupid bastards, I've done my job, now you get on with yours.' On occasions, when he made one of his more dramatic interventions, when he came from nowhere to shut down danger, I would shake my head and think, 'How on earth did you figure that out?' It was a form of envy really. I knew that as long as I played, I wouldn't have that ability to seize on something so quickly and act so sharply—and ruthlessly, if necessary. When Jimmy Murphy hammered out the need to win the tackle, to always be first, he might have had Nobby in mind. Nobby did the hardest thing in the game, he got you the ball, and, as Jimmy used to say, 'All the rest is bloody easy.'

As the team progressed in all areas, Matt Busby again recognised the need to strengthen the goalkeeping position. Pat Dunne, a £10,500 signing from Shamrock Rovers, an enormous fee for a goalkeeper in those days, had ability, but when the

Old Man finally measured the level of it he felt that he needed a bigger, stronger presence, and also someone less erratic, as a contender for the old place of Harry Gregg, who in his best days had always been both ferocious and strong. Alex Stepney, the big Londoner, was quite different from Harry, but he brought the assurance of a natural shot-stopper. He never dominated his area, wouldn't come out ten yards to catch a ball, but we recognised early that he would do well for us. Not only did he get his hands to the ball at crucial moments, he also held on to it—which is a basic but vital reassurance for any team.

We could not have been stronger at left back. You could have scoured Europe and South America and still not found a full back as quick and as sound as Tony Dunne. When I played, reluctantly, on the left wing, we would always have a chat about 'taking the runner', often an overlapping full back. My job was to take the full back if he indeed looked as if he was going to be the runner, and it was something I could also do when playing midfield. Tony's speed and understanding meant that we were rarely inconvenienced by a sudden break; it was an important part of our increasing strength and it was something I was proud of; something to ease the paranoia I sometimes felt about the level of my contribution off the ball.

It was the speed of Tony Dunne that lingers most strongly in the memory, however. You could lose count of the number of times he overtook a man on the ball. It was something he rarely brought to attack, but then we were not exactly short of options in that area. Like Nobby and Bill Foulkes, Tony was a key underpinning of the 'team of stars'.

David Sadler would emerge as another important element as the team built towards its ultimate

European triumph in 1968. He came to Old Trafford as an outstanding young prospect, a boy from Kent who had been pursued by all the major teams, and it was clear that he was a thoroughbred the moment he arrived at the club. However, David wasn't the first naturally gifted player to suffer from his own virtuosity. Because of his elegant touch, he came to us as a centre forward, which in my opinion was not his natural position. To me, he was a classic central defender, an intelligent reader of the ball. However, there was no opening in the middle of our defence when he arrived with considerable fanfare. It had been sealed up by Foulkes and Stiles.

Bill Foulkes played for England at right back, but I have to say he never looked completely at home in that position: the cleverness of a good winger tended to undermine his confidence and this would sometimes lead to the kind of lunging which can draw free kicks—or leave the rest of the defence exposed when the commitment to the tackle is made unsuccessfully. What Bill Foulkes was, however, was a natural born pillar at the heart of a defence. He was maybe the hardest physical specimen I ever encountered on a football field. If he happened to clip you with his arm during training it was like being hit by a rock. You would cry out with the force of it, 'Jesus Christ, Bill!' Accompanied by the Nobby Stiles radar system, this Bill Foulkes was an immense asset; there was his strength and height and a tremendous love of the battle, which would be absolutely vital to us reaching the European Cup final.

When this happened, it was a moment so crucial to the history of Manchester United that it demands, and will receive, more attention than the passing references in this chapter, but maybe at this point it is relevant to say that it sprang from the perfect understanding Bill Foulkes developed with Nobby Stiles. There was no way Bill could be drawn out of his fortress of central defence, and after Nobby had made one of his seek-and-destroy satellite runs he was obliged to scamper back into the defensive lines. There were two reasons for this. One was his own deep awareness of his function. The other was Foulkes's piercing yell, 'Get back here, you little bastard.' In the middle, Foulkes showed no trace of the uncertainty that sometimes came to him on the flank. He was fast into the tackle, rarely missed anything in the air—you would see opponents wince as they bounced off him—and there was never a moment when he was tempted to try to look good by dwelling on the ball. There would be no flowing pass. Just some basic delivery of the ball accompanied by a grunt of satisfaction.

Foulkes, my World Cup team-mate George Cohen and Tommy Banks of Bolton Wanderers, were a breed of defenders who at that time could bring tears to the eyes of skilful, nippy little forwards. I would have hated to have played against Bill. It would have been something to recall in terms of bruised limbs and battered spirit. You would look at someone like George, and, say, well he's not a classic international full back, there isn't a lot of touch there—but he was such a wonderful competitor, fast and hard, another guy you didn't really want to go near on the field. When clever little wingers like Brian Pilkington of Burnley or Joe Haverty of Arsenal came into 50–50 situations with such men, you could only cringe and feel deep pity.

As the Old Man shaped his last team, he recognised the need for one more piece in the jigsaw.

He needed a strong new element in midfield, something of the order of Davie Mackay at Spurs, or the generalship of Johnny Giles, which would emerge later alongside the bite of Billy Bremner at Leeds. He settled for Pat Crerand from Celtic. I heard later that the other contender was the Scottish virtuoso Jimmy Baxter, a player of genius on the field but one whose reputation for ill-discipline off it would have made any manager think twice. It was said that Busby took his dilemma to Denis Law, who knew both players from the Scottish team. Denis recommended Crerand for his brilliant ability to pass the ball long and penetratively, and for his immense competitive instinct.

After accepting the obvious fact that Paddy would never break any speed records, it was clear soon enough that he brought huge value to the team. Around him it seemed a few sparks were always flying. In training, he could be quite ferocious in opinions about who was doing what, and how effectively. He and I were not always doting team-mates (for Crerand there was the unassailable problem that not only was I English, I also played for England), but he did have a warm heart, and with his warring instincts and his passion for Manchester United he became an integral strength of the team. It was also a great help that he could put the ball on a sixpence from fifty yards.

In the build-up through the sixties, it was clear to me that Matt Busby had achieved the last football ambition left to him after he accepted that he had to go on as manager after Munich. It was to rekindle not only success on the field, but a certain kind of playing, a way of saying the game wasn't solely about winning and losing but also lifting the spirits of *all* those who watched the game, not just those who were there for partisan reasons. For me this is one of the great differences between the football of the past and the game of today. In the sixties there were still so many who had the spirit of those Arsenal fans that day we beat them at Highbury in such an unforgettable match. The Old Man wanted to cater for that longing to see beautiful football.

He differed from Stan Cullis, a hard and brilliant maker of a formidable, winning team; the Old Man wanted to win, but also wanted to entertain, and of course he had achieved that with the '48 team which won the cup so brilliantly but had to wait until 1952 to get their hands on the league title. In the sixties, the team of the Big Three—and the Big Four—were racing ahead of that old schedule. The cup fell to us in 1963, the title in 1965. Equally important to the Old Man, and to me I have to say, is that Manchester United were no longer trying to live with their past.

We were making football that apart from winning matches was also lighting up the sky. A glow had come back to the environs of Trafford Park and it had nothing to do with the fire and the smoke and the sulphur of the factories. We had made it clear that once again Manchester United could be a great side.

CHAPTER 16

# DENIS, GEORGE AND ME

I do not like to think of myself as a boastful person, but sometimes you have to be honest. You have to put aside false modesty. So I have to report that when people started reeling off phrases like 'the Big Three', when the names Law, Best and Charlton were linked so frequently and so naturally, it did come to me that I had become part of football history.

This was not something I stepped back to consider later, as a little dust gathered on a shoal of headlines. It was deeply thrilling at the time that it happened, with the excitement of the fans becoming a little more apparent each time we ran on to the field, because for me the records, and the emerging of aristocracy in football, had always been so fascinating from a boyhood watching the great names and keeping company with Wor Jackie Milburn. It was something that would never pall down all the years.

Having put aside the frustrations of playing out on the left wing, where sometimes I used to look at the old clock and swear that it had stopped, I was more confident in my ability than ever before. The results for the team were increasingly solid, and this meant the expectations placed on Denis, George and me had rapidly become more an inspiration than a burden.

We went about our football in contrasting ways, Denis sending sparks and flames up around him, George going on his amazing runs with trickery and courage that just welled out of him, me with my liking for the bold pass and the big, swirling shot. We had one abiding thing in common. We loved to score goals.

About the town and the country you had the growing sense that football fans had a feeling they just had to see us play. If they didn't, they might miss George finding a full back to his liking, or Denis producing flashes of lightning, or me profiting again from Jimmy Murphy's advice to hit the ball hard and early when I felt I was in scoring range.

We brought different qualities to the field, separate abilities, but as each game passed they seemed to become a little more complementary. Of course there were times when George disappeared on his own flight of fancy, when somebody like me might scream fruitlessly for him to pass, but then the chances were that when he was in that vein he would do something utterly unforgettable. It is also true, as he claimed from time to time, that I too could be selfish when I had the ball at my feet. It can be a fine dividing line, anyway, between confidence and inspiration and a failure to understand the needs of the team at any particular moment, and for three or four years no doubt the most important point was that all three of us were able to deliver the best of our talent.

What the fans loved most about Denis Law, I believe, was his incredible aggression and self-belief. There were times when he seemed to define urgency on a football field—all that some of his most brilliant interventions lacked were puffs of smoke—and always there was the gleam in his eye, and the courage. They never made a big centre half who could induce in Denis even a flicker of apprehension.

One of the most amazing things I saw was his decision to take on big Ron Yeats—he man described as the 'New Colossus' by his Liverpool manager Bill

Shankly. Denis scarcely came to the big man's shoulder, but he was in his face throughout the game, chivvying, needling, always at the point of maximum danger. I remember thinking, 'This is ridiculous, impossible', and for anyone else but Denis it certainly would have been. Such a performance would be born of instinct and then, when the physical going became increasingly rough, it would be a point of honour that he stuck to his task. Among his greatest admirers was United's fierce rival Bill Shankly, who valued all aspects of football talent but held the battling, fighting nature most highly, and it was why he spoke with such reverence of the young, spindly Scot who walked into his life when he was manager of Huddersfield Town. 'The kid was a phenomenon,' enthused Shankly.

There was a period around the mid-sixties when Denis was free from injury, and then we saw the full scale of his brilliance. He was an awesome sight as he went into the dangerous places, daring a centre half or a goalkeeper to blink. He got up to incredible heights and when he did so the defenders knew they couldn't afford half a mistake. The semblance of a slip was all he needed. The ball would be in the back of the net and his arm would be shooting skywards.

One result was that if I ever found some space on the right or the left, I always knew precisely what I had to do. I had to get the ball to the near post; never the back one because Denis would not be there. If I could get the ball to the near post, Denis was guaranteed to sneak half a yard, and when it happened the result was inevitable.

This was a strength, almost an expression of himself as a player, that Denis retained even to the end of his long and painfully injury-prone career. I

At home with my mother and brothers Gordon, 10 and Tommy, 7.

Fishing with Jack in the North East. Not sure I've quite mastered my casting technique.

National
Service.

Wilf and me with Eddie Colman's grandfather, who made
me feel very welcome in Manchester.

Dave Pegg and Tommy Taylor. Both lost in the tragedy of Munich.

On the tarmac at Ringway airport, heading to Belgrade, 3 February 1958.

. . . Bill Foulkes led the team out against Sheffield
Wednesday, 19 February 1958.

Jimmy Murphy leads us out at Wembley, 3 May 1958.

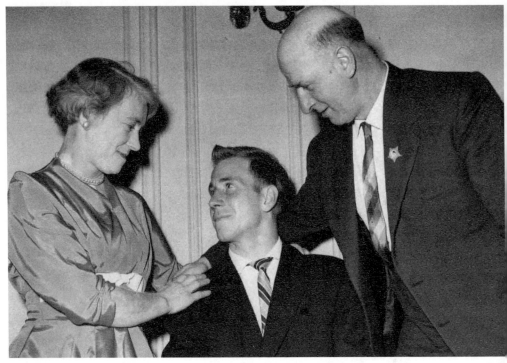

With Mum and Dad at the reception after the final.

Manchester greeted us magnificently, 4 May 1958.

Wembley, 25 May 1963, FA Cup final.
Manchester United 3 Leicester City 1.

David Gaskell, Tony Dunne, me, Paddy Crerand, Noel Cantwell, Albert Quixall, David Herd, Johnny Giles, Maurice Setters.

Not sure Harold Wilson appreciated my choice of karaoke at the reception.

The shining light of my life.

Grandsons Robert and William.

Granddaughter Emma.

## European Players of the Year

*Back row, l-r*: Paulo Rossi, Lothar Matthaus, Igor Belanov,
   Oleg Blokhin, Karl-Heinz Rummenigge, Michel Platini,
   Hristo Stoitchkov, Forian Albert, Johan Cruyff, Denis
   Law, Bobby Charlton, Gianni Rivera, Josef Masopust
*Middle row, l-r*: Allan Simonsen, Franz Beckenbauer, Luis
   Suarez, Alfredo di Stefano, Eusebio, Raymond Kopa
*Front row, l-r*: Jean-Pierre Papin, Zinedine Zidane,
   Ronaldinho, Luis Figo, Andriy Shevchenko

remember that, at a very late hour for both of us, we played in a testimonial match for Bill Foulkes. They brought the old guys back for the game and, in the tradition of testimonials, the full back gave me a little room to go down the right side. As I prepared to cross, I saw a red shirt moving towards the near post and I knew it had to be Denis. As I made to centre the ball, I thought, 'Oh, I remember the ones he used to like.' I hit it to the near post and there, of course, he was, connecting and sending the ball just an inch wide. The Old Trafford crowd roared in a way it hadn't done all night. Denis had made them remember some of the best of the past.

I also felt a wave of emotion. It is not often that you can conjure so clearly and vividly something that has begun to recede into memory. We were both in our late thirties, both contemplating the second half of our lives, but in one precious moment we were back to the pinnacle of our days. What had moved me so much was that the moment had been so spontaneous, springing as it did from our knowledge of each other and our different powers.

The aspect of Denis that I could never understand, and which I suppose made the sharpest contrast in the way we approached the game, was that he refused to be involved the moment he wasn't playing in a match. If he was injured and had to leave the field, he would shower and go home immediately, perhaps with the outcome of the match far from decided. It was the same when substitutes were introduced; if Denis was replaced, that was the end of his afternoon. He wasn't making any statement of anger or resentment. He was just saying that his work and his interest were over. He would rather be back in his house in Chorlton cum Hardy. This lack of involvement if he was not on the pitch was true even for the biggest games—when United played in the European Cup final in 1968, Denis was in hospital having a cartilage operation. He claims to have had a few beers—and fallen asleep.

If I had to pick a single, dominating aspect of his character, apart from the tremendous commitment which marked his play, and which set him apart as much as his dramatic talent, it would be his sheer Scottishness. I know all Scots aren't the same, but I do love the way so many of them see a love of their country as something at the heart of their existence, and how it has always been so passionately expressed on the football field. Often there is a show of toughness, and quite a bit of bluster, but you don't have to be so perceptive to see that at its core is deep pride in their people and a tough view of the world.

When Nobby and I were helping England win the World Cup, Denis made a point of playing golf. Whenever we played Scotland, Denis made sure to kick us both and call us 'English bastards', within the first minute or so of the match. It was as though he had been obliged to make a statement and, having done so, he could then get on with the game.

I believe that it is part of the Scottish education in life, if not officially in the schoolroom agenda, to compete with most determination against the English. The result in football was that even when some English supporters were making a reputation for strident, riotous behaviour across the world, they had little appetite for visiting Hampden Park. The English fans, like the players, knew that no quarter would ever be given.

When I played my first game for England in Scotland I remember the bus journey from Troon up to Glasgow. It seemed that there was scarcely a house where someone wasn't hanging out of a window shouting the Scottish equivalent of, 'You'll get nowt today.' Sometimes we did, sometimes we didn't, but there was always one certainty: if there was ever a Scottish deficit, it would never be one of the heart. Down the years I formed the impression that no one embodied this national pride more strongly than Denis, and on my visits to his country there was always at least a hint that he was regarded as the most patriotic Scottish football player of them all. I know that this image for him will always be a matter of the deepest pride.

Nowadays, I see a certain mellowing in the fierce Scot. He comes down to the club more frequently, and I get the sense that he is pleased to see that his standing remains so huge. He had a battle with prostate cancer a few years ago, and maybe that slightly softened the ferocious edge of the nature that made him such a fantastic player.

Still, I do not expect all of his mysteries to disappear in the years of his maturity. His humour might become a little less edgy—and scathing—and he might be a little less of the loner, but at his heart, I suspect he will always be the same old Denis: a man who played his football, and lived his life, strictly on his own terms.

George Best, of course, kept so much of his mystery right up to the end, when Denis and I sorrowfully boarded that train to London on a cold, grey day in November 2005.

I had met Denis at Stockport station after calling him to discuss George's situation against the background of reports that he was unlikely to survive his latest health crisis. Denis had already made one visit, and warned me that George was indeed at a low ebb. It was unlikely that he would be able to take much in.

233

It was as Denis said it would be. George, surrounded by his family, had slipped into something close to a coma. One of his sisters said he might be able to hear me, and I spoke to him with the greatest sadness. I whispered to him as I had to Duncan Edwards and Matt Busby all those years before in Munich, but I felt that so much of my old team-mate's life had been, and was still, set apart from my own experience and understanding.

I wished some things at the core of George's life had been different. However, the time for judgement had long passed. When he finally left us, meaning so much to so many people, it was enough to shut your eyes and remember all the best of him—and of that there was so much that went beyond any disputes we might have had about the way a professional footballer should operate for the benefit of both himself and his team. Our relationship had grown warmer in later years, and the pain and frustration of the premature ending of the most beautiful and natural talent I had ever seen was tempered by the fact that we had shared moments that would have brought pride and joy to any footballer who had ever played the game.

To be honest, his first performance for the team, in a league match against West Bromwich at Old Trafford in September 1963, does not linger in my mind. I'm sure he showed some nice touches, but the overall impact was not overwhelming. It was when he returned to the team a few months later, against Burnley at Old Trafford, that you began to see all that he would be. We had been beaten badly at Burnley a few days earlier, and the Old Man was determined to shake up the team. Bringing back the seventeen-year-old George was his boldest stroke and it paid off gloriously. Long before the end, I felt pity for my friend John Angus, the Burnley right back who I had got to know on England duty. John was not so much overwhelmed as tortured. George was like a kid's dribbling dream that day. The crowd was stunned, then rapturous, and when it was happening I recalled a conversation I had had with one of the coaches at The Cliff training ground a year or so earlier. He had said, 'We have a lad in the reserves who is bloody good. He'll be playing alongside you guys soon enough.' I made the slightly cynical reply, 'Well, they say that about a lot of young players—let's wait and see.' I didn't watch George play in the reserves, partly because I reckoned that, if he was as good as he was being described, I would be getting a close look at him soon enough. You could see it all in the game against Burnley—the speed, the balance, the nerve, the close control—and the fans loved every second of it. Supporters like nothing better than to see a winger beating a full back to the point of humiliation, and it was a day when they received full value for the price of their tickets.

Going down to London with Denis, I could not help but recall an earlier train journey—one I made with George from Cardiff after we had played in a Uefa representative match, at the time when his reputation—and, much more than that, his celebrity—had reached a peak. This was at the beginning of the phase when the main topic of conversation at Old Trafford often concerned George's whereabouts the night before—and at roughly what time that night had ended, and in whose company.

Sometimes I would get the story from the horse's mouth. Training then, for all the growing success of the team, was nothing like so intense as it would be

235

today. Around the little red track at Old Trafford, the players would at first mingle together, do a bit of jogging and then, perhaps after half an hour, the trainers would come out and some more formal work would be done. In the meantime, however, you might have found yourself with a team-mate discussing what they had been up to over the previous few days or, in George's case, invariably, the nights. Once I said to him, 'Well, what was the programme last night?' He told me in some detail. He had been to various bars and clubs, and then finished up in his favourite watering hole, the Brown Bull in Salford. As he related the progress of his night, and I thought of my own life back home in Lymm, I was a little stunned by the comparison and I could not help saying, 'George, maybe one day they will put you in a bottle in some laboratory at Manchester University.'

On that train journey from Cardiff I remembered that Norma and the girls were away, and I asked George what he was doing that night, imagining that another spectacular tour of Manchester was about to unfold. When he said, 'Oh, nothing really, maybe I'll go somewhere for a drink,' I asked him if he would like to get off the train in Warrington and come to my house for a bit of supper. Norma had told me there was a bag of frozen scampi in the fridge and I had the idea—it turned out to be a little optimistic—that I could make a decent meal out of it for Geroge and me. To be honest, I was a little shocked when George said yes.

It was a strange and in some ways poignant evening. George was very taken with our dog, a Chow, and he was full of questions about how it was being married, about having a dog and domestic life in general. For some reason, I formed the idea that he was intrigued by the possibility of getting married himself, that it might just represent another way of life that could offer him something he maybe wasn't getting in his endless whirl of clubs and pubs and parties; that not least, perhaps, he wanted a little peace.

From the moment he walked into the house he was full of questions. It was as though he had thought to himself, 'Well, who knows, I might pick up a few things from old Bobby Charlton.' He wanted to know about everything, the running of the house, the running of the family, the keeping of the dog, the garden. As the evening wore on, I saw a different George, inquisitive, warm, and maybe a little insecure in himself. It made me think that behind all the glitter and the headlines here was just another young man trying to find his way in life.

Eventually, I drove him into town. The scampi had not been a towering success but I got the feeling he had enjoyed his visit to another world—and it was interesting that soon afterwards he bought himself a dog. He also had a house built in the Cheshire suburbs—though accompanying newspaper stories said that it was designed by him, and it was radically different from the conventional detached house he had visited in Lymm. Also, amid much publicity, he acquired a Danish girlfriend, Eva Haraldsted.

It was enough, certainly, to encourage my belief that George might indeed be considering the idea of getting permanently hooked up. Partly, I suppose, I thought this was because his life seemed to me to be stretching out towards a quite predictable futility. Of course he told the famous joke about being in the hotel room with Miss World and champagne and a fistful of cash, and the waiter asking him where it had all gone wrong, but there were days when you had to suspect that he was in search of something he might never find.

Stories about our differences were often taken as fact, but the truth was they were exaggerated. I didn't agree with some of the things George did, I didn't think his lifestyle was compatible with being a professional footballer, but for a while at least I accepted that he was doing extraordinary things on the field. As long as this was so, it was maybe understandable, if not right, that Matt Busby refused to lay down an iron hand of discipline. I couldn't see that there was much I could do, other than follow the Old Man's approach. This could be summed up simply enough; take the best that George had to offer—and live with the rest.

So often, of course, living with George was a glorious existence, and it started with that amazing performance against my Geordie friend John Angus. He sold that excellent full back so many dummies it was staggering to think he was still just seventeen. There were so many passages of play like that, most famously when he destroyed Benfica three years later in the Estadio da Luz in Lisbon, and all of them reminded you that apart from anything else George Best had a constitution that was hardly believable.

This was no doubt the reason that the Old Man mostly—until the very end, when George's behaviour made the situation untenable if the club was to retain any pretence of discipline—took a lenient view of so many of the transgressions. For me, certainly, an important factor in my decision not to get involved in any of the often heated debates within the club was that at the peak of his success George, when he trained or played, never fell short of what you would expect from one of the world's outstanding footballers. Of that time I cannot recall a moment when George did something on the field that made me think, 'Uh-oh, George overdid it last night.'

When eventually he did become a little ragged in the mornings, when his absences from training were more frequent, and finally you could see that he was beginning to lose some of that brilliant edge, my own overwhelming reaction was one of sadness. Partly, it was because the fans loved him so much, had set him up on a pedestal so high, that when he came down, as he must, the disappointment would be terribly cruel. Down the years when we spoke about this, it was the one thing that he never denied. It was true, he conceded, that his way of life had robbed millions of fans of a pleasure that, when you consider the normal span of a playing career, was much too brief. As his life progressed, when maybe a drink was more important, maybe a girl was more important, it made you think that you don't get truly great players so very often, and if you do it's heartbreaking when, as a result of their own actions, they don't fulfil their potential.

When he left Old Trafford at the age of only twenty-six, I was seeing a real tragedy, for football and for him. I couldn't believe that a player of all his gifts was so soon leaving the big stage, where he was loved so much. Maybe in a way my argument is weakened when you recognise that, whatever had happened, the public really could not have adored him any more than they did—and continued to do so in all the years since he stopped playing.

Today, when I park my car and go to my place at Old Trafford, and see parents taking their children to watch the likes of Wayne Rooney and Cristiano

Ronaldo, I am always reminded of the faces of the kids of the sixties. You could see on them the anticipation and excitement when Georgie Best was playing. But then, suddenly, he was no longer there. You had to regret it, as you did the fact that in his prime George never had the chance to perform in a World Cup. You can only speculate on what that exposure would have done for his legend. Yet, here again, you come to the reality that, like Diego Maradona, another ultimate talent whose life has often careered off the rails, George Best could hardly have gone any deeper into the hearts of his admirers. In the eyes of the Argentinian people, Maradona will always be a god—as will Georgie Best for all those who saw him play.

When I look back on a life that was too brief, too troubled—whatever bright light George attempted to shine on it at times—I share that sense of wonder, sometimes disbelief when I think of how good he was and all those improbable things he achieved under such immense pressure. Rightly the goal he scored against Chelsea—as he ignored scything tackles from some of the toughest, most ruthless ever to play the game—is seen as the embodiment of so much of his ability. It showed courage, resilience and a skill that simply could not be tamed. That was the hard side of him, the one that could see him clouted so hard he wobbled but refused to go down; but then there was also all the delicacy which came out when, say, he chipped the ball over a goalkeeper, exhibiting sublime execution gauged to the very inch.

He set a standard that people talk about even now, and I suspect this will always be so, as long as there is film of him, because what they see is something that, for all the talented players of today, they do believe is no longer available. They don't see anyone who is quite like George Best. I spent quite a large part of my life explaining how it was to play with Duncan Edwards, and now it is the same with George. One day, of course, there may be another Duncan, another George, but the bar was raised so high by those players, that when someone like a young Ryan Giggs or Rooney or Ronaldo step forward, unfavourable comparisons are invariably made, and those who remember George, and the dwindling number who recall Duncan, are quick to defend their idea of what they think of as football perfection.

I carried all those memories of glory and sadness when I walked into the hospital room with Denis. I thought of my perhaps naive belief that George might have been kindling thoughts of a different, more stable life that night I made a mess of the scampi. I smiled, for a moment, at the time I yelled at him repeatedly to give me the ball when he weaved across the field in a match against Nottingham Forest. I remembered how I called him a 'selfish little bugger' as he hogged the ball—and was then obliged to shrug my shoulders and shout, 'Great goal,' when he finally stroked it into the net, a grinning, cocky, defiant matador of a footballer, once again delivering a sword stroke that could not be parried. I thought of all the controversy that had surrounded the last years of George's life, of how some had complained that because of his lifestyle, his repeated failures to stay on the wagon despite the most serious possible warnings from leading doctors, he did not deserve the transplanted liver he was given that might have gone to someone who had not so relentlessly imperilled his own health. But then I thought that life creates extreme cases, and did anyone in football know

241

anybody whose experiences of joy and sadness, and the ability to create such emotions in other people, had been quite so profound?

I had spoken to him a few times when he was drinking in the early days, but even then I wondered if there was really much I could say which might have any effect. Later, when we met at functions, I asked him about his health, and on several occasions I told him how many people wanted him to come out all right. 'George,' I said, 'You wouldn't believe how many people out there want you to get better.' But even as I said it, I suspected that he really wasn't on the same wavelength. In the end it didn't matter how many good wishes he received, how many prayers were said on his behalf, there was only one person who could make him better. I'm sure there were times when he did try—when he got the hard warnings, and when at one point he had pellets inserted into his stomach that would make him nauseous when he had a drink—but maybe there was something inside him that in the end made it impossible.

In the hospital I saw the pain on the faces of George's family, but I also saw how proud they were of the son and brother whose life was ebbing away. After he died and a memorial was held at Old Trafford before a game (poignantly it was against West Bromwich Albion, his first opponents), I was asked to say something. It was not a time for a long speech; you couldn't trust your emotions beyond a few words, and what I said in the stadium filled with admirers, many of whom had only seen a film version of his brilliance, reflected the essence of my feelings. It was that through all the pain and, to be perfectly honest, a certain sense of waste, we were left with one simple statement of our feelings. It was to offer thanks that we had known him and been spellbound by the brilliance of his football. That was his great legacy, a picture of genius that would surely never die.

When I heard that the club had commissioned a bronze statue of George, Denis and me, to stand outside the ground on Sir Matt Busby Way, I told George's father Dickie that nothing could fill me—and I was sure the same was true of Denis—with more pride. For just a little while, there in the hospital room in London, the three of us had been united for one last time. When Denis and I walked away down the corridor we didn't need to say that, along with George, we had left behind the greatest of our football times.

CHAPTER 17

# UNFINISHED BUSINESS

Even as a teenager, George Best's status was unquestioned. He was the light of Manchester United's future, one which would shine most luminously on a March night in Lisbon in 1966. That was when his celebrity, and maybe the shape of the rest of his life, was made in the 5–1 defeat of Benfica. But while recalling the excitement of the night and all those that would follow, it would be negligent to ignore, amid all the dawning glory, the wonderful contribution of another winger. It came from John Connelly, a vital force in the championship-winning season of 1964–65 which carried us back into the European Cup.

John scored the third goal in that thrilling performance at the Estadio da Luz, but it wasn't some random goal from a member of the supporting cast. John may have spent just two full seasons at Old Trafford after signing from Burnley in the spring of '64, but that had nothing to do with the consistently high level of his play. Like Nobby Stiles and Bill Foulkes at the back, he was one of those ingredients a winning team cannot do without; he mixed the cement, he made the bricks—and sometimes he would throw one straight at the heart of the opposition.

Like John Giles before him, John Connelly had a strong belief in his value as a player—and, also like Giles, he felt it deserved a better reward in his wage packet. This brought him into conflict with the Old Man. It was not something I was drawn into, and no details came my way, but I had a sense of this professional's nature—and knew the way things had always been done at Old Trafford—and I thought trouble was inevitable.

Nobby provided one insight when he told the story of the time he, Alan Ball and John got into a little trouble with Sir Alf Ramsey during the build-up to the World Cup. They had slipped away for a pint at the local pub after a day of work at the Lilleshall training centre in Shropshire. Alf was furious and Nobby and Alan were very contrite. John, though, much to the anguish of the other two when the three of them were hauled before the England manager, was much less repentant. He said that no great crime had been committed, no curfew had been smashed.

While such players as Nobby and I, so immersed in the club from boyhood, were happy, or at least resigned, to take what was offered when United felt it necessary to recognise our progress, both for United and as World Cup winners for England, Connelly again was more defiant. He argued his case for better money, as Giles had after the 1963 cup victory. His position was that, apart from being involved in England's World Cup squad, he had made a major contribution to the growth of the team. He pointed out that he had scored twenty goals in all games in the season of our first run to the title in eight years, and then another thirteen in the following season that saw us in fourth place but surprisingly beaten in the European Cup semi-finals by Partizan Belgrade.

We were a top team again, unquestionably, and Connelly was a vital factor. Another point that he latched on to—without too much difficulty, it has to be said, because it was common knowledge in international circles—was that United were notoriously low payers when compared to some of the other top clubs.

When you look back, you see it was reasonable to think that the climate was right for better rewards, for him and for the rest of us. There was no doubt that the team had moved up several levels as serious contenders for the major prizes. United now had a perfectly balanced attack. Best and Connelly could play on either flank. Best could bring a glow to the sky at any moment. Connelly was more predictable, but this was not a matter for relief in any of the defenders who had the job of marking him. They always knew what they were getting when they faced Connelly, and inevitably it was hard and unrewarding work. In those days there was a small group of talented wingers who had learned that in an increasingly physical game they could not afford just to take knocks, brush themselves down and return to the action. They had to make their presence felt as ruthlessly as they could and Connelly elected himself to this tough group of survivors which included Terry Paine of Southampton and Johnny Morrissey of Everton. In my view, though, Connelly was the best in this category. He wasn't afraid of leaving his foot in and this was never a secret; it produced instant respect in any marker.

Connelly was perfectly equipped for this survival game. He was strong and quick, and I rarely saw a winger who was happier to take on the challenge of unnerving a full back. He could beat a man well enough, but he was never inclined to stay around to admire his handiwork. If he had a chance to move on goal he was not reluctant to do so, as his scoring showed eloquently enough. His greatest contribution, however, given the finishing potential of his forward colleagues, was to get to the bye-line and cross accurately. He was so willing to do this for the full ninety minutes that I was surprised when he suddenly disappeared, signing for Blackburn, where he had some good years.

His departure shouldn't have been a mystery, not even to me. John undoubtedly had a spiky quality and, like Giles, he was to learn that at Old Trafford the voice and the judgement of Matt Busby were not wisely questioned if you wanted to make the United experience a long one.

No doubt another contribution to the situation was John Connelly's origins. A native of the rugby league stronghold of St Helens, as a footballer he grew up in Burnley, winning a league title for the town which was so clannish I sometimes thought it might declare a republic at any time. The Burnley lads always stuck together. I remember when Old England used to play against Young England before the FA Cup final, the Turf Moor contingent would always form their own table: John Connelly, Gordon Harris, Ray Pointer and John Angus. They peered out at the rest of the world quite suspiciously, as though they felt that if they kept together, they could hold off all comers, and for a few years they did so quite brilliantly. In those days no team in the land went to Turf Moor, set in a bowl of the moors, with easy hearts.

Whenever I'm in East Lancashire I try to visit John. Until recently that usually meant calling into the fish shop he ran in Brierfield. It was called Connelly's Plaice, and he never apologised for that. As a magistrate, he was not afraid of administrating tough justice, and he would tell me how some of his regulars would come in and complain if they had been up in court and John and his colleagues had

247

found them guilty and given them a stiff fine. But it never seemed to affect his popularity in the area. He was known for what he was at Old Trafford: a tough professional who always came to work with the most serious intent.

It was the same with David Herd, another who, while being a bit of a loner and never drawing too much attention to himself, was a key reason why United emerged so strongly in the mid-sixties. His father Alex was a star of Manchester City in the thirties, a family story that had an extraordinary chapter when they both played for Stockport County, one on his way out of football as the other was coming in. When he came to us from Arsenal he immediately joined up with Nobby, Shay and me in the group he christened the Big Four.

Mostly we played cards in a non-serious way, usually Kings or cribbage. We were never mistaken for high rollers on our way to Las Vegas. Nobby and David were most handicapped. It was during one of our sessions that Harry Gregg observed that Nobby's eyesight was so bad he could scarcely see the cards. It was only when Harry reported this to Matt Busby that Nobby went to a specialist and was given contact lenses—maybe one of the most significant moments in a career which would turn out so brilliantly after some years of struggling to establish himself in a regular position.

David's problem was that, despite all his enthusiasm, he couldn't play cards. He was perhaps the worst cards player I had ever seen. What he could do so much better, however, was lead an attack with speed and power and a withering shot.

Law and Herd complemented each other superbly, a fact which is illustrated perfectly by the latter's

248

productivity in the four seasons that followed his two-goal contribution to the cup victory in 1963. In those seasons we won two titles and finished runners-up once, and Herd's efforts were utterly vital. In the first campaign, when Law was at times unplayable and scored a stunning total of 46 goals in all competitions, Herd, while playing nineteen games fewer, found the net 27 times. In 1964–65, Denis scored 39, David 28. The following season saw Herd overtake Denis, who, while playing three games fewer, had 24 goals against Herd's 32. In the second title year, Law was back in front with 25 goals against 18, but he played in seven games more. In other circumstances, in less glamorous company, David Herd would surely have become something of a folk hero, a component of a famous partnership.

David's fate, though, was not to be one of the fabled heroes of football. He did his job brilliantly, but he was almost destined to operate in someone else's shadow. He often bore the brunt of criticism from the terraces when things didn't go so well, a result, maybe, of all the praise that lapped around three of his team-mates, but it never seemed to take any edge off his determination. He was always the same: as eager to play cards as badly as he was to score goals so regularly and so well.

The power of his shot was the most amazing aspect of his talent. He was particularly ferocious during the warm-up. His shots would threaten the health of the goalkeeper, and sometimes injured hapless fans cowering behind the little wooden fence behind the goal. Once, he was so keen to play that, in his enthusiasm, he injured himself before a game. Mostly, though, he was strong and selfless and, like John Connelly, one of those players destined to impress no one so much as his fellow professionals, who could see during a match what the fans on the terraces might miss: the level of effort and the technical scoring ability. There's a thin line between a performance which looks exceptional but which is actually down to a kindly run of the ball and one which demonstrates true technique. Sometimes you need to share the pitch to appreciate that.

Our success in the cup and then the league brought back the component that I had missed so acutely in the battle to recover from Munich: a return to the European theatre. We had built ourselves back into the upper echelons of English football, but the great lure was still those foreign fields where it was as important as ever for us to make our mark.

When Bill Shankly opened the gates to Europe for Liverpool for the first time with the title win of 1963–64—when they beat us by the four points which went to them after a 1–0 win at Old Trafford and a 3–0 triumph at Anfield—I felt like a hungry urchin with his nose pressed against the window of some glitzy restaurant. It was a reminder of that feeling I had in the army camp in Shropshire when a plane flew overhead, and I imagined it carrying other, more fortunate, players to Europe. Football's greatest adventure was again going on without me.

I would call Liverpool for tickets for their European games, and they would always oblige. Shankly would know terrible disappointment in Europe, most devastatingly when he and his team claimed that Internazionale Milan had been cruelly favoured by a Spanish referee in their semi-final tie at the San Siro in 1965, but he laid down the standards, and the tradition, which would bring so much success in the tournament that I ached to be part of once more. However, that longing did not prevent me from enjoying their European nights at Anfield. It is a long time now since anyone with Manchester United close to their heart has been able say that a night in that ground was fun, but in those days no one with any feeling for the game, or working-class humour, could say otherwise. The Liverpool fans appreciated a new level of football and responded with great wit. Nowadays, five European Cup victories later, the Liverpool fans may not be so funny, at least not when United are visiting, but the memory of those distant nights is something that still fills me with warmth. Then, it would never have occurred to someone like me that attending a big game of one of your fiercest rivals might not be the wisest thing to do. There was never a hint of hostility.

One night at Anfield, that came much later, stands out vividly. It was the one when I was able to study, at greater distance than usual, the talent of my great rival Franz Beckenbauer. Liverpool beat Bayern Munich 3–0, but it was still fascinating to study the style of the emperor of German football. The quality that struck you most was his confidence, the aura he threw up around himself. Everything he did seemed to suggest that all he needed to do was move into another gear to leave everyone for dead. It wasn't true. Beckenbauer didn't slip through the gears like some high-powered Mercedes-Benz. He couldn't do that—but what he could do was exploit a fantastic football brain, an innate awareness of where to be at any given moment. On this particular night, however, Liverpool were too good even for a player well on the way to proving himself one of the most influential in the history of the game. They were wonderfully quick and drilled, a team who seemed born for such nights of football drama.

When I looked at Liverpool in that first European season of theirs, I realised we still had work to do at Old Trafford. In Shankly they had more than a manager. He was a messiah whipping up both a team and a great city, and whenever you saw him, or heard about his latest outrageous statement, you knew that he, and Don Revie at Leeds United—and then a little later, Joe Mercer and Malcolm Allison at Manchester City and Brian Clough at Derby—were going to provide the most formidable opposition to our attempt to remake the Old Trafford empire.

The eccentric passion of Shankly was underlined for me by my England team-mate Roger Hunt's version of the classic tale of the Liverpool manager's pre-game talk before playing Manchester United. The story has probably been told a thousand times in and out of football, and each time you hear it there are different details, but when Roger told it the occasion was still fresh in his mind and I've always believed it to be the definitive account. It was later on the same day, as Roger and I travelled together to report for England duty, after we had played our bruising match at Anfield. Ian St John had scored the winner, then squared up to Denis Law, with Nobby finally sealing the mood of the afternoon by giving the Kop the 'V' sign. After settling down in our railway carriage, Roger said, 'You may have lost today, but you would have been pleased with yourself before the game. Shanks mentioned you in the team talk. When he says anything positive about the opposition, normally he never singles out players.' According to Roger, Shankly burst into the dressing room in his usual aggressive style and said, 'We're playing Manchester United this afternoon, and really it's an insult that we have to let them on to our field because we are superior to them in every department, but they are in the league so I suppose we have to play them. In goal Dunne is hopeless—he never knows where he is going. At right back Brennan is a straw—any wind will blow him over. Foulkes the centre half kicks the ball anywhere. On the left Tony Dunne is fast but he only has one foot. Crerand couldn't beat a tortoise. It's true David Herd has got a fantastic shot, but if Ronnie Yeats can point him in the right direction he's likely to score for us. So there you are, Manchester United, useless . . .'

Apparently it was at this point the Liverpool winger Ian Callaghan, who was never known to whisper a single word on such occasions, asked, 'What about Best, Law and Charlton, boss?'

Shankly paused, narrowed his eyes, and said, 'What are you saying to me, Callaghan? I hope you're not saying we cannot play three men.'

The beauty of the story for us, soon enough, was that Shankly was protesting too much. While no side is ever complete—Pat Dunne in goal had some fantastic games in the first championship year, but his consistency did not inspire total confidence—the fact was that we were unquestionably nearer to producing eleven strong pieces of the jigsaw than at any point since Munich. Despite the strength of the First Division, and our unfulfilled desire to taste the European game, we were getting back some of the old swagger in that 1963–64 season. Indeed, there were times when you had to believe we had a whole team's allocation of it packed into Denis Law.

We were progressing at pace, with a growing swell of opportunities coming our way, although we failed to take advantage of them all. West Ham United, then Leeds, running and tackling endlessly in their

253

promotion year, beat us in the FA Cup semi-finals of 1964 and 1965, and there was crushing disappointment when we failed, in '64, to exploit the 1963 cup final win over Leicester which returned us, a little too nonchalantly in the end, to Europe in the Cup-Winners' Cup.

At first things went well. We drew and then won in the legs against Willem II. Then Tottenham, defending their crown, were swept aside 4–1 at Old Trafford after beating us 2–0 in the first leg of the quarter-final at White Hart Lane. Spurs suffered a terrible blow when Dave Mackay broke his leg after colliding with Noel Cantwell, but then we lost Maurice Setters for some time with a head wound. Danny Blanchflower had gone, but Spurs were still full of quality with men like John White, Cliff Jones and Jimmy Greaves. David Herd scored the goals that drew us level on aggregate and though Greaves pushed Tottenham into the lead again, I was able to respond with two goals in the last ten minutes. I had the feeling that we would soon have our hands on a piece of European silverware—not the one we craved, the European Cup itself, but something to announce that we were winning again on the foreign ground we once pioneered.

However, in Lisbon, just a few miles down the road from the Estadio da Luz where George would change the scale of his career and his life in another two years, Sporting Lisbon ambushed us at the Alvalade Stadium. George scarcely got a kick. Nor did the rest of us. Sporting, trailing 4–1 from the first leg, beat us 5–0. No one could look back on this night with any satisfaction, and least of all poor Maurice Setters. After the game he stumbled on the marble floor of our hotel lobby in Estoril and injured his knee.

This left the door open for Nobby Stiles, who for so long had been in search of a settled first-team place. The Old Man received a word in his ear from Jimmy Murphy: Norrie, as the Old Man always called Nobby, was perfectly equipped to replace Maurice alongside Bill Foulkes, and make the position his own. It meant that Nobby's professional life had—for him just as profoundly as George's would also do—changed in Lisbon. He was not destined to be a star of the discos or the boutiques, but he would make his name as an English folk hero. As so often in football, a mishap for one player makes the future of a team-mate. The door opened for Stiles—and he went through and closed it behind him more smoothly, more emphatically, than he would ever do anything else in his life.

I have already expressed my love for Nobby, my admiration for him as a man and a competitor, but maybe it is time to give some of the flavour of what he brought to us on a permanent basis, something beyond his almost psychic reading of an opposing team. He made me laugh so hard that the tears ran down my face, and the sportswriter Hugh McIlvanney once wrote that compared to Nobby, Inspector Clouseau was 'blessedly adroit'. No one could accuse him of over-statement.

Nobby didn't say good morning. Instead, he always reported a catastrophe. A typical offering was: 'You'll never guess what I did this morning, Bob . . .' I would agree, and then he would say something like, 'I pulled the garage door off.' We heard that one on more than one occasion.

He excelled himself when we arrived in Australia after a long flight which had made several stops. For the trip I had borrowed an expensive camera, which I had put in one bag, and in another I'd placed some duty-free items, including a bottle of brandy I had bought on the way out from England. At Sydney airport, I asked Nobby to look after the bags while I went off to the duty free shop. When I got back there was only one bag, and it didn't look right. It wasn't. The brandy bottle was broken and the camera was floating. Nobby was quite agitated. He said, 'It's your bloody fault. You shouldn't have left them with me.' I said, 'Fair enough Nobby, but just out of interest, could you tell me, please, what happened?'

Nobby said he had thought it stupid that I had a small amount of stuff in two bags. Why not put all the items into one bag? Of course it made perfect sense—right up to the point that Nobby smashed the bag against a chair.

Another time, he described one memorable scene in Market Street, a main thoroughfare of Manchester, as if he was a pure victim. 'Some silly bugger banged into the back of my car,' he reported. Of course he leaped out, but the other driver pointed at Nobby's bumper and said, 'Look, I don't think I've done too much damage.' They both bent down at the same time to inspect the bumper—and they nutted each other. Apparently a large crowd gathered.

When he moved to Middlesbrough, I was able to follow the trail of disaster whenever he appeared on television. A plaster on his neck told me he had cut himself while shaving. If he had one on his forehead it meant he had had a problem getting in or out of his car. A plaster on the nose suggested he had walked into a door or maybe a set of French windows. Stories would be swapped around the dressing room on an almost daily basis.

Because I shared a room with Nobby from time to

time, with both United and England, the law of averages said that I would have the best story, and the truth is that the airport performance was really a relatively minor example of his destructive potential. Far more extraordinary was his performance one morning when we were returning from England duty in London. We were sharing a room in a hotel near Euston station and had slept quite late. When I awoke I realised we had scarcely an hour to get on the train. I didn't need to shave so I was quickly into my clothes. To help with the job of rousing Nobby, I switched on a little radio attached to the bedroom wall.

As he got out of bed he said we needed some light and walked over to the window to draw the curtains. When he tugged them they fell to the floor. He then complained about the noise of the radio and reached to switch it off. On cue, it fell off the wall. Then he went to the washbasin. He collided with the glass shelf where you put your shaving gear and soap. Everything fell down. All this action was compressed into no more than five minutes. It remains a mystery how Nobby was able to make the short journey to the station without the help of an ambulance crew.

On that flight down to Australia he reported that he had quite a number of relatives there. However, he was going to avoid them. His theory was that they must have been in a huff when they decided to emigrate. Yet one morning in Brisbane I walked into the hotel lobby only to see Nobby in the middle of a great crowd of people. They all wanted to know how it was back in Manchester—and particularly in their part of it, Collyhurst. They were all relatives.

Uncannily, when Nobby went out to the field he became one of the most business-like footballers I would ever see. His timing and sense of space and movement were simply phenomenal, something which you couldn't help but reflect upon when sometimes, after a game, you had to get down on your hands and knees to help him find a lost contact lens. Once, he had to implore the head groundsman to keep on the floodlights. He desperately needed to see a glint in the grass.

With Nobby such a force, both as a lynchpin in defence and a character in the dressing room, and with the sense of a team growing so steadily, the title wins of 1965 and 1967 were surely the signal that the European drought would end soon enough. It was an intoxicating thought, but there was more frustration of the kind that had come to us in the game against Sporting Lisbon in 1964.

The following season we were knocked out of the Inter Cities Fairs Cup by Hungarian club Ferencváros in a semi-final play-off, but that disappointment was nothing compared to the blow that hit us at Old Trafford a year later—we had been convinced that 1966 was the year we were supposed to win the big one. We had thought that it had been written in the sky above the Estadio da Luz when we thrashed Benfica in the quarter-final, when the Portuguese team, who had never been beaten at home in the European Cup they had won twice, presented the European Player of the Year trophy to the great Eusebio.

Benfica had bristled with confidence despite their 3–2 loss in the first leg. Estadio da Luz, after all, was a fortress: in nineteen previous European Cup ties at the ground they had won eighteen and drawn one, scoring seventy-eight goals in the process. They had appeared in four of the five previous European Cup finals. A tremendous roar greeted the first whistle.

From that moment it was George Best's game, football history will always be sure about that, but in fact the whole team functioned beautifully.

More than forty years later, soon after George's death, Denis Law and I spent a nostalgic morning together at The Cliff training ground. We communed with the ghosts of the past and, as you sometimes do on such occasions, we considered when our old team hit its highest level of performance. When did everything fit together most perfectly? When did we understand most completely what each of us was about? We agreed very quickly it was that night in Lisbon when we tore Benfica apart. Georgie ran riot, but then so did the team. Every pass seemed to find its target. Every run seemed to have a point. We were unstoppable—and surely we would remain so in the semi-finals against Partizan Belgrade?

Of course it would have been impossible to come up with a match that carried any heavier load of emotion. For Matt Busby, Harry Gregg, Bill Foulkes and me going back to Belgrade was like retracing footsteps that never ceased to haunt us. In footballing terms Partizan were not so special, certainly not as good as the team we had come so close to dismantling on that frozen pitch in the first half of our last game before Munich, but we were caught in a strange, almost eerie listlessness. There was also the problem of George Best. The destroyer of Benfica had picked up a cartilage injury in an FA Cup match against Preston, but the Old Man, conscious of the mystique that George had created in Lisbon, asked him to go into the game with his knee strapped. However, when Best missed an early chance that in Lisbon he would probably have converted with his eyes closed, it was clear that the gamble would fail.

259

Partizan scored early in the second half, taking a quick throw-in which we claimed was ours, and we were never able to get back in the game. Denis Law drew a fine save from the goalkeeper, and then hit the bar, but that was the extent of our chances. We lost 2–0, and if it was the kind of deficit that had been swept aside in the past, with the Stretford End willing their visitors to defeat, there was perhaps now a sense that a team from Belgrade, for one reason or another, might never be party to our happiness. This feeling was evident not least in the eyes of Matt Busby. He made the usual pronouncements, in the bowels of the stadium after the game and at Old Trafford a week later, but maybe the word Belgrade and the thought of once again confronting a Serbian team had provoked an old dread.

At first the theory looked vulnerable enough as we swarmed all over them in the second leg, but Partizan defended as though they were manning tank traps. Paddy Crerand and a Belgrade player were sent off for fighting, which was to our disadvantage in that we missed the bite of his long passing. Nobby Stiles scored in the seventy-third minute, but it was no good: the curse of Belgrade could not be lifted.

A few days later we lost yet another semi-final, to Everton at Bolton in the FA Cup.

For the Old Man it was revisiting old disappointment, old pain. He knew the team was strong and talented, and more competitive than it had been at any time since Munich, but after Lisbon he had been convinced that it was finally his time to win the prize in which he had invested so much more than mere football ambition. Defeat by Everton was a blow, but it was the one by Partizan which hurt down to his bones. In the dressing room he sighed, and submitted to a wave of doubt and depression. 'We will never win the European Cup now,' he said.

Very soon, Nobby and I would be celebrating our part in winning the World Cup for England—but it did not disguise the fact that we were left with some unfinished business. There was one last burden placed on our ambitions. It was, of course, to prove the Old Man wrong.

# CHAPTER 18

# FORGING TEAM SPIRIT

Old Trafford, 18 March 1967: it should have been a day to cherish, one of those you remember warmly when you look back on a campaign that ended in success. We beat Leicester City 5–2, George Best made some wonderful runs, I scored with a low shot, Denis Law chipped over my World Cup team-mate Gordon Banks quite beautifully, and the new blood of substitute David Sadler flowed strongly as he headed in the fifth.

Yet not even the news that Burnley, leaping out of the pack as their days of power began to ebb, had ambushed Liverpool and helped strengthen our place at the top of the league could drive the chill out of the dressing room.

The wider picture might come into focus somewhere along the line of the twenty undefeated games which would carry us to another title—and open up Europe once again—but for the moment all any of us could see was David Herd lying on the pitch seriously injured.

David, as he so often did, had given us the perfect start against Leicester in a match vital to our long-term prospects. He scored inside two minutes. It was a routine reward for his hard running and powerful shot. Then he broke his leg. You could see it was a bad break by the way he went down and then the look on his face.

I had seen it happen to John Doherty, Wilf McGuinness, and now David Herd. Inevitably, there are two reactions. You are first reminded of your own

262

good luck, then of how brittle the football life, like the human body, can be. It means that you are obliged to take every day, every game, as it comes, and be grateful that it has passed, if not successfully, at least safely.

Such thoughts dominated the dressing room as we showered and reflected on how easily it could have been any one of us in David's place at the hospital as a doctor examined the damage and offered the most hopeful words he could muster for a man who, so soon after the exhilaration of scoring in front of a vast crowd, was suddenly looking into a future which offered not a single guarantee.

Like so many of the other victims down the years, David said he would fight his fate. He did that, as you would have expected of such a committed professional, but his courage could only take him so far.

He never made it back into the team. He missed the most glorious passage of a side he had done so much to make strong and confident, and what might have been a superb climax to a fine career became a losing fight against the heaviest odds. He went, briefly, to Stoke City, and then played for Waterford in the League of Ireland. Finally, and just for a year, he managed Lincoln City.

David Sadler, who had substituted for David Herd after he was carried off, again took Herd's place in the next match, the one at Anfield that everyone said could well decide the championship. Liverpool had their strongest side: Lawrence, Lawler, Hughes, Smith, Yeats, Stevenson, Callaghan, Hunt, St John, Strong and Thompson. This—with the possible exception of the Leeds United of John Giles, Billy Bremner and Norman Hunter—was the most relentless team in England, and you could see on their faces that Bill Shankly had not been in one of his more whimsical moods when he gave the pre-match talk. You could also see this in the way the Liverpool manager bustled his way down the corridor which, before it reaches the pitch, displays the intimidating notice, 'This is Anfield.' As if you didn't know. Apparently there were no jokes, this time, about the need to overcome just three men. Still furious about the loss to Burnley, Shankly said his men were in danger of throwing away the title they had won so convincingly the previous season—with a six-point margin over Leeds—if they did not 'fight like men'.

Liverpool's response was to produce one of their trademark performances, full of running and pressure. Ian Callaghan provoked a brilliant save from Alex Stepney. Then Ian St John flattened Stepney in a collision on the line. Tommy Smith was coming into his prime, tackling and moving forward quite ferociously in following Shankly's version of the instructions Jimmy Murphy always used to hammer into my ears. For Tommy, the advice was always the same: make your presence felt, show them you're on the field. Translation: establish physical and psychological dominance from the word go.

The Old Man had told us that he saw this as a classic test of our determination to inject into our game a little of the steel that he believed had become such a vital factor in the game, both in England and in Europe—something we may have lacked to a crucial degree when sliding out of the European Cup in Belgrade the previous year. He was not disappointed. Stepney was defiant on his line and the back four of Tony Dunne, Bill Foulkes, Nobby Stiles and Bobby Noble seemed capable of mopping up the pressure until midnight.

264

Everyone agreed that the goalless draw was our moral victory. We had proved that we could slug it out in the trenches as well as score pretty goals, and there was a lot of satisfaction on the team bus rolling home down the East Lancashire Road. It is the way of football to celebrate great victories, to make them the milestones of any career, but sometimes a deeper pride comes from knowing that you have come up with a result under the heaviest pressure. It strengthens you in a way that is never true of a flurry of goals against opposition which, deep down, you know has been wanting in some vital area of the game.

Though I had been as unable to provide a cutting edge of counter-attack as either Denis Law or George Best, I still felt this had been a good and significant day. We had achieved our basic ambition of frustrating a Liverpool we knew would attack us from the first whistle, and both Matt Busby and Jimmy Murphy seemed pleased with the level of effort. Jimmy had passed on his usual insight that footballers never suffered heart attacks because of hard work and he was quick to say that we had shown enough energy—and spirit. There had been some evidence of the mettle of champions.

It was a theory confirmed in the penultimate match of the season at Upton Park, where we completed our twentieth unbeaten league game with a 6–1 trouncing of West Ham. My World Cup team-mates Bobby Moore, Geoff Hurst and Martin Peters suffered as painfully as Gordon Banks had at Old Trafford, but once again one of our most extravagant attacking performances was achieved under a shadow; in fact at the end of this occasion, after goals from George Best, Denis Law (2), Paddy Crerand, Bill Foulkes

265

and me, there were two reasons for gloom working against the elation we felt at landing another title.

At the end of the match there was fighting on the terraces, some of the worst, it was said, ever seen in an English football ground, and though the disease of football hooliganism was still in its teething stages, there had been earlier evidence that the days when a man could take his family to a game without danger might be on the point of disappearing. It was depressing to think that the times Jack and I had enjoyed so much at St James' Park and Roker Park might soon belong to another, all but forgotten culture. Hooliganism is a threat which has come and gone and then returned down the years since then, but if there is one common duty for all in football it is to be vigilant in a way that perhaps none of us were when the problem first began to take deep root in the sixties.

The other reason for sadness was the absence of Bobby Noble, who at twenty-one had been playing so well that he had kept my friend Shay Brennan out of the side. Bobby, a Stockport lad, was not the most elegant full back you ever saw, and there were also stories that off the field and away from the club he liked a good time, but he had all the qualities of a great defender. He was especially suited to meet the new demand of Matt Busby for a United who defended and tackled as hard as it attacked elegantly. Two weeks before the decisive performance at West Ham, Bobby had been involved in a car crash while driving home after a game with Sunderland. Like David Herd, he insisted he would win back his place, but when he came back to work he made a shocking discovery. His head and chest injuries had taken away his natural understanding of how to play the game.

There had been other prices to pay for the championship win which Matt Busby had made such a priority. However, when you considered how cruelly David Herd and Bobby Noble had been cut down, a 5–1 League Cup defeat by Blackpool, and Norwich City's 2–1 fourth round FA Cup win before a huge crowd at Old Trafford, didn't seem quite so disastrous. As it turned out, in fact, these slip-ups almost seemed pre-ordained, as though for us there could be only one major challenge—the title and beyond.

For Matt Busby, as his eyes turned to Europe again, there was one great encouragement. He had reason to believe once more that his team, despite the setbacks, had shown a capacity to grow stronger after the kind of disappointment which had threatened to be so crushing in Belgrade. The suspicion then was that something as vital as reasonable hope had died in the Old Man that gut-wrenching night in Serbia, but such fears had surely been banished in the campaign which followed, before the final break-out at Upton Park—the classic pattern of winning at home and drawing away.

This is something that doesn't just sprout overnight. It is a collective understanding of the strengths and weaknesses of team-mates, a willingness to fight, to grow strong at the points of vulnerability. There had been plenty of those down the years, not least in the run of semi-final defeats, but there was also a sense that we could come back with our self-belief undamaged.

It was certainly a satisfying time for me to reflect on the course of my career. I would be thirty in a few months and though my enthusiasm for the game was as strong as ever—as were my ambitions—I already had plenty of reasons to be grateful for all the circumstances that had drawn me to United and their special vision on how the game should be played.

I had been part of three championship-winning teams, won one and lost two FA Cup finals, plus played in more semi-finals than I cared to recall, and had reached two European Cup semi-finals. I had also just been voted European Player of the Year, a great honour but one which I also accepted on behalf of the England team who had won the World Cup and a Manchester United team which had once again proved that it was still a major force in the game.

It meant that with the Old Man and Bill Foulkes, the only other survivor of Munich still playing in the team, I was left with just one unfulfilled goal. We had to make another run at the European Cup, we had to put right the losses against AC Milan, Real Madrid and Partizan at the last but one hurdle—and we had to make good on that promise we had all made to ourselves at various stages of our recovery from the air crash.

Ten years on, which if we could do it was not so long down the road of a football club, we had to make a proper monument for the men who died in Munich.

In the summer of 1967, we had reason to believe that the coming season might just see the completion of five years of growth which, taken overall, was not so difficult to measure. At Wembley in 1963 some of the chemistry had been in place; now, two titles and a near miss in Europe later, we could look back on some great days—and great matches—with considerable pride. There was a bit more fibre—and maybe devil—about Manchester United. We could see where the doubts had been engaged and countered and where, after some failure, we had made our strongest efforts to reassert our status as a leading team.

Many would have chosen the eruption at the Estadio da Luz as the most compelling evidence that we were indeed able to compete again at the highest level, but in the matter of forging the team's spirit my favourite example was not one match but three. All of them were against Sunderland, who, though it was hard to believe for much of the time, were still a Second Division team in 1964. That status, though, was obviously a temporary condition when we drew them in the quarter-final of the 1963–64 FA Cup. Under their tough and experienced manager Alan Brown—who had earlier built a reputation for iron discipline in shaping Burnley into a major force in the land—Sunderland had invested heavily in young players and were moving back to what they believed was a right dictated by their history: a return to the First Division which had been their constant home from the nineteenth century until they were relegated in 1958.

Sunderland won the league title six times before they were relegated. Now, everything about them, and not least the fervour of their vast support, said they were impatient to be back where they belonged. All three games, I believe, pushed forward the understanding of football in all those who saw them—and in all those who played.

Brown was fighting out the Second Division championship with Leeds United's Don Revie, and there wasn't a hint of an inferiority complex about Sunderland when they came at us so strongly at Old Trafford. Their confidence was well founded. They moved the ball with conviction, and when they ran into forward positions they did it with a bright optimism. They had strength in all areas of the team. Jimmy Montgomery, as he would prove so spectacularly nearly a decade later, when he defied a then mighty Leeds United in the 1973 cup final, was a goalkeeper of both nerve and great agility. In the middle of their defence, they had a glamorous giant, the handsome, elegant Irishman Charlie Hurley, who even in the Second Division was said to be one of the country's best-paid players. He had both talent and aura, and in Sunderland was nothing less than a cult figure. Nick Sharkey, a product of a good youth system, was building a reputation as a striker; another Irishman, Johnny Crossan, was recognised as one of the most skilful players in the game, and out on the left George Mulhall was a winger of craft who had been capped by Scotland.

This was a team who were right to believe they could offer more than hope and speculation, and just before, and after, half time they proved it with devastating effect. First Mulhall headed in a cross from his fellow winger Brian Usher, then Crossan ran from the halfway line to beat our goalkeeper Dave Gaskell. Maybe it was because of my tribal origins in the North East, but I had rarely felt so drawn into a battle, and there was some relief when Hurley, of all people, headed into his own goal.

In the first half, despite the quality of the opposition, we had probably assumed that our firepower, which had carried us through a crisis at Southampton in the third round, then swept us by Bristol Rovers and Barnsley, would again be the decisive factor. The result was a performance which was not as disciplined as it should have been in defence and we paid again, just five minutes after Hurley's own goal, when Shay Brennan fouled Crossan and then had to watch him score the penalty. With four minutes to go, we were still 3–1 down and you could sense the resignation seeping from the Old Trafford terraces. But this, we seemed to be saying, just wouldn't do. We raised ourselves for one last push and in the 87th minute I did something rather extraordinary. I went in for a corner and headed it home. We won the ball at the restart and swept down on Montgomery again, this time with George Best finishing the move for 3–3.

Four days later the battle was resumed at Roker Park in circumstances that would prove quite unforgettable. If anyone had ever doubted the passions that football could release in my corner of the country, they needed to be in the little streets around the old stadium. The official gate figure was 46,727, but gates were knocked down and some estimates had the crowd as high as 90,000—with another thousand, finally, locked out.

Sunderland didn't have a ticket system and it was a case of first come, first served. As we travelled from our hotel to the stadium, it seemed as though the whole world wanted to see the game. Apart from local pride, it also said something about the rise of Manchester United back to some of the old levels of appeal first created by the lovely football produced by the team of 1948. It took the team bus an hour to inch round from one side of the ground to the other.

Again the pressure was immense out on the field— and again we struggled to stay in the tie. Nick Sharkey scored five minutes before half time and it took us half an hour to equalise, Denis Law winning a vital half yard against a defence which until then hadn't offered an inch. The noise generated by all those fans crammed into the dark, and what must have been extremely dangerous, terraces was amazing. It was though we were playing beyond

271

ourselves, carried on by the fervour of the crowd and an unwillingness, after so much effort, to abandon the fight.

Extra time was inevitable—and yet another ordeal for us. In the first minute, Maurice Setters lost control of the ball in the rain and it squirted past Dave Gaskell. With two minutes to go, we were heading out of the cup we had won so convincingly less than a year before. Then, as Sunderland was building to a roar that would surely have swept down across the River Wear and along the coastline, I repeated my unlikely deed of the first game. I headed another equaliser. The ball came to me in the air in the box, but I cannot say it was a particularly assured nod of my head. The ball went in a slow arc over the line, with just the tips of Jimmy Montgomery's fingers away from stopping it.

In the second replay at Huddersfield, before 54,952 ticket-holding fans, Nick Sharkey again put Sunderland in the lead, two minutes after half time. However, this time there was a factor beyond the discipline and the work ethic the old general Alan Brown had injected into his team. Denis Law, returning to the ground where he had first beguiled Bill Shankly, announced he was in a familiar place and was taking charge. No one could do that more imperiously, and his first goal came a minute after Sharkey's. His hat-trick was completed in the 61st minute. Phil Chisnall interjected with one goal and David Herd made it 5–1.

Sunderland deserved better than that score-line after putting so much effort—and skill—into the three games, but they would have some reward when, after so spectacularly signalling their intentions to return to the top flight, they fought on and shared promotion to the First Division with Leeds a few weeks later.

For us what came after was only anti-climax: a 3–1 defeat by West Ham down the road in Hillsborough, and second place to Liverpool in the league. But then maybe sometimes there are other measurements to be made: when the team bus pulled away from the Leeds Road stadium, the arena Denis Law had reclaimed so brilliantly and where, after the fight of our lives, we had finally come out on top, I said to myself, 'Well, if you ever wanted to watch football, or play football, it could never get better than this. I will never forget these three games.' That still holds as true today as when the final whistle came on that muddy field in Yorkshire.

I remember the matches quite separately and for different reasons. The first one carried the shock of struggling to compete with a second divison team, even though it was one of obvious talent and managed by one of the early pioneers of modern, organised football. Brown was a difficult, often inaccessible man, but he imposed standards and won many admirers, not least another coaching revolutionary, Malcolm Allison, who produced a wonderfully dynamic Manchester City team.

The second game at Roker distilled everything I believed was true about the potential of football to capture the imagination of the ordinary working man. There was a fever in the moist air.

The third game was made to look one-sided, but at least half of it wasn't. It required us to drive ourselves forward as we had never done before—and would rarely be asked to again.

Looking back, the semi-final defeat which then came to us against West Ham—a team we had beaten

2–0 on their own ground a week earlier—was not such a disgrace. Bobby Moore had one of his best ever club games, and when we called on the last of our reserves—one step from a return to Wembley—we found they had gone. They had been drawn out of us by Sunderland three times in nine days, and when we travelled to Hillsborough it was to try to cross a bridge too far. However, I would never believe all that effort had been misspent.

# CHAPTER 19

# THE FOOTBALL TRIP OF OUR LIVES

One day recently I was sitting alone in the Old Trafford stands, facing the Stretford End and taking in the sweep of the empty, beautifully manicured green field as I thought of the old days and old games. Suddenly a burst of action flared in my mind's eye: light summer rain was falling as Denis Law won the ball at the goal-line to the left of the near posts and made off irresistibly down the left side. When the full back, Tottenham's Joe Kinnear, came to challenge, Denis went by him as though he didn't exist.

It had been wonderful and unforgettable to see. I had been out on the left, but moved inside to create the space that would accommodate Denis's run. Brian Kidd, who at eighteen was making a statement of talent that might rush him to glory at an age when I had still been fretting over my chances of getting to play just one game at the highest level, had already announced an easy ability to slip his marker, and he did this again, perfectly, before inviting a pass. Denis laid the ball into Kidd, who quickly rolled it across the front of the eighteen-yard line and into my path. The shot swirled past Pat Jennings, one of the greatest goalkeepers of all time.

The movement had lasted no more than five or six seconds. I had made my run without ever being near the ball. The Spurs defence, which was also manned by players of the quality of Dave Mackay, Mike England and Cyril Knowles, had not come near to closing the hole made for me by Denis Law's charge and the movement of young Kidd.

It was a lovely moment—and an encouraging signal in a Charity Shield game that introduced the season of 1967–68 which, whatever else it produced, required us to win the European Cup.

In one way, though, the passage of play which was so thrilling to be part of, and which I have always been able to recall so vividly that it might have happened yesterday, was something of an illusion in what it said about the future of Denis Law. For three seasons largely free of injuries he had been unstoppable, and now it seemed, when maybe it would matter more than ever before, he was still in the richest vein of his career. Unfortunately, however, the sweet and biting simplicity of Denis's impact on that game against Spurs became progressively elusive through the season, initially through disciplinary problems—he missed nine matches after a fight with Arsenal's Ian Ure, a climax to some volatile reactions to heavy tackling which had plunged him into controversy when an opponent's jaw was broken in a flare-up on the summer tour of Australia—and then, more seriously, through injury.

He would play just three games in our European Cup campaign, and two of them were in the formal business of the tie with the part-timers of Hibernians of Malta. By the end of the season, Denis would be in a hospital bed after a knee operation.

There would be other disappointments. We were ejected from the FA Cup in the third round, losing by the only goal, which came fourteen minutes into extra time of a replay against Spurs at White Hart Lane. Also, in a tremendous race, we let go of our title on the last day, losing 2–1 to fifteenth-placed Sunderland while Manchester City, having won at Tottenham a few days earlier, claimed the championship in a thrilling 4–3 win at Newcastle. It didn't help that City's Malcolm Allison's after-match reaction was less than modest. He said, 'Next stop Mars?'

We, however, still had to face our most pressing reality. Our next stop was in Madrid, at the Bernabeu, for the second leg of the European Cup semi-final. It was not inter-planetary travel, just the most important football trip of our lives.

Little or nothing in the campaign had proved easy—even the Maltese had held us to a goalless draw on their flinty pitch—but the harder it got, the more determined we became. Losing the cup was unfortunate, mislaying the title careless, but no one wanted to consider the possibility of surrender in Europe.

In the second round in Bosnia, Sarajevo tested our resolve in the only way they could. They were a team of limited ability, but, like most Balkan sides, they lacked nothing in resolve—or physical ruthlessness. The tackles were flying in, sometimes thigh high, and Alex Stepney did well to stop a shot from the striker Musemic on the line. It was a small miracle that the only casualty was the Sarajevo winger Prodanovic. He left after half an hour.

Stepney's goal was besieged in the second half but the defence—the polished young Scot Francis Burns (keeping Shay Brennan out of the team) and David Sadler (replacing the injured Nobby Stiles)—made the vital tackles and held their nerve. John Fitzpatrick, whose career would end prematurely when he injured his leg in a collision with John Giles, also gave us some iron. Bill Foulkes was, well, Bill Foulkes, the same old piece of English granite.

This was no gradual re-introduction to the more

competitive edge of the European Cup. We were back in the middle of the type of battle we had lost in Belgrade two years earlier, but this time we headed off the ambush. There were no goals, only the prospect of another highly physical collision at Old Trafford. No one was disappointed.

The Bosnians, if anything, were even harder when the bell rang a second time. Three Sarajevo players were booked and the midfielder Prljaca was sent off for chopping down George Best, a fate that could also have befallen the victim when he lashed out at the goalkeeper, Muftik. Fortunately for us, George escaped—and proceeded to send us through, putting in a cross that could only be pushed to the feet of John Aston who scored, then scoring himself in the sixty-third minute.

It said everything about the Sarajevo effort that they refused to accept that their massive and, it has to be said, unscrupulous application had failed, Delalic scoring with just two minutes to go. In the dressing room we all agreed we were relieved to have survived tackling which the Old Man described as 'the most disgraceful I have ever seen'—and also any disciplinary action following some scuffling in the tunnel, when some of the emotions of two fierce games came surging to the surface.

It was rarely easy fighting on Europe's Eastern front, and the draw committed us to another exercise in survival. Katowice, home of Gornik Zabrze in the Silesian coalfields of Poland, was the next challenging venue. It was said, correctly, that even in March the wind there could feel as though it had blown all the way from Siberia.

Only once before had we known such demanding conditions in European action—at the start of our last campaign, against Vorwaerts in East Berlin. That was a Denis Law night. He scored one, brilliantly, and made another for John Connelly. It had been bleak going through Checkpoint Charlie, Frank McGhee, the *Daily Mirror* sportswriter, lightening the mood only briefly when he signed an entry form at the border in the name of James Bond, but it scarcely prepared us for the conditions over which Denis prevailed so memorably at the Walter Ulbrecht stadium.

He was missing, however, in Poland where we had to defend a 2–0 lead given to us at Old Trafford by a Gornik own goal and one from Brian Kidd just a minute from the end. This might not sound like the toughest of challenges, but we carried a lot of apprehension into the tough industrial city of Katowice, which is invariably the location for key Polish international matches because of the frenzied support supplied by the coal miners. In winter they warmed themselves on heated vodka.

No one felt the edge of tension more than the Old Man. He had always been superb at disguising his deepest feelings when he knew the world was looking at him, but the tension he carried visibly was probably inevitable. He was just three matches away from his great goal, a European Cup final that would be played, so helpfully for us, at Wembley. This was a fact which made it all the more unthinkable that we should stumble at this rugged outpost of the game—but of course we did think about it, and it didn't help when we looked out of the window of the bus carrying us from the airport and saw huddled figures in ice-bound streets.

We also knew that Kidd's late goal had given us a flattering win in the first leg. The Gornik defence had played with great resolution, and if George's shot hadn't flown in off a Polish body after an hour our increasingly desperate assaults on their goal might well have been contained. There was no question the Poles could play with bite and skill, and in Włodzimierz Lubanski they had one of the world game's most celebrated forwards. At Old Trafford he had been a brooding threat; in front of his adoring public, we feared he might well produce more.

The concern of some of the lads stretched to the food that would be offered at the hotel. They had brought little stoves to warm up cans of soup, a decision which proved embarrassing when we were fed perfectly adequately in the big dining room. However, there was no doubting the chief menace to our progress into the semi-finals—the cold that froze the thought processes as well as the limbs, plus a pitch surface that made almost every basic move a kind of Polish roulette.

We were shocked when we saw the pitch on the eve of the game. The snow had been crushed flat and into a hard pack. Matt Busby agonised over whether to press for a postponement, but the view of some players—which was expressed most strongly by Paddy Crerand and had my agreement—was that if conditions were indeed extremely difficult they would probably suit us better than Gornik. It was they who had to force the issue, get the ball into our net at least twice, and when you tested the pitch you realised immediately that it was a virtually hopeless task, even for a player of Lubanski's skills.

In the cruel wind, that view was soon confirmed. Moving the ball from one end of the pitch to the other took an age, and almost invariably moves broke down as one forward after another fell or slid out of control when challenged by a defender.

Lubanski became increasingly frustrated as the fans cheered hopefully whenever he touched the ball, but for him all contact was brief and fruitless. With Bill Foulkes missing, much was expected of David Sadler when he moved back alongside Nobby Stiles, and he met the challenge superbly—as did all of a defence in which Francis Burns was continuing to impress with his speed and neat touch. When the Poles scored, after seventy minutes, it was from one moment of defensive breakdown, Alex Stepney being penalised for obstruction in the box and Lubanski's striking partner Lentner running on to the free kick. It meant twenty minutes of intense pressure as the wind cut through us, but, fortunately, Gornik had had their moment of penetration.

I discovered that the night offered one last threat to some peaceful sleep when I finally went to my hotel room, warm at last, in the early hours of the morning. Almost immediately, the phone rang. It was my friend and accountant, Reuben Kay, who had joined us on the trip. His voice was agitated when he told me, 'Bobby, somebody's after me. My phone keeps ringing and when I pick it up someone keeps saying, Comrade Ten, Comrade Ten.' I went to Reuben's room, calmed him down a little and took him to the reception desk in the hotel. It didn't take long to identify the problem. The culprit was someone seeking George Best's autograph. He had got hold of the wrong room number.

It was a small reminder of how football, back when the Berlin Wall seemed like a permanent statement about the divisions of Europe and the world, had the power to draw people together, however confusingly at times. Recently, when a

Russian intelligence man was poisoned in London, I was reminded of Reuben's anxiety in the small hours of the Polish night—and also of another curious affair that came at around that time, after the BBC rang me up one day to say that one of their Russian correspondents was anxious to meet me. They wondered if I could give him a few hours of my time. I said that I was going to watch a match at Burnley that night; if he cared to catch a plane, I would pick him up at the airport and take him to Turf Moor. We could talk on the journey and at the match.

When his interviewing was done, the Russian said, 'I know you're going to see your friend, the great goalkeeper Lev Yashin in Moscow when you play in his testimonial match, and I wonder if you could give him a present from me?' It seemed a little odd, but when I agreed he handed me a pen. I never knew a pen could be so heavy, and I thought to myself, 'Well, what am I going to do now?' I didn't want to make any kind of fuss; Lev was a personal friend and I worried that I might cause him some embarrassment in those Cold War days by going to the police with this strange object. So I took the 'pen' to Moscow, though not without a twinge of misgiving, and duly presented it to the great man. It was curious that when I explained it came from a Russian BBC man in London, he didn't say a word, just slipped it into his pocket, almost as though it was something he had expected. But from whom? Could it possibly have been M?

Unlike Frank McGhee of the *Daily Mirror*, however, I had no yearnings for a career in espionage, a fact which struck me again on another visit to Moscow. I received a call from a Russian, who said, 'My friends and I want to arrange a meeting with you.' I told him that, as he knew where I was staying, he should come down to my hotel. 'Oh, no,' he replied. 'We want to see you outside the Bolshoi Ballet.' I declined, quite sensibly I think.

For some time playing football in Eastern Europe had been both an adventure and a mystery. Moscow, Belgrade, Budapest, Prague, Warsaw, they were fascinating places if you wanted to venture, however carefully, into another world. My charming and somewhat eccentric friend, Geoffrey Green of *The Times*, perhaps did it with less care than most of his colleagues or the players of Manchester United and England. Sometimes he arrived at an airport, almost invariably dressed in his Russian old leather coat, carrying not much more than his prized banjo. Once, though, he took this to the extreme when he arrived in Budapest without a passport. The Hungarian officials were aghast that someone in those days had expected to walk into their tightly secured country without even a slip of paper to say who he was. Of course, he was the talk of the airport bus that back then would carry both the players and those who wrote about them—but one of his colleagues, who was at the time muttering that this was so typical of Geoffrey, was soon quite shocked when he looked out of the window. There, flying past us, was a government limousine—with the football correspondent of *The Times* sitting serenely in the back seat.

Geoffrey Green was one of those characters who bring a little spice to life. For someone like me, who always, whether successfully or not, tried to do what I thought was expected of me, he was operating on a rather different planet. He went his own way, in his own style, but one of the things I always liked about him was his obvious passion for football. It showed in his beautiful writing and conversation, which might occasionally be quirky but was always filled with warmth and humour.

Once, on a long flight from South America, I wandered to the back of the plane in search of a cup of tea. As was often the case, my team-mates were sleeping while I fidgeted in my seat, bored or a little tense depending on my mood and the quality of the flight. Geoffrey was in the galley and he wasn't drinking tea. He was sipping a whisky and was plainly in a very good mood. 'Bobby,' he said, 'can you believe I'm sixty and my young wife is going to give me my first child! I want you to be the godparent.' I said I would be honoured, even though I didn't quite know what godfathers were supposed to do. Geoffrey duly named my goddaughter Ti, because he had referred to her as It before she was born, which even Geoffrey knew wouldn't do for a young lady.

Once at a football writer's dinner his speech was very short. He simply produced a record player and put on Louis Armstrong, one of his favourites, intoning, 'What a wonderful world'. His presence always helped to make it so—and he could certainly have played it again on the hot, tense night in Madrid when Manchester United finally fought their way through to the final of the European Cup.

We led 1–0 from the first leg, with a fine goal from George Best, but even though Real were no longer the force that had swept beyond us eleven years earlier in another semi-final, with Gento their only surviving player of the great team, the narrow advantage left us uneasy. Denis Law had briefly returned to the European theatre that night, but he knew he was fighting a losing battle against a knee injury, and after the game he had been told he needed to go to hospital for an operation. For the away leg, the versatile David Sadler took Denis's place in the forward line and Bill Foulkes was brought back to the middle of defence. From the Old Man came the eternal advice: play naturally, pass accurately—and, above all, play without fear.

The best advice in the world would have counted for nothing, however, if Nobby Stiles had not simply refused to be beaten. His defiance grew through this most vital of games to an extraordinary degree and before the end, decisively, it had touched us all.

Two years earlier he had become a hero of the nation when he brilliantly curbed the threat of Portugal's Eusebio in a World Cup semi-final. That was the performance that persuaded our team-mate George Cohen that the Football Association should make a video and offer it to all young players as a classic lesson in how to defend. Now, in the Bernabeu, Nobby produced something more than a technical masterpiece. He persuaded all of us that defeat simply wasn't an option, and he did it from a position that, from any other perspective but his own, would have looked pretty hopeless.

It was not just that we were 3–1 down at half time. Amancio, the hero of a crowd of 125,000, was running free. He was also arrogant to the point of provocation, needling us and playing to a great gallery that greeted his every touch with the most excited anticipation. Later Nobby revealed that his taming of Amancio—the key to the game—was not entirely legal.

He reported that after the Real player had kicked him, off the ball and without a word from the Italian referee, he had taken football law into his own hands, throwing a punch that escaped the attention of the officials—if not the booing crowd—and rattled the Real star. I didn't see the punch, but Nobby said that one of our team-mates' reactions could just be heard above the din: 'Fucking hell, Nob,' he exclaimed. Nobby's contribution amounted to so much more than one piece of villainy, which he justified by saying that he had feared he might break down with injury at any moment because his leg was tightening a little more each minute with the effects of the illicit kick. Nobby had had heat treatment at half time, but he was concerned that Amancio's speed might embarrass him in the second half, and that the Spaniard's advantage had been created quite unfairly. It was a version of football justice to which no one in our dressing room, perhaps not surprisingly, could raise an objection.

We were desperate at half time, really quite distraught after seeing our lead vanish under goals from Pirri, Gento and Amancio, with our only riposte an own goal forced off the defender Zoco. Matt Busby buried his own feelings of disappointment, insisting that we could get back into the game. He kept pointing out that on aggregate we were only one goal down. His encouragement wasn't all that comforting when we thought about what faced us: a Real side made confident by their goals and the extraordinary level of support from the vast crowd. Their cockiness was underlined as we walked back down the tunnel to the pitch. Some of the Real players, with Gento involved, made it clear that they considered the game won and there was something of a confrontation, with Nobby, naturally, to the fore.

He was magnificently defiant. The man who was christened Happy because of his tendency to moan would not let us feel sorry for ourselves. Despite his injury worry, he made a series of brilliant tackles, and that changed the entire mood of the game. Suddenly, we were thinking, 'The little sod is winning everything'—and the opposition were beginning to argue among themselves. At half time, when the Old Man had said we needed only to score one goal, we had nodded our agreement—but had thought, 'Oh, yes, boss, but have you noticed how they are playing?' Now we were beginning to feel differently, although the immense heat was a constant worry.

When David Sadler, who had been pushed forward in pursuit of the aggregate equaliser, scored twenty minutes into the second half, the Bernabeu fell into a shocked silence. It was a softish goal—it only rolled into the net—but its impact could not have been greater. Nobby was emphatic now, 'Come on, come on, you bastards!' he shouted. 'We can win it now, we've just got to keep the focus.'

He was right, of course, but saying it is not always the same as doing it, even though there was no doubt that we were now in charge. Just before we had equalised, the ball ran out of play to the little wall that kept the crowd back. One fan picked it up as I ran, obviously in a hurry, to retrieve. The Spanish supporter went to send the ball away from me down the line, which, with no ball-boy around, would have lost precious time that was becoming more vital by the second. I said to myself, 'Just keep it cool, just walk . . .' It was quite strange really. As I slowed and walked towards him, he kept the ball in his hands. Then, when I reached the wall, he just handed it to me.

It was one of those little psychological moments that can be so important at a vital stage of a game. My fear was that if I'd kept running, the fan would have kicked the ball away, and with me chasing after it, everybody would have thought we were panicking. It was the last thing we should do. Nobby had convinced us that we could still win.

Three minutes after Sadler's equaliser, George took the ball down the right side to the dead-ball line. I was running in from behind as he pulled the ball back into the box, and as I looked across I saw a red shirt. My instinct was, 'This is a chance.' Then, in a flash, I saw that the person on the end of the pass was not Brian Kidd or David Sadler or John Aston. Of all people, it was Bill Foulkes—the granite man, the rock of the defence, but unquestionably the last man any of us wanted to see running on to a George Best cross twelve minutes from the end of a match that could possibly destroy, one last time, our chances of ever winning the European Cup.

How can I describe one of the most important goals I would ever see? Maybe Bill will settle for 'exquisite'. Those of us who expected to see the ball balloon high on to the terraces behind the goal were instantly heaped in shame. Not only did Bill Foulkes score, he looked like a striker of the ages, tucking in his shot so easily, so unanswerably, that the goalkeeper Betancort, who had shown brilliant reflexes in the first game at Old Trafford, could scarcely move.

Foulkes was buried in red shirts led by Nobby Stiles.

Later, I was unable to join Norma and my friend, Dave Thomas, the golfer, and his wife, for a dinner of celebration. I couldn't move from my room because of a bad case of dehydration. The conditions had been so humid, and in those days they didn't let the players have water. Today's footballers are overwhelmed with water bottles, but back then you were obliged to carry on and hope you didn't collapse in extreme conditions. When the final whistle went I fell to the turf. I couldn't muster the energy to kiss it, but I did think, at a moment I would never forget, 'It's ours now. We are going to win the European Cup.'

# CHAPTER 20

# THE EUROPEAN CUP FINAL, 1968

The certainty was a dangerous feeling, maybe—at least it could have been if at any point before 29 May 1968 at Wembley Stadium I had forgotten one of the first lessons a professional must learn—that you are never going to win a game by right; when you kick off, nothing of the past matters, nothing about reputation—and certainly not just deserts. Still, on the flight back from Madrid I couldn't get out of my head the idea that the European Cup might well have been sitting next to me. I couldn't stop thinking, 'We've won it in Madrid—we've won it in a place which matters so much to the club and to me.' I just couldn't see us losing a European Cup final against Benfica at Wembley—the place where Nobby had jigged so ecstatically when we beat Germany in the World Cup final two years earlier, where I couldn't hold back the tears when I embraced another team-mate, my brother Jack.

The Old Man's genius for motivation, his ability to calm or inspire his players in the simplest terms, would surely never operate in more favourable circumstances.

The European Cup, I have always reckoned, was much harder to win than England's World Cup. The World Cup ran over just four weeks, and we had the advantage of playing all our games at home. It takes effectively two years to win the European Cup and that's a long time—Manchester United knew better than anybody how hazards can rise up suddenly and strike you down. For Matt Busby, however, the challenge had now reached its easiest point. We were playing on our own soil, and anyone who glanced at our history knew that no club and team ever had greater motivation.

Apart from the memory of Munich, and our duty to those who died there to play to our very limits, there were the semi-final defeats of '57, '58 and '66, against Real Madrid, Milan and Partizan. Added to those focal points was the fact that for some of us this was possibly our last—and certainly our best—chance to win the great trophy.

Bill Foulkes, Shay Brennan—who had returned to the team in Madrid because of worries that Francis Burns might struggle against the guile of Gento—Pat Crerand and I were all approaching that point when we had to wonder how many opportunities were left. It was something I'm sure was also occupying the mind of Denis Law, denied the possibility of a great climactic moment in a brilliant career as he prepared to enter hospital for a vital operation at the age of twenty-eight. If I felt any touch of doubt as we approached the final, I chased it away with the thought, 'Well, this is it—if we don't win it this time, we will never do it.'

Before the final we stayed at Great Fosters, a country house hotel in Surrey where the first Queen Elizabeth was supposed to have entertained some of her men friends. It was an interesting place, with secret passageways—ideal for the discreet romantic assignations of a ruling monarch I thought.

Every minute of the day, and quite a bit of the night, was dominated by our thoughts on the game. In our bedroom Shay Brennan and I tried to relax, but every time we opened our mouths we would find ourselves babbling about our chances in the final. On the night before the game, however, there was a diversion. As we lay in our beds, staring at the ceiling and trying, and failing, not to think about the match, we heard a ghostly cry very close by. We knew immediately it was Nobby Stiles, but at first we didn't realise he had found one of the secret passageways. He had discovered it led to our room and, quite miraculously when you thought about, he eventually appeared wrapped in a sheet.

When he got over his disappointment that we had recognised him straight away, he was less than flattering about Good Queen Bess's hideaway. 'What a bloody place this is,' he declared while sweeping his hand for dust across the wooden frieze above the fireplace. Naturally, he took out a huge chunk of the history-laden wood. Shay and I reckoned it had previously gone unmolested for about five hundred years. Nobby tried to repair the damage, but we managed to persuade him that it was probably not a good idea.

In the morning we strolled in the countryside, again not very successfully attempting to keep our minds off the game. In the afternoon we watched the Derby on television, along with the millions of people who had decided once again to put their money on Lester Piggott. Even to me, someone who didn't know much about horse racing, the great jockey seemed to have pulled off a masterpiece of timing on the back of Sir Ivor. We could only hope, on a day that seemed to be lasting forever, that we could touch his levels of professionalism.

We didn't fear Benfica. We had, after all, beaten them twice when we met in the tournament two years earlier, the second time so momentously in the

292

Estadio da Luz. That alone, we felt, gave us a big edge psychologically—but it was something we couldn't afford to rest upon. They had some very good players, and one great one in Eusebio. Nobby once again had been given the job of marking him, and he was being asked to reproduce his masterful performance for England in the World Cup semi-final. Rightly, the Old Man reckoned that he was the only man fully equipped to do the job. He was given the usual instructions, which by now he probably knew by heart: shadow him, jockey him, don't give him the chance of a crack on goal and, as often as you can, keep him on his left foot.

Eusebio was the overwhelming threat, he was so quick and strong and had such a good touch, but Benfica did have other strengths. Jaime Graca and Coluna in midfield were clever, strong players, and there was plenty of pace and skill on the flanks in Jose Augusto and Antonio Simoes. If they were given half a chance, the wingers would look for the tall Jose Torres, who had plenty of goals in him. We went over all this again and again, among ourselves and with the Old Man and Jimmy Murphy, but however many times you felt you had covered the ground, the nearer the game came the more you dwelt on the possibility of things going unaccountably wrong.

It was a sticky day and I hated nothing more than playing in humidity. The certainty of this was playing on my mind a little, and from time to time I found myself saying, 'Oh God, what if something goes wrong, what if Eusebio gets away from us, what if one of us makes a stupid mistake?' As captain I felt a heavy responsibility. I had to do everything that was expected of me, and I had to make sure the others didn't forget their responsibilities for a second. In the end, all you could guarantee was that you would run, on and off the ball, until you were ready to drop. If we ran with their players, if we never left them alone, it would be difficult for them. Perhaps it would be impossible.

The greatest fear was of the unexpected and it was a little worrying that the gangling Torres was such a freakish height and so capable of doing something unpredictable. For Nobby and me, however, there were so many points of reassuring familiarity after the World Cup semi-final victory. We would be playing the same 4–3–3 formation, against the same set of wingers, and the beauty of it for us was the simplicity of tactics which Alf Ramsey had imposed on England and the Old Man now hoped would benefit United. Our three midfielders, John Aston on the left, me, Paddy Crerand on the right, playing behind George Best, Brian Kidd and David Sadler—who was also required to pick up Eusebio when Nobby took up a more withdrawn position—could be forwards or defenders. It depended entirely on who had the ball. It would have been more complicated if Benfica hadn't played such orthodox wingers.

Beyond tactics, though, there was something that we had to absorb completely—Benfica were not exactly short of motivation themselves. They had been humiliated by us in front of their own people, and this was, they were no doubt telling themselves, the perfect chance to heal the wounds that were still raw after just two years. It was a point we learned later, that my counterpart Coluna, the captain of Portugal and a man of fierce pride, had been hammering home.

What they couldn't have anticipated was that their right back Adolfo would be injured so early. I felt really sorry for him, even though you could see immediately that it opened up a vast advantage for us—a point that John Aston, who was putting in the most effective performance of his life, repeatedly made clear by knocking the ball past him and racing down the flank. Adolfo was a tortured figure, hobbling in pursuit. It was almost embarrassing. At one point I was saying, 'Just give the ball to me, and I'll give it to John Aston.' Playing without our 4–3–3 structure, Benfica couldn't adjust to support the stricken Adolfo.

As we developed our huge edge along the left side of the field, a thought did strike me that was detached from the nitty gritty of the game, and it is a thought that has stayed with me. Adolfo was in a terrible situation, but he remained a most honourable player. In his circumstances, most players—and maybe this is even more true today—would have leaned on Aston, tried to level off the odds with some tripping and holding, stopping him, indeed, with any means at their disposal. (For anyone detecting a little inconsistency of reaction here on my part, I know it is true my friend Nobby confessed to an unscrupulous act against Amancio in Madrid, but then, I did think the circumstances were different. Nobby had feared that he was going the way of Adolfo now, that he would be lost to the team not because of the random luck of football, to which Adolfo had fallen foul, but because Amancio had deliberately tried to take him out of the game. So, I could say that Nobby had merely been rearranging natural justice.) However, I had the good feeling that always came to me when I played against Portuguese players. I felt that their view of football was almost gentle, as pure as any I had observed: they wanted to play football—they wanted to win, but they also wanted to do it well and with grace. Yes, it is true that back in the World Cup they had been accused, with Hungary, of kicking Pelé out of the tournament, but then that was a matter between Portugal and Brazil, the mother country and the uppity colonials; that was family business. I also have to say that, judging on their most recent appearance in the World Cup, the ruling ethics of the Portuguese team are a little different—and rather less uplifting—these days.

At Wembley the game was flowing strongly in our favour, and as a contest it might have been over if Sadler had been able to take a couple of chances, but as it was we had to be happy with the way it was going. In the first half they had created scarcely a single chance, and Bill Foulkes was again putting in a fantastic performance. At thirty-six, he knew this was a defining moment of his career—and his life—and his commitment was more than impressive. It was moving. He was giving away around five or six inches in height to the deceptively clever Torres, but he battled him for every inch of advantage. He knew that he had little chance of winning the ball in the air, but he made the practical decision to make everything uncomfortable for the tall man. He wouldn't allow him the space or the leverage to place his header—Torres would have to reach too far or stretch back. He couldn't set himself to truly menace Alex Stepney's goal.

I wasn't worried about our full backs. If Shay Brennan or Tony Dunne found themselves in any difficulty, they were immediately supported from midfield. We had a flexibility that stifled Benfica—and gave us the chance to strike on goal early in the second half.

For once it was David Sadler, rather than John

Aston, on the ball out on the left, and I made my move. No dart to the far post in pursuit of some towering header for me. Instead, my preferred option was the decoy run, and that's what I did now. I was looking to create a little space in their defence, but instead of being involved in a diversion I was in at the kill. The ball came at heading height and the goalkeeper Jose Henrique was exposed. I just helped the ball into the back of the net. 'That makes the job quite a bit easier,' I remember thinking.

At half time the Old Man had been calm and consistent: 'Keep doing what you're doing boys, be patient, keep passing.' Passing was the key. The humidity was as bad as I'd feared, and the more possession we had, the more running they had to do. The demands on their legs had of course been exaggerated by Adolfo's situation. I'm sure today's players would find it incomprehensible that we were expected to run so hard for so long in such sapping heat, and without the possibility of substitutes.

We were bearing up well enough under the inevitable pressure that came from Benfica once they had slipped a goal behind, but we still had worries. The law of averages said that Bill Foulkes couldn't frustrate Torres for the entire ninety minutes, and it would only be when the final whistle sounded that we would be able to put away the fear that Eusebio might erupt devastatingly from almost any position on the field.

The first possibility came to pass with ten minutes to go. For the first time Torres beat Bill cleanly in the air, leaping up and nodding the ball down. Jaime Graca was racing in and as I watched I thought, 'Oh, no, this is my worst nightmare.' And so it was. I couldn't see him missing and he didn't.

Naturally, all the Benfica players, except perhaps poor Adolfo, were given new life. Suddenly, they had a real chance of avenging the bad night in Lisbon. For us the time had passed for some great surging statement of superiority. As captain, I would have been mad to say, 'Right, let's charge at them.' Looking round, on this steamy night, you could see that everyone was labouring in one way or another. Socks were rolled down. Every one of us was tired and some were near exhausted. Then the worst case scenario was upon us.

Later, Nobby explained the crisis from his place at the heart of it quite vividly: 'Antonio Simoes broke quickly with the ball after Shay Brennan had gone forward in an attack. I was tracking Eusebio, with Bill Foulkes behind me guarding Jose Torres. Shay was making his ground back and Tony Dunne was out on the left. We had gone forward—and we're now paying the price with the score locked at 1–1. As Simoes played the ball forward, I made my decision to go for it—and break up the attack at source. I thought that Simoes had pushed the ball too far forward, and if I could get to it first I could shut down the danger. I was reassured that the ever dependable Foulkesy was behind me. What I didn't know was that, just as I set off, Torres made a run that dragged Bill out wide. So there was no one behind me, and before I could get in the block Simoes knocked it by me. As I turned I was horrified to see Eusebio bearing down on Alex Stepney's goal.'

I couldn't help thinking how many times we had discussed and fretted over this possibility—and now it was happening. 'Not again,' I groaned. Not another failure to achieve the great ambition. Not another invitation to a thousand regrets. Before such giant and painful reflections, however, there was the burning thought: if there is one person you don't want to see running through with only the goalkeeper to beat, it is Eusebio.

In such an awful situation, there was just one encouragement. It was a hint of body language from Eusebio: he was saying that he too was feeling more than a little pressure. He seemed to be thrusting, even lunging, a little bit too much. Normally, he would have kept the ball down, he would have taken his time and picked his spot, but he was hurrying, and when he thought he was near enough to shoot, he blasted it. Nobby had a tendency to kiss his team-mates in moments of triumph—most famously demonstrated to a global audience when he landed a smacker on George Cohen after winning the World Cup—and, had Alex Stepney merely parried Eusebio's effort, Nobby's enthusiastic embrace would have been entirely justified. But Alex did so much better. He held it cleanly.

Though all of us were, to various degrees, affected by tiredness, we were still quite pleased by the prospect of extra time. When you looked at Benfica you could see they were very close to their limits of endurance—almost certainly nearer to theirs than we were to ours. We were never afraid to play to the last minute of ninety—or to go beyond. It was a matter of English pride that had surfaced so strongly for Nobby and me when we faced extra time in the World Cup, and now it was with us again. 'Look, they've gone, they're knackered,' said Wilf McGuinness when he came on to the field to give some encouragement. I heard him telling Nobby, who had run endlessly in his effort to contain Eusebio, 'Come on, Nob, another half an hour and you're home.'

The Old Man was keen we didn't sprawl on the pitch during our little respite. 'If you lie down, boys,' he said, 'you may stiffen up, and if that happens you might not be able to start again.' I remembered Alf Ramsey making a similar point after Wolfgang Weber had forced England into extra time two summers previously. 'Come on,' said Alf. 'You've got to get to your feet *now*. If they see you getting up before you need to, they will think you're all right.'

Now, looking over to Benfica, it was easy to remember Alf's point. The Portuguese were down and just about out. They didn't look ready to run the extra mile. I had my socks down around my ankles, like Nobby, but it seemed obvious that if we scored they would be unable to come back at us. When Alex Stepney held Eusebio's shot it was almost certainly their last hope of taking the game away from us.

Two minutes into extra time, our weary legs found new energy and our optimism was confirmed. Stepney kicked downfield and as the Benfica central defender Cruz struggled to control the ball, George Best was on him and carrying it away, free and closing on Jose Henrique's goal. As he dribbled the ball around the goalkeeper, I found myself shouting, 'Knock it in, knock it in!' Eventually, in a second that seemed like an eternity, George sent the ball towards the net. Jose Henrique struggled to get back, but he couldn't get there in time. George had done it.

'That has to be it,' I thought. I just couldn't see them coming back, certainly not after Brian Kidd scored another a minute after George's breakthrough. Kiddo headed a corner against the goalkeeper and, when it came back to him in the air, he just managed to squeeze it under the crossbar. I couldn't see the fans out there in the dark, but I could hear them. I could hear the joy and the first singing. I had to hold back the tears that would make my eyes sting when I thought about what this meant. It was all over now. We only had to guard against any stupidity. Nobby and I agreed there was one priority: to keep hold of the ball. We kept running when we had to, avoiding ambitious passes, and playing the ball to each other with infinite care.

We were doing that competently enough to banish all Benfica's hope. They battled to cover the ground, but it was clear they couldn't do much more than go through the motions. Then, when I scored again with twenty-one minutes to go, we really began to believe that the game was over. Brian Kidd took the ball past a Benfica defender, skipping over a rash tackle that no doubt was the result of exhaustion, and once again I moved for the near post. Really we were in a comfort zone by this stage, and when Kiddo played the ball to me, rather than send it across the goal I thought, 'Well, OK, thank you,' and just helped it into the net, looping it over Jose Henrique. The score was 4–1.

It was a beautiful feeling. It was triumph and deliverance all wrapped into one, but the deepest emotion would take a little time to well up. For the moment we had enough to do in getting to the finish. The contest was over, but we still had to play out the time. We still had to drag our bodies around and forget how much had been drained from us this night.

When the final whistle went my strongest sensation was worry for the Old Man. He really was, I felt, an old man. He had been through so much, and this was unquestionably the pinnacle of his football life. For days he had been reminded of the meaning of the game, the legacy of Munich and how his boys had died in pursuit of this trophy. So many people

301

believed that this night was *for* him and *about* him, and it was natural, I suppose, that everyone wanted to touch him at the end of the game.

When I got through to the Old Man, a great crowd of people, including some supporters, were holding on to him. Even though I was so tired, I started to drag them off, one by one. 'Get off, give him some room!' I yelled. Later I thought that was maybe a little bit rude because the fans only wanted to express their happiness, but I was concerned that he was being buffeted one way and then another.

Eventually, he got to his players and hugged them. To be perfectly honest, I cannot tell you precisely my feelings at that moment. Fatigue certainly. I do recall what it meant to embrace team-mates like Bill Foulkes, Nobby Stiles and Shay Brennan, who had been involved in this quest for so long—and maybe especially Bill because, like me, he had been on the snowy airfield and seen Matt Busby down and his team, our friends, destroyed.

I know there was an understanding that something was over, something that had dominated our lives for so long. I walked to the dressing room and drank two bottles of beer, downing them in a rush, one after the other.

# CHAPTER 21

# GATHERING STORM CLOUDS

I would have been wiser to seek out the water that had been denied us out on that sweltering field, but when somebody reached out with a bottle and said, 'Here, Bobby, have a beer,' I took it gratefully. I thought, 'Right now I'd drink anything.' There was an unfortunate consequence, however. As soon as Norma and I got to our room in the Russell Hotel, where the greatest celebration of all my time at Manchester United was about to unfold, I fainted.

It was exactly as it had been in Madrid after the semi-final. Repeatedly, I tried to fight off the effects of dehydration and also, maybe, the huge accumulation of feelings that had built up in me, but each time I thought I had steadied myself, I fainted again.

Finally, I said to Norma, 'You'll have to go downstairs, because there are so many people celebrating and it will look strange if I'm not there. I want to be with them so much, but look, I can't walk to the door. I'll lie down for five minutes, and as soon as I can I'll join you.'

Later, Nobby—who eventually went off to Danny La Rue's club, a favourite place of his, with Shay Brennan—speculated that really my problem was an emotional overload, that maybe I couldn't trust myself to cope with so many deep private thoughts and memories on such a public occasion, washed in champagne and illuminated by a thousand camera flashes.

When I thought about it, I could understand why

303

Nobby might think that—and it was true he had come to know me very well over the years—but the facts were plain enough. Three times I got off the bed to face the world, three times I went to the door with the best of intentions—and three times I fainted and had to pick myself off the floor. I wasn't alarmed, however. I just thought this is how it is when you reach the end of something so important to you, and when you are utterly drained physically. Later, Pat Crerand said that he had been much the same. He, too, could hardly trust himself to put one foot in front of the other.

When Norma came back to the room, she said that there were many old United players down there in the big, lushly carpeted room beneath the chandeliers, and added, 'They were all wanting to see you.' This made me a little sad, especially when I recalled the saying of Joe Mercer, who declared with a glass of champagne in his hand, 'Footballers should always celebrate their victories . . . you never know when the next one is coming.'

Mercer's philosophical warning was to prove particularly appropriate to me as the next few years confirmed the suspicion that if we were ever going to be crowned champions of Europe, it had to happen in that spring of 1968. Lying in that hotel room, however, none of that concerned me. Although I know I would have enjoyed the celebrations downstairs, the pats on the back, being the centre of attention, in truth it wasn't that important. What mattered, deep down, was that I'd taken the chance to fulfil my dream when it had been given to me.

Certainly I was pretty sure how I would feel in the morning. We had done something that ninety-nine per cent of players could only fantasise about. It was the last chapter of an amazing story and one I knew, in my thirty-first year, would never be surpassed in my playing career.

People still ask me what the dominant feeling was when I travelled to our West End hotel from Wembley Stadium. Honestly, it was more than anything complete exhaustion, but maybe that is only part of the truth. Maybe deep down there was that other sense, one that said that even if we hadn't drawn a line under the past, in some ways closed the door on it—which of course could never be done completely—at least something important had indeed changed. Perhaps it allowed us, finally, to think that in the future, however much of it was left to us as players contending for the great trophies, we were now responsible for ourselves and not those we'd so tragically left behind.

Nobby and I missed the great homecoming, the scenes of joy in Albert Square, Manchester, in front of the town hall. We had to report for England, which, speaking for myself, was in some ways a relief.

Just as I had been relieved after Munich that I did not have to experience the ordeal of the funerals, of saying farewell to so many friends in public and in a state of mind where I couldn't really begin to trust my emotions, maybe there was an echo of that when Nobby and I said farewell to our United team-mates and told them to give our regards to our happy old town. The guts of the story had been played out.

Certainly the feeling of satisfaction had indeed come with the dawn, and the knowledge that we had accomplished our mission and it was all that I had hoped it would be. If I stripped away all the history, the special circumstances that had been rooted in my thoughts for so long, I was still left with something that

305

any professional would treasure for the rest of his days. Eleven years after that first collision with the great Real Madrid, I was a champion of Europe.

The great thing was that we had got there after all those disappointments. All those anguished thoughts about what might have happened if, say, two years earlier the Partizan goalkeeper had not made that great save from Denis Law, could be put away once and for all time. We had done the job that had been asked of us, and that we had demanded from ourselves, and now we had to move to another phase of our football lives. That it would prove to be something far from what we might have hoped when the champagne corks popped in the Russell Hotel was something we coped with on some days better than others.

However, running through every game I played, every choked-back bout of frustration, was an enduring sense that I was one of the last men in the game with any reason to complain about whatever cards might be dealt me. You take the best, you do as Joe Mercer said, you celebrate it and store it against the worst the future can bring, and then you always play the game as well as you can.

For me, playing the game was in itself the greatest reward, the biggest incentive to face another day on the balls of my feet. Winning trophies would only ever be a bonus. As long as I could say that—and it would be so for another few years—I could live with the downside of the glory, the truth, as Geoffrey Green was never shy of citing, that into every life a little rain must fall. It just happened that the two games we played early in the new season, against the Argentine side Estudiantes in the World Club Championship, added up to a bit of a torrent.

306

Many felt that, in view of the state of Anglo-Argentina football relations after the scarring of the World Cup quarter-final, the Old Man would have been wise to have turned down the chance to win a title that for many was at best an irrelevance and at worst a potential ambush of football values—a situation produced almost entirely by the long failure of the European and South American football cultures to come to any solid ground of mutual understanding.

Twenty-four years later, at a Fifa committee shortly before the 2002 World Cup in Japan and South Korea, I learned there had been a frightening lack of progress against cheating and unfair practices. Indeed, there was a widening disregard for what I have always thought of as the fundamentals of the game when it is played properly: respect for the game, yourselves and your opponents. Sepp Blatter, the president, said to about twenty former players gathered around a big table, 'We've got another World Cup coming up in a few months' time. Could any of you tell me what you most want to see to make it a good tournament?'

There was silence around the table until I pressed the button for the translation and said, 'One thing I would like to see is players not trying to get each other in trouble by feigning injury, by diving in the eighteen-yard box and holding on to each other—if we could rid the World Cup of this type of behaviour it would be a tremendous start. As an ex-player I hate to see these things. They are spoiling football for everyone, and especially all those fans who support the game . . . stopping this is what I would most like to see.'

An old South American player said, 'But, Bobby, don't you think, as a professional, that if we can get away with creating an advantage for our own side, we really should be applauded?' Sepp Blatter steered us away from a confrontation, saying, 'Let's stick to the rules,' and moved the discussion on from a subject that was guaranteed to cause major division, and possibly a serious row.

We can be sure the late Jock Stein would not have been surprised by the exchange. He tried to persuade his friend Matt Busby to abandon the idea that United should follow in the footsteps of his Celtic team, who twelve months earlier, and after their brilliant European Cup victory over Internazionale Milan, had been involved in two riotous games with the South American champions Racing Club of Buenos Aires. Stein railed against the kicking and the spitting his players had been exposed to, with scarcely a hint of protection from the referee. The Old Man valued hugely the opinions of Stein, but in his ideal of a world of football that flew beyond borders, and prejudice, he was still unshakeable. Even after a scouting mission to Argentina which proved to be terribly uncomfortable—he picked up a bug and spent almost the entire flight home locked in the tiny toilet cubicle—Matt Busby was emphatic. The adventure must go on. Unfortunately, the adventure was almost exclusively an ordeal, both in Buenos Aires, where we played the first leg, and then at Old Trafford.

Nobby Stiles was ranked second only to Alf Ramsey (following the manager's charge that Argentina had played like animals against England in the World Cup) as a leading public enemy in the view of fanatic elements of that football-mad nation, and he bore the brunt of the hostility when we arrived in South America. As he has ruefully recalled down the years, the Argentine fans had produced a series of banners for their greeting to us. One said, 'Denis Law—El Rey [the King]'. Another declared, 'George Best—El Beatle'. Nor did I have any reason for complaint. My banner said, 'Bobby Charlton—El Campeón [the Champion]'. Nobby was much less pleased when he saw, 'Nobby Stiles—El Bandido'.

Nobby growled, 'Fucking charming,' as he climbed into the team bus to a chorus of catcalls and boos. He knew, like the rest of us, that Jock Stein's reservations were almost certainly about to be confirmed. It wasn't as though the World Club Championship was exactly a glittering prize; it was a novelty then, and it is still something quite marginal all these years later. Still, the Old Man insisted we could get through it successfully, and that if we helped to give the trophy some significance, it would in the end be for the good of the game. My feeling was, 'Well, the boss seems to want this, and if we're involved we might as well make the best of it—and win another trophy.'

I hadn't been to Argentina before and so many people who had were telling me, 'You're heading for the most hostile place any footballer could go.' But then I thought, 'It's something we'll get used to.' Soon enough, though, we realised that this would not be a formality. I had to have three stitches after a kick on the shin from a defender we had christened Dracula but, as anticipated, the real nightmare was Nobby's. He acquitted himself with great discipline, and application to the play, despite all kinds of provocation, including a head butt from Carlos Bilardo, who would later coach Argentina to their World Cup win in Mexico in 1986.

The way the script was shaping it was probably

inevitable that Nobby would be sent off, though in the event the circumstances were quite shocking. The dismissal was a complete injustice in view of all that had gone on before. The referee didn't give us any protection, and nothing in the way of 50–50 decisions, and Nobby no doubt reached breaking point in the second half when he made a perfect run through an offside trap to pick up a pass from Paddy Crerand. Though the linesman's flag stayed down, the referee immediately blew for offside. Nobby protested and gestured towards the linesman, then turned to me and said, 'We'll get nowt out of this.' The referee called Nobby to him and asked him what he had said. It was then that my friend sealed his own fate. He said in my direction, 'He can't fucking see and now it turns out he can't hear.'

On the journey home it seemed fair to congratulate ourselves on bringing away a deficit no worse than a single goal and, even though we would be missing Nobby in the second leg, we had to be confident that we could outplay them at Old Trafford.

This belief was supported by some striking circumstantial evidence. It seemed that the transatlantic flight had worked a remarkable transformation on the disposition of Estudiantes. They were staying near my house in Lymm and all the locals seemed to be agreed: the Argentinian players were perfect gentlemen. They posed for pictures with local schoolchildren, and waved and smiled whenever they left their hotel. One Lymm resident wondered, 'What's all this nonsense about them being thugs and animals—really, they are lovely.' One of them came round to my house with a photographer from the *Manchester Evening News*. He suggested that it would be good for the match if we proved that really the players of both sides were, despite what happened in Buenos Aires, quite the best of friends. I posed for a picture including Norma and the girls as we received a 'delegation' in our front garden. We were presented with flags. It was all so amiable there might have been a temptation to forget, at least to some extent, quite how hard it had been in South America, how hopeless the prospect of making a worthwhile game had so quickly become.

Then the second leg started and the first thing that happened was 'whack'. They were coming at us again with all that unscrupulous fury they had displayed back home in the Boca stadium. Once again we were plunged into mayhem. From the point of view of winning the game, as opposed to avoiding a full-scale riot, Ramon Veron (the father of Juan Sebastian Veron, the wonderfully skilled player who was never able to deliver his best in his short stay at Old Trafford) put us in a critical position after just six minutes. Veron was known as 'the Witch' in Argentina and it was not hard to understand why. Like his son, he had tremendous skill—indeed it seems like a South American birthright—and he also had an equally freely distributed mean streak. Estudiantes had caught us on the break, as we pursued the aggregate equaliser, and Veron coolly put the ball past Alex Stepney.

In the hands of a Yugoslav referee, the game never quite descended to the depths of violence and skullduggery seen in Buenos Aires, but it was plain enough that neither team would finish with eleven players. George Best was sent off, with the defender Medina, in the last minutes, a fact which over-shadowed Willie Morgan's late goal and filled the following day's newspapers with headlines about soccer scandal and shame. Had a reporter been in the

311

tunnel, there would have been even more substance to the claims that inter-continental club football was probably an irredeemably dangerous enterprise. Nobby Stiles, who was sitting in the stands, reported that he rushed down to the dressing room when, at the final whistle, he saw the big Estudiantes goalkeeper Poletti dashing off the field with what seemed like the clear intention of challenging George, but by the time Nobby got down to the tunnel his role as protector had already been taken, not for the first time, by Paddy Crerand. Paddy, who was proud to have come from one of Glasgow's harder schools of self-protection, was attacking the goalkeeper with some relish. By now, the Old Man was no doubt reflecting on the wisdom of his South American adventure. He stepped in between the combatants, sighed, and said, 'That's enough of that, Paddy.'

For Matt Busby, as he headed into a season that would see us finish a deeply mediocre eleventh in the First Division, knocked out of the FA Cup in the sixth round by the rising power of Alan Ball's Everton, and lose our grip on the European Cup in the semi-finals against AC Milan, it may well have been the moment when he finally decided that maybe he had had enough.

It was around this time that he surprised me one day with an invitation to join him on a golf trip to Scotland. There was a Bing Crosby tournament at Turnberry, he said, and he would like to go up for a few days. To me, it was almost unthinkable that a player should go off with the manager like this, but he was insistent and I couldn't see that I had any alternative but to say yes. I socialised with the Old Man much less than some of the other senior players, but I had never refused a request from him throughout all my days at Old Trafford either, and it plainly wasn't the time to start. We had been together so long now, and I got the impression that he had a lot on his mind. What it mostly was, I learned soon enough, and it confirmed that earlier suspicion of mine that deep down he had become drained and made weary by the constant need to be setting standards—and winning trophies. Maybe victory in the European Cup had indeed signalled to him that his active life's work had reached a natural point of closure.

As I drove up to Scotland, we talked about the good and the bad times of the past, and the uncertainties of the future. He talked about the weight of pressure on the manager of Manchester United, the sense that you always had to be one step ahead, always moving forward.

Naturally, I left most of the talking to him. He asked me my opinion about his possible successors, but the only name he himself mentioned was Dave Sexton, who had been doing some tremendous work with a young and talented Chelsea side. I said that Sexton seemed to be an extremely good football man, and a very strong and decent character, but really that was all I could say. I never saw myself as a kingmaker, certainly not then when I was still playing.

It did occur to me that maybe he had something in mind for me. The mere fact that he had decided we should spend a few days together on our own provoked that thought, but I was certainly not inclined to make any claims for myself. I never had, and never would, have ambitions to manage Manchester United. However much I loved the club, and wanted it to do well, I just couldn't see myself

313

taking the reins. I hadn't thought of the job, or still less trained myself for it, and the mood of the Old Man didn't provide any new incentive. He made it clear that in some ways he had gone on under sufferance, out of a sense of duty—and also that no obvious successor had announced himself.

It was good to spend some time with the great man who had been such a powerful influence in my life, who had set the standards that I had always tried to follow, but it was sad, too. I think he felt that as far as he was concerned the best of his contribution had come and now, most probably, gone. He lamented the fact that there was no obvious candidate to take on his mantle, leaving him to go, finally, with an easy heart, knowing that his work was in strong and safe hands.

Looking back, it is some comfort that towards the end of his life he did have the clearest indication that the search he was embarking upon when I drove him to Scotland had almost certainly ended in success. As we were playing our golf and musing on the future, a very different football man was contemplating the end of his playing career, and concentrating his mind on the challenge of becoming a great manager. It would take more than a decade for the strength of the former Rangers centre forward Alex Ferguson to truly emerge, and for Manchester United those years would be uncertain and often difficult ones, but the great bonus was that, when he did eventually arrive at Old Trafford, the ambitions and dreams inspired by Matt Busby remained as intense as ever.

For me, though, the drive home from Scotland, despite the restlessness and concerns of the Old Man, brought no change in my view of football: I trained, I played and I thanked God for an existence which had met all of my boyhood hopes. My basic ambition was the same as it had always been. I would wake up in the morning lifted by the knowledge that I still loved to play football more than anything else, and that I would be safe for as long as this was true.

But then, I suppose, you can detach yourself from certain realities only for so long. I reckoned I had a few years left, give or take the size and the menace of the clouds that were now, as probably anyone could see, beginning to form over what I had seen as the unbreakable citadel of Old Trafford.

It meant that I had a very simple option. I had to take the best of what was left—and live as well, and as uncomplainingly, as I could with the rest.

# CHAPTER 22

## THE OLD MAN STEPS BACK

Although I shared the growing concern about what would happen after the now inevitable abdication of the Old Man, the rest of my football life remained on a diet of hopefulness. The ebbing of belief that we were still a major force would be spread over a few years. It is one of the great aspects of football—hope is usually one of the last casualties.

As I pushed into my thirties, I could congratulate myself that I was still playing the game for a living at the highest level. I couldn't imagine doing anything that would be better or more satisfying, and certainly there was nothing that could be more enjoyable on a recurring, daily basis. Yes, I was moving into the wrong end of my career, but I still felt good when I did my work on the training field and went out to play.

I was also still deeply involved with the now knighted Alf Ramsey's England and many said we were stronger than in 1966, with players like Colin Bell, Francis Lee and Alan Mullery pushing hard for their places in the Mexican sun of the 1970 World Cup, when we would have good reason to believe in our chances of defending our title.

At home, it was true that there was a feeling that the United team really had only one way to go unless it was dramatically refitted by Sir Matt Busby—who, on top of his other concerns, was still reluctant to plunge all the profits into the transfer market—but some days did see a flaring of hope. These were days when the fingers on the clock seem to flick back magically a year or so; when the old chemistry stirred.

With the exception of a taut night in Brussels, when Anderlecht attacked our 3–0 first-leg lead (explosively created by a revived Denis Law) so strongly that we were happy to edge through on a 4–3 aggregate, in general we eased our way through to the semi-finals of the European Cup.

In the league George Best, assisted mainly by new signing Willie Morgan from Burnley, helped us travel back to the peak of the mid-sixties in an 8–1 demolition of Queens Park Rangers—a performance that, despite the weakness of the London team, provided enough momentum for us to play our way out of a dawning threat of relegation. There was also a burst of promise in the fifth round of the FA Cup, when Birmingham were thrashed 6–2, but that particular tide turned against us soon enough when we met Everton in the next round.

Of course there was still much quality in our team, but there was also considerable wear and tear. Nobby, for instance, was being betrayed by his knees, submitting to a serious operation and then endangering his recovery in his enthusiasm to be playing again. Perhaps, like the rest of his older team-mates, he had an anxiety to prove that he was as good and as strong as he ever was. John Aston, who had looked so indestructible in the European Cup final, broke a leg against Manchester City just at that point in his career when he had truly established himself as a significant player. He fought his way back, but he was never quite the same and soon he was being transferred to Luton Town. Brian Kidd suffered a scoring block and suffered his first injuries.

However, when you looked at the personality and

the confidence of the team, perhaps the most serious indication of a problem was the fact that as captain I was beginning to be asked by some of my team-mates: 'What's happening with George?'

The truth was that George Best, though still just in his mid-twenties, was making less and less effort to conform to the basic requirements of a professional footballer; if he wasn't absent from training, he was late, and though, when he did appear, his extraordinary physical resilience was as apparent as ever, the effect was inevitably distracting. He was beginning to operate on his own terms.

However wonderfully he performed on Saturday afternoons, George was a member of a team and his sense of the responsibilities of that had slipped to a degree dangerous to both him and anyone who was trying to impose some basic levels of discipline at the club. That was still the Old Man's job, but my position was, to say the least, delicate.

I understood the frustrations of those players who argued that there should be only one set of rules, and that they should apply to everyone, whatever the level of their talent—but then I also tried to look at the situation through the eyes of the manager. George—helped by that extraordinary capacity to live his life on his own terms and yet so often brilliantly disguise the effects—could still ravage any opposition in his unique way. Even if you worried about his prospects in the longer term, for the moment it was still plain that we could not easily jettison such a talent.

The problem with George was progressive throughout the reigns of three of the men who succeeded the Old Man—Wilf McGuinness, Frank O'Farrell and Tommy Docherty; all of them would face the dilemma of measuring genius against the

318

need to install discipline that covered everyone at the club.

George would, down the months—and not least in the spring of 1970 when he was caught with a girl in a hotel room by Wilf on the day of our FA Cup semi-final replay with Leeds United—work himself into the core of United's growing crisis. He was hard to live with, in some professional terms, but could we live without him?

The question was increasingly to the forefront of our affairs—and it would become particularly so, for example, when you considered the height of the hurdle barring our way to a second straight appearance in the European Cup final. Success in the semi-final would have quite dramatically obscured the extent of our slippage as one of the strongest teams at home and abroad.

We would have liked to take our chances against two of the other three survivors in the competition, Ajax of Amsterdam or Spartak Trnava, the champions of Czechoslovakia, but instead we drew the most formidable team: AC Milan, our conquerors in those desperate post-Munich days.

Polished and prompted by Gianni Rivera, a star of the Italian national team, Milan played the classic Italian game, rock solid in defence and always looking for breaks. They did maximum damage on two of them, their second goal of the first leg coming from their Swedish international winger Kurt Hamrin, who was also involved in the dismissal of John Fitzpatrick, found guilty of kicking the Swede off the ball. Nor did it help when Nobby was forced to limp out of the match.

By now, we knew that the Old Man was about to surrender the reins at Old Trafford. He had gathered us together one day after training to say that he felt it was time for him to step down from running the team, though he would not be walking away; he would still be involved with the club and still willing us on into new challenges. This was the most powerful of incentives. What better parting present could there be than another European Cup?

At Old Trafford, we threw ourselves at Milan, but their defence—in which my old World Cup final opponent Karl Heinz Schnellinger had recovered some of the poise he had lost when trying to curb the amazing energy of Alan Ball at Wembley—were as defiant as they had been in San Siro. After the first game, the odds were always going to be severe, but at the very least we could run ourselves into the floor. Denis Law had a goal disallowed and with the Milan defence so strong and unforgiving the disappointment of that was compounded. However, after seventy minutes George Best once again demonstrated why the Old Man had decided to turn away from any zero tolerance policy with regard to his time-keeping at the training ground. George took on the Milan defence and won, before playing me in so that I could score from an acute angle.

Naturally, we laid siege to the Milan goal but the *catenaccio*—the bolted door of Italian defence—had been slammed back into place. It was immovable in the face of all of George's wiles, Denis's lunges and my attempts to break it down. Afterwards, Sir Matt—like Alf, he too had been knighted in the wake of the outstanding moment in his career—shook our hands and thanked us for our efforts.

Perhaps no football man on earth had learned to walk with such grace along the fine line between the greatest of success and disappointment—and if this, as he then believed, was his last competitive match in charge of the team who had become the centre of his life, at least he had the satisfaction of seeing a fighting effort. If, undoubtedly, we were not the team that had run so hard and played so well in the Bernabeu a year earlier, it was clear that he realised we had fought that reality as best we could.

What no one, including the Old Man, could know, was that what had happened against Milan represented a pivotal moment in our history. Manchester United finally stepped down, for the best part of the next two decades, from that status that had first been achieved in the years after the war when they became the team that carried a special aura whenever they walked on to the field.

Of course there had been the lean time after Munich, but that was an inevitable interlude created by the most tragic of circumstances, and the truth was that if the accident was devastating, it also added to the mystique of the club. The drama of United had moved on to another level where resurrection, rather than the mere gathering of trophies, became a great and compelling goal, but now, at the end of the sixties, there was another kind of problem. It was the need to reignite the club and also set new targets and standards.

The problem was that Sir Matt Busby had made it clear that resurgence was a burden he could no longer carry, although it was one that was being accepted by hungrier, and maybe less wounded managers like Bill Shankly (for a few years more) and his successors at Liverpool, by Brian Clough at Derby County and by Malcolm Allison a few miles across town at Manchester City.

The Busby legacy was a huge pressure on the managers and players who followed. Eventually of course, men brimming with talent and confidence would arrive in the shape of Bryan Robson, Roy Keane and, in his unique and somewhat eccentric way, Eric Cantona. Most thrilling of all, there would be those heirs to the original Busby Babes: Ryan Giggs and Paul Scholes, David Beckham and Nicky Butt and the Neville boys. But before that there would be the desert, one made all the more barren by the raids on the peak of Europe by Liverpool and Nottingham Forest, and then by a team who had lived in our shadows for so long, Aston Villa.

One of the problems, I believed, was that we started to buy inferior players. We went into the market, I sometimes thought, almost for the sake of it without any real guarantees that we were improving our squad.

Down the years a series of managers failed to make the breakthrough and the extent of the problems they faced is surely illustrated by the quality of the credentials they brought to the job: O'Farrell, Docherty, Dave Sexton and Ron Atkinson all arrived at Old Trafford with big reputations and solid bodies of work behind them, but none of them could achieve anything like United's former glory.

First, though, there was the ordeal of my friend Wilf McGuinness. As a player, Wilf had suffered the most terrible disappointment, but in some ways it seemed that this was mere preparation for the trial which came to him when the Old Man told him that he was going to take a back seat and was putting him in charge of the day-to-day running of the team.

Wilf lived for United, he had fought his injury with exceptional and moving courage, but he failed to succeed in a challenge he plainly felt carried awesome responsibility. Maybe that in itself was part of the reason, maybe it was because he did find it precisely that—awesome.

There was also the fact that whoever it was who arrived to take up Busby's mantle would have faced massive pressure. Taking over from the Old Man wasn't just a question of producing a series of good results. It was also about style—that famous aura that was now so frequently being called into question whenever we struggled on the field. There were indeed some tough days out on the pitch. Sometimes, as a midfielder, I felt that I was permanently defending rather than attacking. I did a lot of running, but rarely did it seem to be in the right direction.

The appointment of Wilf turned out to be a trauma for him that stretched out eighteen months before he was relieved of his duties at the tail end of 1970. Famously, tragically, the shock of being told that his leadership of the club to which he had devoted so much was over, caused him to lose all of his hair. It was painful to see Wilf go down because here was one of the great enthusiasts. He had been a great friend to me when we were lads, and played in the England Schoolboys team, and he had made me part of his family life.

There were stories that Wilf changed when he got the job, that he tried too hard to separate himself from players he had been so close to before his elevation, but I didn't see it that way. He knew he had to alter his relationships with the players; we knew that too; but if that was straightforward enough when you thought about it, it was not so easy in practice. I could only sympathise with the difficulties he faced in his new role—and wonder, given his background in the training set-up, whether he had been placed in an impossible situation.

Wilf had to make some authority for himself, and it would be unfair on him now to forget the huge problems he faced. No longer could he come into the dressing room with his jaunty banter and maybe a new joke; he had to develop, instantly, a certain distance—and making distance between him and people he knew and liked and admired for their football ability could never come easily to him. Certainly I reject some suggestions that he was particularly hard on me. It didn't fill me with joy that one of his first moves was to drop me, but leaving me out of the team was, I reckoned, maybe one of his rites of passage as the new boss of the dressing room. There was one story that he had me doing press-ups in front of the other players and that it was an act designed to humiliate me. Nonsense. That wasn't Wilf's nature at all. I once did have to do press-ups in the dressing room, that's true, but only as a routine punishment that any of us were subjected to if we were late. Sure, I faced the good-natured taunts of my team-mates—but I was only on the receiving end of something that I had been happy to dish out in the past. There was no problem at all. It was good banter.

Later, he did say that, maybe when he was appointed, he should have fought the Old Man harder for more influence in such a vital matter as transfer dealing, the key to any club's future. It seemed that he pushed for the signing of three players who he believed would have the quality to provide the club with a new core of strength and ambition—Colin Todd, the young defensive star of Sunderland who were sliding back to the Second Division, Mick Mills, the tough and skilled full back of Ipswich, and Malcolm Macdonald, who had become something of a scoring sensation with Luton Town. For one reason or

324

another, however, Wilf received the thumbs down on each proposal. It meant that he had to try to lift the team, and meet expectations which anyone would have found oppressive, without the power to truly shape his own destiny.

It must have been tremendous pressure, and sometimes you could see that he was under great stress. On one of our better days, when we beat Manchester City in the FA Cup at Old Trafford—after Wilf had had to face the psychological warfare that Malcolm Allison waged so skilfully in the media, knowing that a bad result might have devastating effects on the faith of both the club and the fans in his ability—his relief filled the dressing room. He was the latest football man inhabiting that perilous ground between success and failure, but no one had done it, at that point in English football, under such a harsh spotlight.

The change, overnight, in Wilf's position could not have been more demanding—and, emotionally speaking, nor could the circumstances of his demotion in December 1970. After home defeats by Manchester City and Arsenal, with the gate dropping to a mere 33,182 for the second game, and then the League Cup semi-final defeat by Aston Villa who were then in the Third Division, the Old Man decided that, however reluctantly, he had to come back to full management. It was a cruel situation for Wilf, but sentiment runs only so far in football. We were eighteenth in the league and confronted by an old nightmare which had previously come in the days after Munich—our first post-war relegation.

While Sir Matt gathered the shell-shocked troops together for a meeting in which he said we were fighting for our own futures as well as the club's,

Wilf returned to his role as second-team coach. Later he went to work in Greece for a few years, followed by managing York briefly and then serving Bury in various capacities including coach and trainer, caretaker manager and physiotherapist.

You could only guess at the depth of his sadness when he went off to make a new life away from that place which had dominated all his professional thoughts and hopes for so long. All you could do was shake his hand, thank him for his friendship and hope that in time the hurt would pass.

Faced by the humiliating possibility of demotion, and no doubt reassured to some extent by the mystical aura that still surrounded the Old Man, we rallied to eighth place by the end of the season, winning eleven of our last eighteen games.

The last stand of Sir Matt Busby as a working manager started with a 2–1 win at Stamford Bridge, where we overcame the deficit caused when Alan Hudson—who with team-mates like Peter Osgood and Charlie Cooke was painting an extremely bright future for Chelsea—scored early in the second half. Denis Law was fouled in the box, Willie Morgan converted the penalty, and then, with just a few minutes left, one of the young contenders, Alan Gowling, ran through for the winner. The Old Man was back, said the headlines, and all the old confidence had been restored to Manchester United. It was a pretty thought, but among the players there was no illusion that Matt Busby was doing anything more than holding the line at Old Trafford as a new search for his successor was launched.

The holding part, at least, was a successful operation and for the Old Man's last match in charge of the team—the final league game at, of all places,

Maine Road—we managed to produce one of our most committed performances of a difficult season. We won 4–3, and for me the scoring line-up still reads like some attempt to recreate a more glittering past: Charlton, Law and Best (2). It was a terrific game, with Francis Lee at the heart of City's fight back after we took a 3–0 lead, and on the way home, amid all the other emotions, I had the satisfaction of feeling that, on his last day as the manager of Manchester United, Matt Busby had almost certainly been reminded of what his work would always represent most strikingly: a willingness to nourish talented players, to give them freedom to express all their ability.

Poignantly, ironically, call it what you like, the outstanding performance of the day came from George Best. He ran, he dribbled, he dipped into his great reserves of genius. On that day at Maine Road, George was once again announcing that he was George—untamable, both on and off the field. He was such a great player that maybe it was inevitable that the growing crisis of his career, and his life, should coincide with the one facing the football club he had lifted so high and so brilliantly.

# CHAPTER 23

## THE BAND CAN'T PLAY FOREVER

One of the charges against Frank O'Farrell, who, like Wilf McGuinness, would be in command for just eighteen months, was that he was excessively suspicious of what he considered the powerfully lingering influence of the Old Man—that instead of embracing the experience and the help of the manager who had created the meaning of Manchester United, he was too keen to draw a line under all that had gone before.

Something else Frank and Wilf had in common was their basic decency; they were good men under pressure that in both cases proved too much, although both argued that they were sacked before they had had enough time and freedom of action to meet the challenge that faced them.

Again my reaction had to be that it was circumstances that worked so damagingly against Frank, as they had against Wilf, rather than any great flaw in his knowledge of the game—or of footballers.

My own approach, even as captain, had been to attend to my own business and try to provide leadership on the training field and the pitch by example. I always attempted to steer wide of the politics of the club, something that O'Farrell later insisted wasn't so in the case of some senior players like Denis Law, Pat Crerand and Alex Stepney.

Also, apart from arguing that the Old Man's retention of his office at the top of the stairs sent out the message that he was still in charge, Frank said he felt undermined by stories that somebody still referred to as the Boss or the Old Man regularly played golf with players who should now be operating under the sole influence of the new manager. It was almost as though O'Farrell saw the mere presence of Sir Matt as some kind of reproach to himself.

There was also the problem that took a sharp turn for the worse at the end of O'Farrell's first season, one that started so promisingly with a rush to the top of the league, before a run of seven straight defeats shattered the idea that the manager had found an instant solution to our problems. The big blow came when George Best took off for Spain, insisting that he was quitting the game. He told a horde of reporters on the beach at Marbella that he was drinking a bottle of vodka a day. Whether that was true or not—and you had to pray that it wasn't—the damage to O'Farrell's authority was heavy. The key to his job was always going to be dealing with George successfully, and here, after a season which had promised much until a late tailspin dropped us into eighth place in the league, was a huge setback.

The manager urged George to remember that there would be a day when he wouldn't have the choice between playing the game maybe better than anyone else in the world and doing something else at which he could never hope to be brilliant. For the moment he was young and handsome and was surrounded by people who enjoyed the light of celebrity he created. It wouldn't always be like this.

O'Farrell's wise words didn't bite home and he was disappointed when George failed to join the team for the opening of a summer tour in Israel. There, our troubles were put into perspective when we reflected that only slightly different flight scheduling would have put us in Tel Aviv's Lod airport when three members of the Japanese Red Army terrorist group took automatic weapons and hand grenades out of violin cases and started firing indiscriminately, killing twenty-six and injuring many more. It was a powerful reminder that sometimes whatever happens within the margins of a football field, or in a club, has to be taken with a certain shrug of resignation. But even with our perspective on life once again properly realigned, there was no escaping the fact that as footballers we were facing some of our most difficult days.

This was proved true quickly enough. We failed to win in our first nine games and the shadow of relegation fell upon us again. O'Farrell complained about the level of press criticism, talking about the 'violence of the typewriter', but then I thought this was probably inevitable. When you were Manchester United, one of the last gifts you could expect was patience. Confidence had drained away with the confirmation that the fears first provoked in the second half of the previous season—when, among some bad defeats, we suffered the humiliation of conceding five goals to Leeds United at Elland Road—could not be easily banished.

Frank had been able to push through a couple of excellent signings in Martin Buchan from Aberdeen and Ian Storey-Moore from Nottingham Forest. Unfortunately, such encouragement was nullified by the latter's injury problems—and the fact that the manager was plainly running out of time at about the same rate suffered by Wilf McGuinness. His third significant signing, the free-scoring Ted MacDougall, who was bought from Bournemouth for £200,000, had scarcely found his way around the corridors of

Old Trafford when the axe fell. It came after another five-goal defeat, this time to Crystal Palace. It was Christmas time but no one was humming 'Jingle Bells'.

It seemed that a little bit of desperation was creeping into a lot of bones and these, I have to say, included my own, which were now thirty-five years old. Certainly there was no doubt I had reached a critical point in my enthusiasm. I no longer felt that surge of expectation which I had always experienced at the dawn of any match I played for Manchester United.

Nobody needed to tell me the extent of the rewards that had come to me, which at this time included a testimonial match against Celtic which raised £45,000, three times more than I had earned in any one season of my career. I had known the best and the worst of days, and was now living through some tough ones; but the job still had to be done, at the very least until the end of this draining season. No doubt Frank O'Farrell would have welcomed the opportunity to do the same but, instead, he went away in anguish that the great opportunity of his career had come and gone. Later, he wrote a book—unpublished for reasons to do with clauses inserted into his severance agreement with United—which was to have been entitled 'A Nice Day for an Execution'.

It was certainly a time when everyone at Old Trafford, including the Old Man, was obliged to examine their performance and their roles in the descent into crisis. Bill Foulkes had decided that it was time to retire. Denis Law would shortly move to his former club Manchester City. Nobby Stiles had already gone.

Once again, I found it impossible to attach

331

individual blame, or at least to apportion too much specific responsibility. Many of the players thought Frank was too remote and there was no doubt about the fact that in one respect his regime was completely different from the Busby way. The Old Man was always approachable. Often he would come down to the training field in his track suit, and always you had the sense that he was weighing the atmosphere and the state of commitment and belief. Frank was more formal. Almost all our day-by-day contact was with the coach Malcolm Musgrove and though he was always agreeable, and full of ideas and commitments, some of the players thought this wasn't enough. We needed more involvement from the new boss.

Once, Frank made an attempt to break the cycle. He gathered the players together and said, 'Well, *you* tell me what is wrong.' Some of the senior players threw their hats in the ring, and the consensus was that there was no doubt the squad needed strengthening if we were to maintain our place in the game, but then the arguments trailed off, and nothing had changed. Our confidence continued to slip away.

Naturally, the arrival of Tommy Docherty was another reason to make me think about how much time I had left as a player. Though he would always treat me with great consideration, he was something of a change from the manager I had known all my professional life. However, if the Old Man had decided that Docherty and his hard driving, and sometimes quite noisy assistant Tommy Cavanagh would bring the style that we needed in our situation, I was ready to go along. But for how long was quite another matter.

The question was really about me, and the strength of my own feelings as to how long I wanted to play, rather than what was going on elsewhere in the club.

In our day-to-day working relationship there was no point of friction between the manager and me, and I think that was seen on every occasion I needed to seek his help. I didn't want any special treatment from Tommy, and he was good to me in the sense that he never even hinted that I was coming from the direction of someone who expected any privileges. 'Aye, come back in a day or two,' he would say when I asked him for the odd leave of absence, perhaps to do something like a personal appearance for a friend. This may seem like a relatively trivial matter, but it is on such details that relationships between a manager and a player can go awry. Tommy seemed to accept that I knew more about my need for good fitness than anyone else, and that I wouldn't let a couple of days off here and there have any negative impact. I appreciated that.

Earlier in his career—and as time went on at Old Trafford it would be displayed again—'The Doc' had shown a more abrasive side of his nature, and when he left United after his five-year stint there would be some familiar swirls of controversy. He lost a libel action taken against Willie Morgan, and his relationship with Mary Brown, the wife of team physiotherapist Laurie, was the sensationally reported prelude to a typically stormy exit. However, these were developments that would come when I was gone. Whatever else was said about Tommy Docherty, there was no question about the fact he knew the game—and how to fight.

For me, though, the most valuable product of his long experience as a player and manager at the top level of club and international football was his understanding of how it was for a player who had to get the timing right in one of the most painful decisions of his life. The truth was, I had found it harder than I could ever have imagined getting to the point of advising Docherty that I had decided it was finally time to walk away. The manager was using all his wiles, his tough professional instincts, to postpone relegation for a year, but for me it was getting progressively difficult on the field. Some days I walked off the pitch thinking, 'I'm not sure how long I can go on.' But then there were some frightening questions: what do I do next? How have I prepared for the days after I retire? And even: how do you go about quitting? How do you turn your back on all those things which have shaped your life?

I didn't consciously pull back in my effort, but sometimes I did have the terrible sense that I was running for the sake of it; all the old optimism, the innate belief that I had the means to shape the outcome of any match, was dwindling. I was reaching the point when Saturday morning was no longer the greatest part of the week: the time when you woke up full of questions about the day's opposition, and how you and your team-mates would perform. With a couple months to go to the end of the season, I finally realised that I was playing my last games for Manchester United. We were playing Birmingham City and I couldn't remember ever running so hard and so long, not even under the whip of Jimmy Murphy. I chased and I chased, but there was nothing there for me, not even one of those sweet moments which had always lifted me. We lost the match and, I do not think it is too dramatic to say, I lost that last belief that, for a while at least, I could still be a United player—which meant of course that I could no longer be a player at all. I just couldn't imagine playing for any other team.

I spoke to Norma, and she confirmed what I already knew when she said, 'Bobby, only *you* can really decide. You know better than anyone else how you truly feel.'

I went to Tommy Docherty and told him I had reached a decision. I said he was the first to know, and as this was something I had never done before, I didn't quite know how to go about it. He said he would inform the board. At no time did he attempt to persuade me to stay on. Maybe he thought that the club were heading for days which demanded a fresh start and a new team with new influences, and that at this stage of my career I was just too strongly associated with the old days. Whatever his reasons, it didn't matter, because in certain situations I can be decisive, and this was one of them. Deep down I was perturbed, even a little scared about what awaited me, but I also knew that, like every player before me, I had a duty to represent only the best of myself on and off the field. If I felt something vital had gone out of my game, and my feelings for it, I had no option but to leave.

Inevitably, the news got out. This meant that the last weeks of the season amounted to a farewell tour. Everyone was very kind, very generous. Wherever I went, someone seemed to have a present for me. My last home game, against Sheffield United, was inevitably poignant and, unavoidably I suppose, I replayed in my mind some of the warmest, most thrilling days of my football life.

I remembered it all, right back to the nervousness I felt in that first game against Charlton, lining up with men who were demi-gods before they became friends, the thrill of scoring my first goal, the wave of pleasure and satisfaction that came when men like

Matt Busby and Jimmy Murphy patted me on the back and said, 'Well done, son, you'll be all right.' I was all right—but the band can't play for ever, and now the music was drawing to a close.

The memories accompanied every step of the way to that moment I pulled on the red shirt for the last time. It was in Verona on a warm night of early summer. Someone said that it was appropriate I played my last game for United in Shakespeare's City of Gentlemen. I took pride in that, because, whatever my effect in football, whether I won or lost, I always hoped that I would bring no discredit to the game that had given me my life. Of all the lessons he taught, I always believed that was the most important one delivered by the Old Man. Whatever you did, however well, however desperately, the important thing was that you never damaged the game, never threatened its place in the affections of those who paid their money to see something that took them away from the difficulties and strains of everyday life.

Geoffrey Green added a tribute that was typically poetic, but I liked to think that it did express something of what I had tried to do. He wrote in *The Times*, 'Bobby Charlton always possessed an elemental quality, jinking, changing feet and direction, turning gracefully on to the ball or accelerating through a gap surrendered by a confused enemy.' It was a generous assessment of my work, and perhaps something that I could keep in my heart, to guard against some of the uncertainties of the future.

On that last of my trips with United—for an Anglo-Italian Cup game—we stayed on the shore of beautiful Lake Garda. The accompanying press were most concerned with the shape of Tommy Docherty's new United, and it was a little strange to read about a future in which I no longer belonged. One story suggested that the manager would follow up his signing of Lou Macari, the forward star of Celtic, with a move for Asa Hartford, another Scot who was drawing a lot of attention as the midfield driving force of West Bromwich. The signing never happened, but the speculation was reasonable. United did, after all, have a vacancy.

As I thought of all the travels of the past, and how all the roads had finally brought me to this beautiful old part of the world, inevitably Nobby Stiles came to mind. I remembered an earlier trip to Italy. We were staying in Florence, killing some time in the hotel lobby, when I said to Nobby, 'Come on, let's take a little walk.' I was looking in a shop window in a little square when I realised that Nobby was no longer with me. I saw a china shop and almost immediately heard a crash. Nobby came running out, straight past me. A few seconds later the owner emerged. When he saw me he said, 'Mr Charlton, will you please tell Mr Stiles that he didn't have to run like a thief. We have accidents like this all the time.'

We didn't win the tournament, that honour went to Newcastle United with Fiorentina as runners-up, but I was able to finish as I began against Charlton in 1956. I scored two goals and played well enough to wonder, if only for a second or two, whether I had made the right decision to retire. It was so hard to think that I would never do this again, and all the emotion intensified in a restaurant later when the players gave me a standing ovation after presenting with me with an Italian clock they had clubbed together to buy.

It was a beautiful object, the centrepiece of a statue depicting the four seasons—something that would have been quite beyond my means nearly twenty years earlier when I peered into the jeweller's window in Zurich before buying my first watch. Inevitably, I choked up when I made my speech of thanks and attempted the impossible task of explaining what all the days I had spent wearing the shirt of Manchester United would always mean to me.

No doubt if Nobby had been there, he would have volunteered to help me home with the clock, but by then I would probably have been wise enough to decline with thanks. Enough to say, maybe, that I carried it back with great care, I put it on display immediately, and it still stands in the middle of my mantelpiece—one of the most important places in the house to me now.

CHAPTER 24

## WHAT NEXT?

The question that had been nagging down the weeks and the months before I made my farewell on that soft Italian night was now, back home in Cheshire, as relentless as the ticking of the beautiful clock on the mantelpiece: what now?

Sadly, for this is something to be filed among my regrets, what happened next wasn't the completion of any attempt to become a qualified coach. I had the strongest sense that any life outside football for me would be miserable, but although I knew this, I hadn't responded in any practical way. Matt Busby wasn't a qualified coach, nor was Bill Shankly, and privately I had always thought that if you were a strong enough character, and if you had been around the right people all your career and tried all you could to learn from them, you probably knew more than could ever be imparted in a lecture room, or out on a training field under the supervision of someone wearing a bib and holding a sheaf of notes. But of course, times were changing.

Nobby Stiles had joined the procession to the Lilleshall coaching centre almost as soon as his knees began to give way, and though he frequently found it a frustrating and exasperating experience, he had battled on. There was no doubt that within the game a network of coaches was creating a new culture, one which could leave you on the outside, however much fame you had won on the field.

I did look at the coaching programmes, but my

first reaction was, 'Oh, God, this will take ages'—a bleak thought and one reinforced when people kept telling me, 'You will have to start at the lowest level.'

Nowadays, of course, the perception is quite different. Someone like Roy Keane, so strong and independent as a player, saw that he would, for all his brilliant experience as a leader on the pitch, be disarmed if he didn't have his coaching badges, and no doubt the training was a factor giving him confidence in his superb opening statement as a manager at Sunderland.

Because of my circumstances, the fact that I had built a strong profile for United and England, I was in quite a bit of demand from outside the game as my playing career wound down, and my friend and adviser Reuben Kay always urged me to take advantage of every overture that came my way. 'Bobby,' he said, 'the most important thing in life is having something to do when you wake up in the morning. You always have to have somewhere to go. When you finish playing, you will still have half your life to live.' I could see that easily enough, but the vital question concerned what I would be doing. Anything that did not involve football loomed for me as a kind of death.

When I made my last farewells at Old Trafford, and felt—if I am honest—a terrible uncertainty about what lay ahead, I had, after taking Norma, Suzanne and Andrea away for two weeks beside a warm, blue sea, no alternative but to wait for the phone to ring. It did, after three weeks.

The chairman of Preston North End, Alan Jones, was on the line. He wanted to come to see me and I said, 'Yes of course.' It was not as though my diary was crowded. Preston North End—I liked the sound of the famous old club, the team of Tom Finney. When he asked me to be manager I had several reactions all at once: new regret at not having worked on the coaching side, a certain apprehension about doing something I had never really considered, but then, dominating everything, was the sheer joy that came at the thought of returning so quickly to football.

I said yes, almost immediately, and maybe it is true that a lot of football men, and not least me, are deep down the purest of dreamers. Certainly my concerns about the coaching situation were pushed back into the margins. Surely I had played enough football, talked long enough with Jimmy Murphy, listened in to enough coaching sessions down the years, had sufficient an education in the game at the sharpest end, that I could do something at Preston?

In retrospect, I suspect I was probably caught up in a little flattery that worked against the uncertainties about my ability to manage, the concerns which in some important ways were well founded. No doubt I went into management a little too quickly. I should have weighed my situation more carefully, but this is wisdom long detached from my mood of the time. My brain was separated a little from my commonsense, and the reason was no mystery. The pressing reality was that I was desperate to feel good again, and, it came to me overwhelmingly, the only way that was going to happen was in football.

Unfortunately, the first season was extremely tough. It finished in relegation, but the board understood that I had inherited a difficult situation with quite thin playing resources, so there was no pressure that I might lose my post. By the following season, we had picked up momentum and I was beginning to see the job as more a pleasure than an ordeal. There was also a quite unforeseen bonus. Suddenly, I was playing again.

I was out with the lads on the practice field one day, and it occurred to me that I was enjoying every minute of it. I was fresh in my mind and my body felt relaxed. I made my passes, I ran easily as I geed up my players and then, when I was walking back to the dressing room, I thought, 'This is ridiculous, we're fighting so hard to get results, I'm doing everything except playing—and I *can* still play.'

I talked to a few of the players and to Nobby, who had joined me as a coach, and everyone's reaction was the same. They said it would be fantastic if I came back. I experienced a great wave of excitement as I rushed to the office to put through the papers for my registration as a player. Driving home, I felt almost boyish again.

In all I played thirty-eight times for Preston and scored eight goals, not a bad ratio for an old-timer roaming around midfield. One outstanding memory is of a cup victory back in my old terrain. We played the famous amateur warriors of Bishop Auckland on a pitch exposed to a bitter wind. As we went out on the field I thought to myself, 'This is nearly as bad as Katowice.' I hammered home to the lads that old Jimmy Murphy law: when you are playing a team of lesser status the most important thing is to run as hard as they do. This, Jimmy always insisted, invariably neutralises their one possibility of success, their chasing and hustling of the more skilful side.

One of our best players, Tony Morley, who would go on to Everton and Aston Villa, profited most from our busy approach, and we won more easily than the 2–0 margin said. I felt I was getting more into the job of management, and playing again was a tremendous release of pressure—and also of some of that accumulation of frustration which had started building when it became obvious that the Manchester United I once knew and loved appeared to be breaking apart.

Naturally, given all my time at Old Trafford, it was not so easy to shake off the particular pain of being involved in such a rapid descent from the mountaintop. There were days when I yearned for the old certainties of that time when, he would later report, Sir Matt Busby would have a wee dram of Scotch before a game, in the blissful confidence that his team would not only win but also demonstrate all that he considered worthwhile in football. In that time when the club was clearly going wrong, I had tried to keep my own counsel, but sometimes you did find yourself confiding some of your worries and fears in a trusted team-mate. In the absence of Nobby and Shay Brennan, Tony Dunne, who had also known the best of times, was most often my confidant. On several occasions we agreed that the going had become harder than we could ever have imagined in the glory of the mid-sixties.

As Wilf McGuinness, Frank O'Farrell, and Tommy Docherty had all battled to reverse the trend, it was as though they were in pursuit of the unattainable when they tried to reproduce the authority of the Old Man. 'It's crazy,' I once said to Tony. 'No one can be a new Busby. His personality was just too big.'

I tried to remember some of the lessons I thought I had learned at United as I went about my business in Preston, and there were days when I did feel, despite my regrets about the lack of coaching qualifications, that I was indeed making a little progress. I liked the atmosphere at Deepdale; it was a friendly club, a genuine football place, and I couldn't complain that the board were ungenerous. I also felt I was learning another side of football, the tougher aspects of the game you miss when you spend your playing career at places like United, Liverpool and Arsenal. At the top level, you take so much for granted: the first-class travel facilities, the fact that you walk a few yards after a match and a luxurious bus is waiting to whisk you away, staying in the best hotels, the way the team can be strengthened when a clear weakness has become apparent. It is why somebody like Alex Ferguson is eager today to send off young lads on loan: when he sent David Beckham to Preston, it was to give him more than the chance to play against mature players; it was also to toughen him to some of the realities of football life beyond a place like Old Trafford.

Recently, I saw a young manager from a lower division club in the reception lounge at United and I asked him how he was doing. He said, 'I'm fine, but you know it is a struggle sometimes. I think I would go mad if I didn't get to see how football is at the highest level, how good it can be. I'm not looking for players tonight, just seeing football as it should be—I'm just recharging the batteries.' The remark took me back to Deepdale and my own battle to adjust to the manager's life. In the end I concluded that if you attempt it without the coaching background—and without membership of that school of football men who, like Alex Ferguson each day, spend so much time talking to each other on the phone, spinning off ideas—you almost certainly need lots of money, and maybe an excessive reliance on the word of agents.

It was the workings of the transfer market that

persuaded me that my position in that second season at Preston had become untenable. The problem was that some of the directors seemed to have started going behind my back. When I confronted them with my suspicion that they were contemplating moves without consulting me, they told me they wanted me to sell a player I didn't want to part with and to buy back one I had already sold.

It turned out that they had already made overtures to Newcastle for the return of Alex Bruce, a small, lively striker who had been sold at what I thought was a very good price. I said that I considered this behaviour unacceptable. Their response was that in order to fund the Bruce signing—which I told them would be a bad move because in football you do not go back on a decision like that—I had to sell John Bird, a big and very capable central defender, a player I regarded as the backbone of my team.

I told the directors that if there was one player in the club we shouldn't sell it was this big lad. I also pointed out that in the lower divisions there were a couple of crucial positions: you needed someone who could really head the ball up front, and someone who could hold a defence together. John had proved he was the latter. I argued my case with as much force as I could muster, saying finally, 'I can't stay here if you sell him.' There was a short pause before one of the directors said, 'Well, we still want to sell him.'

I told them I was sorry, but I couldn't operate on those terms. I wasn't disillusioned as I left Deepdale. I had been around football all my life and I knew what it could do to people. The good and the bad that it could deliver. No, my feelings had mostly to do with what I had learned about myself. Maybe I had been right to be suspicious of my aptitude for the job when I drove with the Old Man to Scotland, and wondered if I was expected to make a case for myself as he pondered over possible successors, but I had enjoyed so much of my time at the club. Most of all I had loved the fact that I was still involved in football.

On the good days I was defying the fears of my family, so deeply embedded in the game, and also the fears that grew in me, as I neared the end of my playing days, that this next stage of my life might be something of a wasteland because, as one of them said, 'Everyone can't run a pub.' But now, maybe, I had to think again. Perhaps I really did have to enter a world which I had never known, the one of work or business which I had been able to escape so easily up to this point. Of course I had a degree of celebrity, people might want me to open a shop or a sports centre, but what would I put at the core of my life which had always been filled by football?

Preston might have been the foundry where I forged the rest of my life, but it had proved not to be so, which of course made for a reflective drive down the motorway and into the leafy lanes of Cheshire. Maybe, if I could have seen into a future where a player not yet twenty could make enough money, if wisely invested, to keep him and his family in luxurious security for the rest of his life, my apprehensions might have been tinged with a certain bitterness, but I doubt it. Whatever happened in the next few months and years, I would always have the great days of my life. I would always have George and Denis in Lisbon, Nobby in Madrid and at Wembley for United and England, and there would always be the image of the Old Man and a time when everything was so fine—and so sure.

One thing I can say for myself is that I have never

been prone to jealousy, which is no doubt something from which I cannot take too much pride when I consider the good fortune that has accompanied me ever since I first realised I could play football better than most of my schoolmates. I think this is true of a lot of players of my generation who had some success. They accept that you cannot change history, that you can only get the best of what is available to you in your own day, and for me that was pleasure and pride.

Certainly I was a little sad when I realised how bitter my uncle Jimmy, who played for Bradford and Leeds, had been made by the fact that his career came several generations before what might be described as the football goldrush. He was the uncle I was least close to as a boy, and perhaps it was because of this that, when we met at a family funeral, I was eager for him to join me for a United game. I said we could see a good match and make up for a little lost time. But he wouldn't hear of it. He tore into the game, saying, 'Bobby, I wouldn't go near a bloody football match.' He was angry about the escalation of wages in the game, the fact that he had missed out on rewards which he believed, when he compared them to those he had received in a long career, were grotesque.

Although my earnings had been modest by the standards of football today, they had been better than those of most of the lads I had grown up with. I had a lovely family, a nice house and a bit of a name. It was not as though I had been thrown in the street after my experience at Preston, and it would have been outrageous to have felt sorry for myself.

My first rescuer was Freddie Pye, a successful businessman who had always been involved with football, and whose passion for Manchester City had never interfered with our long friendship. Freddie called me to say, 'I have a travel business, Bobby, and if you would care to be a director maybe we could try to use your name—but come in anyway, you're my pal.' I thanked him and said I would be along. Then I got into my business suit, walked to my car and started the second half of my life.

The company had three shops, and though in time the business would become difficult, especially with the arrival of the internet, I was grateful for the chance to do something which would give me both an income and also a little time to plot my future.

It didn't take long to realise, however, that I wasn't going to make a fortune out of the travel business, and that I had to shape something more for myself. Though football management hadn't worked for me, no more than it would for the majority of my World Cup team-mates with the notable exception of my brother Jack of course, the game itself was impossible to push away from the centre of my thoughts. Somehow, I never stopped hoping I would get to be part of football again, and then perhaps my world would return securely to its axis.

Freddie Pye had opened the first door for me, then, by chance, the BBC took me through the second. They invited me to do some commentary and features during the World Cup of 1978 in Argentina. When I was there I was asked, with Alfredo di Stefano, to present an award at half time during one of the games. This coincided with a remarkable coaching session involving some young boys, who displayed astonishing ball skills.

The BBC made a short film of di Stefano and me watching the lads, and when I returned home people were saying, 'Wow, I saw you on television with those little South American kids. Weren't they fantastic?'

I agreed but added, 'There is no reason why our boys couldn't be like that.' This is how the Bobby Charlton Soccer School was born; how I found a way to be a working part of football again.

The more I thought about it, the more I could see how there was a vacuum in the way we taught our kids to play football. There was a missing element— the fun, the sheer enjoyment of playing the game. I remembered my grammar school days when our sports master was really the geography teacher. He was a good man, but undoubtedly he did the job under sufferance. It wasn't his passion. Freddie Pye was once again a great supporter. I asked him if he would be interested in helping me form a company and he readily agreed.

My business sense might not have been particularly well developed, but I could see clearly the potential of a project that could be organised for the five or six weeks of summer school holidays when, I thought, so many parents must be fed up with so many people telling their kids what not to do.

The surge of excitement was tremendous, the strongest I had felt since I had put away my boots. I contacted Ray Whelan, a staff coach at the FA, and he gathered together some of his lads. I told them, 'I want to do something for the kids in this country, but in my situation it has to be commercial. It's got to be a proper business, but there is one thing we have to guarantee . . . that you will make sure these lads improve as footballers—and enjoy themselves at the same time. I insist they have a good time.'

Perhaps inevitably, I received a lot of hostility from the Football Association: how could I dare to do this? I wasn't a qualified coach, I hadn't gone through the system. But I told myself once again, as I'd done before joining Preston, that I was not without a little background, I had played a few matches, had been around people like Matt Busby, Alf Ramsey and Jimmy Murphy, and maybe I could pass on a little bit about the meaning of football. At the FA no individual came out against me openly, but it was made quite clear there would be no co-operation—and certainly no blessing. Indeed, I heard later that messages went out from the old Lancaster Gate FA headquarters saying that the Bobby Charlton Soccer School was an outlaw organisation, and could not be supported by anyone attached to the ruling body.

It was not a deterrent. We organised rooms and playing fields at the universities when the students were away, and I stressed that everything we laid on for the boys, including prizes, would be to do with either watching or playing the game. One night we put on a film featuring Diego Maradona and it was great to see so many enthralled faces.

I had a standard speech at the start of a week's session. I told the boys that I was not their father or their teacher, but if anyone was caught swearing or stealing, or doing anything to be ashamed of, his parents would be asked to take him home immediately.

It was magical to see it all take off. Quickly, we expanded into the Easter holidays as well, and Ray Whelan had no difficulty in hiring qualified coaches, mostly schoolteachers eager to earn some extra money. There was no shortage of big sponsors like TSB, British Gas and Sharp, and soon we were able to offer scholarships through the sponsors. Prizewinners got the chance to play under the supervision of Real

Madrid and Barcelona coaches. A young lad from Essex won one of the prizes and his reward was a trip to Barcelona, where Terry Venables was the manager. Terry was taken with the boy's skill, and when he moved to Tottenham he tried to sign him. The boy was David Beckham.

Reflecting now, I suppose part of my enthusiasm for the school was that it took me back to my boyhood; I remembered it so well, and as football was so much part of it, it was as if I was winning some of it back. I could identify so easily with the pleasure of the lads when they worked on some exercise that they enjoyed, and I was thrilled with their response to my idea of installing six tests at different stages of the week, with points going into an aggregate that would produce the big prizewinner. The tests were about skills, just skills. You got extra points if you put the ball in the top corner of the net, if you passed the ball so accurately you hit targets with both feet, and especially popular was a juggling exercise.

Influencing all my ideas for the school was the memory of my own feelings when I was young. I used to daydream about what might happen—and what I might say—if by some miracle I met somebody like Len Shackleton. There was also the reality of all I had gained from the time given to me by Wor Jackie Milburn. So I asked what all these kids coming to school really wanted from me, what did they expect? The answer was that they would want to see a lot of me, not just at the start and finish of the week but all the way through. So I went every day. I loved it.

The potential, first created for me by that little passage of film made in Argentina, was clearly immense. The exchange scheme with Real Madrid and Barcelona was expanded to Benfica, and then it seemed that we could go almost anywhere in the world. We went to America, to Australia and then, most excitingly, to China. While we were there we were told that the football authority wanted to send a squad to Britain to prepare for the World Youth Tournament, which was being held in Scotland the following year. I talked to Coca Cola and British Airways, and they agreed to sponsor the trip. I organised some games for the squad, and one of them was at the ground of Witton Albion. I was late for the game, arriving at half time. When I went into the dressing room I was amazed to see all the Chinese lads sitting on the floor, sticking acupuncture pins into their knees and their ankles.

I had the idea of setting the six tests for the Chinese boys, and offering the prize of three months in Manchester with United for the lads who finished in the top two places. I had talked to Alex Ferguson and he had approved the idea. Impressively, every member of the Chinese team, even the goalkeeper, beat the best score achieved by any British boy, including the 1988 winner David Beckham. One of the winners, a little lad called Su Mao Zhen—of course we knew him as Sue—eventually became a Footballer of the Year in China and now he is involved in their Olympic programme. Unfortunately, he broke an ankle while in Manchester and had a pin inserted. When he returned home, the Chinese doctors wanted to remove the pin but he insisted it stayed. Later, he handed me a little book that told the story of his three months with Manchester United.

It was a wonderful adventure in football for 'Sue'—and one of the many rewards that flowed to me from a business which was successful in every way I could have wanted. Eventually, the operation became tougher because a lot of local authorities looked at our business and said, 'We can do that.' When one of the companies who took us over, Conrad PLC, the leisure activity firm, were in turn bought out by Sheffield United, it signalled the end of my connection in all but name with the Bobby Charlton Soccer School. It was a sadness, but there was really no alternative. I couldn't be a director of Sheffield United as well as Manchester United.

It was in 1984, eleven years after I'd left with my heart in my throat, that I received the invitation to return to United as a director. Apart from the soccer school which had given me such pleasure and reward, my focus on professional football had necessarily shifted about in the years since I had parted with Preston. I had scored eighteen goals in thirty-one games for my friend Shay Brennan's Waterford United in Ireland, had played a little in the South African league and was then a director and, briefly, caretaker manager at Wigan Athletic. From time to time I was a pundit for BBC television. I had enjoyed it all because it kept me involved in the game; it maintained the flow of my lifeblood. But nothing had touched me quite like the call from Old Trafford—the one that asked me to come home.

# CHAPTER 25

## COMING HOME

The first overture for a return to Manchester United came a few years before I joined the board in 1984. It was made by the chairman Louis Edwards, who had been such a strong supporter of the Old Man. He came up to me after a game, put his arm around my shoulder and said, 'Come back to Old Trafford, Bobby . . . come back to where you belong.'

I had felt a flush of the old excitement, as though time, having in some ways stood still, was ticking again, but I could see straight away it wasn't right. It was a warm sentiment from the man who had long held the title 'Champagne Louis' for the enthusiasm of his celebration of our triumphs in the sixties, but it was also a little foggy. Maybe a sentimental whim, a longing for a return to happier, less complicated days, I speculated. I had to ask the hard question: 'Doing what, Mr Edwards?'

The chairman replied, 'Well, you could do the public relations.' I told him I couldn't see myself in that role. I was a football man, and if I had value to the club I felt it was in putting my playing experience at the disposal of the board of directors. As a manager at Preston, and in all my years as a player at United, I had learned that the men who really knew how to run a club, who understood all aspects of the challenge, were almost invariably those who had grown up within the professional football ranks. The supreme example for me was, of course, Sir Matt Busby. They are the ones who have learned in all their years in the game something that quite often escapes the most successful businessmen. It is quite fundamental: football will never be quite like any other business. This was something that was not often reflected in the boardrooms of the game, I told Louis Edwards— and when I think about it today, it seems remarkable that of all my contemporaries I can think of only two who graduated to the place where the big decisions are made: Dennis Tueart, a Manchester City director, and Martin Peters who had a spell on the Tottenham board.

As it happened, my return came four years after Louis had died and been succeeded by his son Martin. In 1984 United were probably more buoyant than they had been at any time since the Old Man had surrendered the reins. Unlike his quiet predecessor, Dave Sexton, Ron Atkinson did not appear so susceptible to the expectations that had besieged all of Matt Busby's successors. Sexton was a deeply impressive football man. He had the respect of his players and there was no doubt he knew more about coaching a team than I ever would, but even from a distance you could see that the need to win trophies facing every United manager was a particularly heavy burden for him. Dave Sexton was an introvert. Ron Atkinson was not. He was happy with the nickname Big Ron, and as confident with the media as Big Mal Allison had been while transforming our rivals City back in the mid-sixties.

Ron was flamboyantly self-confident, believed in having players of quality, was plainly happy with a squad which included Bryan Robson, Norman Whiteside, Paul McGrath and Gordon Strachan—and there were times when the performance of his team was so good, and so in keeping with United's

355

tradition, that on several occasions I said during board meetings, 'I think we should put our appreciation of the team's performance into the minutes.' Later Ron said we did not get along, but I was never conscious of any antipathy, and certainly I was never aware of any particular friction between us when he appeared in the boardroom.

I liked the adventure of his football and there was plenty of evidence that United were moving back into the elite of the game. He won his second FA Cup in my first year on the board, and if the club ached for its first title win in nearly two decades it wasn't as though the goal now seemed so remote.

However, one hard truth of football is that potential, even when it is backed by sometimes spectacular promise, has a limited shelf-life. There is also the argument, much favoured by my brother Jack, that however good a manager, his best effect is limited to just a few years; after that his style can became a little too familiar. The fear is that players start to say, 'Oh, we've heard all that before.'

I don't know if this was the reason, but in 1986—five years after his appointment—it seemed that Big Ron had hit a wall. In 1985, he appeared to be flying, winning the cup again after the triumph of 1983 and then launching a brilliant campaign in the new season. Ten successive league wins swept us to the top of the table. However, the spring was filled with disappointment and we finished fourth. Then the new season brought no encouragement, a string of poor results leaving us fourth from the bottom.

Some time before the plunge I had had a discouraging experience, seeing something that made me worry about the future of the club. It came when I went to a reserve match at Sheffield United. It's not always easy judging players in reserve football, but the overall effect was depressing. As we drove back over the Pennines, I thought to myself, 'Well, I can't see any of these lads ever being in the first team.' That had sounded a warning; then, when the results went wrong again, it was something I went back to in my mind. Where were the young lions who were going to give us new life, new impetus?

There was talk of a drink culture building among lads like Paul McGrath and Norman Whiteside. In the boardroom the talk, predictably maybe when you consider the extent of the slide away from so much promise, was of a new manager. Some of it concerned Terry Venables, who was coming under pressure at Barcelona after the brilliant feat of leading his club to a title triumph over Real Madrid. I respected Terry, of course. He had an impressive record as a coach and a manager, a big aura, and after his time at Barca there was no question about him being intimidated by the challenge at Old Trafford. However, once the decision to part with Ron Atkinson was made, I was quite open—and emphatic—about who the new manager should be. 'It has to be Alex Ferguson,' I declared.

That summer I had been doing work for the BBC at the World Cup in Mexico. Alex was the caretaker manager of Scotland after the sudden death of Jock Stein at Ninian Park in Cardiff during a qualifying game. At the Scotland–Uruguay match he was on the touchline before the game, saw me and came over to talk through the fence. We discussed the tournament prospects for a while. It was a brief but enjoyable exchange. He seemed to be filled with intensity and pride that he had been chosen by his country to step into the shoes of the great man. When we parted we said that no doubt we would see each other back home during the course of the season.

He had been doing a brilliant job at Aberdeen, one that I had followed more closely than most in the English game because of my interest in Scottish football, something that started when I was a boy growing up so close to the border. I had seen him in action, driving Aberdeen to performances that smashed the stranglehold of the Old Firm, and I had heard the stories of how he had tackled his first managerial stints at East Stirling and St Mirren. He had gone into the streets with a microphone to whip up the fans. He was part-evangelist, part-fighter and there was never any doubt about either his ambition or his ability to inspire his players.

An encouraging sign for us at Old Trafford was that he had made it clear that if he was ever to leave his Aberdeen fortress it would not be along the road to Glasgow for one of the two big jobs in Scottish football, Rangers or Celtic. He didn't think he would be improving himself at either Ibrox or Parkhead. But what about Old Trafford? Well, he had more than hinted in one newspaper I read that this would be quite a different matter.

In the boardroom there was a strong feeling for Venables. I said that I understood it well enough. Terry was a marvellous coach who as a player had represented his country at every level. He was another football man of high profile and character who commanded attention and respect in his players. Some of our directors emphasised Terry's confidence, his easy manner in front of the television cameras. He would be more than a football manager. He would be a personality who refused to be dominated by all that had happened in the past.

I conceded all of that, but then I made the case for

Alex Ferguson. I pointed out the unique scale of his achievement in Scotland; no domestic club could think seriously of taking on the Glasgow powers and beat them, but that was the mission that Alex had declared on his first day at Aberdeen.

Aberdeen were not supposed to beat Real Madrid in the final of the Cup-Winners' Cup either. I asked my fellow directors if they had seen Ferguson on the touchline when Aberdeen scored their great victory in Gothenburg. I said he had lived passionately every moment of the game, charging on to the pitch, filling his players with his self-belief. 'Never mind, Real Madrid,' he seemed to be saying. 'This is my team, this is Aberdeen.'

I do not want to make too many claims for myself as I look back on this phase which would be so vital to the shaping of a new United. Ferguson was operating so brilliantly and passionately in north-east Scotland, not on another planet, and I wouldn't begin to say that I had discovered a talent that was not visible to anyone who cared to look. Certainly I didn't feel I was fighting an uphill battle on behalf of Ferguson. I just felt it was necessary to make an old player's point as strongly as I could; an old player, that was, who had long experienced the special demands and forces of Old Trafford.

I believe, however, as all the talk—and the headlines—swirled around the question of who would succeed Ron Atkinson, that my role on the board as an ex-player, as someone who knew the importance of a manager who could truly lead a squad of players, was a significant factor in the argument.

Soon enough—and despite the fact that some of his early signings were not greeted as great successes, and that we had to wait until his fifth season to land a major trophy—I was convinced there would be no regrets. Alex Ferguson showed something you can't teach and can't learn. It is something you are born with, some determination that is established not in a football stadium but in the womb. He assumed a right to victory in every match—and if it didn't happen, you knew his resolve would not fade but redouble.

For me, and more of my colleagues in the boardroom than a lot of reports suggested, there was never any question of firing the manager before the great logjam of frustration was swept away. However, there was a strong belief within football that the Ferguson regime was in danger of going down at the turn into 1990; indeed, the day of his fall was nominated with great certainty in many newspapers. It was supposed to be the inevitable consequence if we were defeated in the third round of the FA Cup at Nottingham Forest. I would have fought any move to dismiss the manager with all the resources of argument I had, but my sense, anyway, was that Alex Ferguson's D-Day beside the River Trent was largely a creation of the media. It all became increasingly academic, however, when Mark Robins scored the goal that sent us into the fourth round—and a series of away ties—before the final replay victory over Crystal Palace.

The rest, stretching all the way to the spring of 2007 when Alex Ferguson delivered his ninth Premiership title, has been an infrequently interrupted passage of glory—a series of triumphs for both the will and the energy of the most passionately committed football man I have known.

Now, looking back, the impression may be of a seamless process, a series of decisions which, like building blocks, created an edifice of success which became inevitable. But of course each change of direction, each commitment to a new player or groups of them, required nerve and judgement, and the instinct of someone who could never be content with any kind of fleeting success.

From my position on the board, I watched fascinated—and supported as well as I could—the work of a man who was developing and underpinning everything that I had strived for, and believed in, in my days as a Manchester United player.

Sometimes we played a little golf together and Alex would talk about an idea he had, a possible move into the transfer market perhaps, but he did it gently; it was as though he was probing to see what kind of reaction he would get in the boardroom whenever he tabled a new plan. It may be something of a surprise to those who haven't worked with him closely, but the Ferguson style of combativeness vanishes when he is away from the field of action. In more than twenty years of working alongside him, and attending board meetings, I have never heard a raised voice or an angry gesture. But then, on the other hand, I have never seen such decisiveness at the helm of a great football club.

Of course the outline of the Ferguson years is imprinted in the awareness of everyone who takes an interest in football, but even now, and as someone who saw the trends developing and the style of leadership unfolding from close up, I find the scale of the achievement quite stunning.

Consider the extraordinary milestones: the breaking up of the championship-winning team of Paul Ince and Mark Hughes, the cornerstone signings of Roy Keane, Eric Cantona and Peter Schmeichel, the explosion of youth represented by a nineties version of the Busby Babes, the titles, the Doubles, the climactic Champions League victory that brought a unique treble, the decision to sell David Beckham to Real Madrid, the arrival of Cristiano Ronaldo and Wayne Rooney and the regaining of the title from Chelsea . . . all of it forms an amazing body of work which has taken United into a dimension which no one could have dreamed of when we shuddered, shook our heads and contemplated the challenge that faced us in the ashes of Munich.

For so many years I was at the heart of Manchester United's effort to maintain its place in football—and in all the triumphs and the disappointments, and the tragedy, there was always one great hope: the return to greatness of my beloved club. To my mind, it has been my last and great privilege in football to have been given a ringside view of the Ferguson years when that great hope became a reality.

Sometimes I sit in the great stadium and marvel all over again at the progress that has been made. I recall the time when a bus-load of fans from the other side of Rochdale arrived one close-season morning to see the first Old Trafford floodlights going up, explaining that they couldn't stay away any longer, and I relate that innocent time to the more recent one when, after meeting the new owners of Manchester United, the Glazer family, I walked across the same stretch of car park to be confronted by supporters in an entirely different frame of mind. They believed that their club had been sold beneath them, that the links with the old United had been snapped. I understood their concerns, but I also pointed out that the world had changed along with football. I said the moment the club turned itself into a plc, it had exposed itself to such possibilities of foreign ownership.

362

I was, frankly, a little ambushed by the occasion. I had left the boardroom with the Glazer sons, Joel and Avram, and other board members and club officials, imagining we were all leaving the ground at the same time, but when I stepped out of the stadium I saw the fans—and that I was all alone. What could I say? Only that as someone who cared very much for Manchester United, I had been assured that the club would move forward along the old way: getting the best players, and pursuing every ambition. I believed Alex Ferguson would be able to continue as before— that he would have the necessary budget to maintain United's position, and also the freedom of action and authority that should naturally be given to one of the most successful managers in the history of the game. The Glazer operation had been depicted as an asset-stripping enterprise, but the fact was that they were in control, quite legally, and it was also true that in Florida their Tampa Bay NFL team had won a Super Bowl. They knew how big-money sport worked.

There was one overwhelming point I wanted to make to these fervent supporters of Manchester United. It was that I shared their feelings for the club—to the point where, if something was done in the boardroom that was fundamentally wrong, and I truly thought went against the long-term interests of United, I would walk away. In the meantime, I would work as hard as I could to maintain the success of the club. I would maintain my support of Alex Ferguson, the man who I still believed was capable of producing the drive and the vision that had turned a club which was worth barely £13 million in the late eighties into one whose value at one point was touching a billion, and which remains one of the most desirable properties in all of professional sport.

Every great football man has a defining moment; the Old Man had his in Wembley in 1968, Alex Ferguson's came in the Nou Camp in 1999. In the end United won their second European Cup—against Bayern Munich—because, even without Roy Keane and Paul Scholes, their appetite and their professional honesty were overwhelming. They were qualities built into the team down the years, and when the winning goals of Teddy Sheringham and Ole Solskjaer went in after the colours of Bayern had been attached to the trophy, and Alex Ferguson ran along the touchline with tears in his eyes and his arms outstretched, you could see the source of the effort which would never be forgotten by anyone who saw it.

It was the kind of performance which can only come from a team when everything is right about their approach, when the dressing room is free of any disharmony, and when each player knows precisely what is expected of him. Down the years this has been the Ferguson bedrock. When the manager decided that for one reason or another players who had previously performed great service—stars like Ruud van Nistelrooy and, most wrenchingly of all, I'm sure, Roy Keane—were no longer able to help in the shaping of team spirit and motivation, the hard decision was invariably made.

Alex Ferguson could have walked away from Old Trafford at any point after delivering the treble of league, FA Cup and Champions League on that astonishing night in Barcelona and been given all the acclaim and the honour that went to the Old Man when he decided that he had done enough in the game. However, when he announced that he was doing so four years ago, I was shocked. It seemed such a waste of a unique competitive intensity which was still not staunched in any way. But then what could I say? If ever a football manager had earned the right to go in what he considered his own good time, it was surely this one. He announced that he had talked it over with his wife Kath and his sons and had decided it was time to sip his vintage wine, pursue his racing interests, and step back from the football life in which he had immersed himself so passionately for so long.

Was it really time to begin the search for the right man to pick up the baton? No, I didn't really think so. Certainly there was no shortage of impressive candidates, stretching from Martin O'Neill in Glasgow to such Italian coaching giants as Ferguson's friend Marcello Lippi—but who knew more about the needs of the club, and who was more capable of meeting them, than the man who had already done so quite brilliantly and, it seemed to me, was still at the peak of his powers?

It was a conviction I nursed and was determined to express at some time when I felt he might be most receptive to my arguments; perhaps when it had truly dawned on him that the great adventure of his life could be coming to a close.

Finally, when his departure as manager was accepted as a formality, with the speculation on his successor raging up to ever new levels, I felt it was getting close to the time when the case against his abdication had to be made with some force.

It was thus something of a relief when we met in the Old Trafford lift one morning and he said, 'I've had a chat with Kath and I've decided I'm staying on . . .'

I smiled, contentedly, and said, 'Surprise, surprise . . .'

# CHAPTER 26

# THE VERY BEST OF MANCHESTER UNITED

In any great tide of football achievement there is always going to be something that most warms the heart of an old player, something that stands on its own in his affection and respect, and of course it is invariably another player. He may not have one overwhelming skill, he may not be without flaw, but there is something in him that relights the fire that once burned so strongly inside yourself. He is a player who reminds you what it was about football that first filled you with so much passion. He is a player whose love of the game, and his commitment to it, glows in every stride he makes out on the field. He has a purity about his game, an understanding of it and a talent for it, which you wish everyone could share. He makes you feel young again—and aching to play as you once were able to do, with the freedom that comes with trust in your body and the belief that if you put enough into it you can achieve anything.

As I approach my seventieth birthday, I have no hesitation in putting a name to such an embodiment of all that I believe is best about football: Paul Scholes.

In these pages I have had the chance to discuss so many great players who have worn the shirt of Manchester United: players I worshipped, then lost with my youth at Munich; players like Denis Law and George Best who I enjoyed so much as team-mates in my maturity; and now, finally, players that I have watched closely in every surge of the Ferguson era. Assessing and grading them all precisely is a difficult, maybe impossible job, but if I am honest I have to admit that in so many ways Scholes is my favourite.

I know that Jimmy Murphy would have loved him. No doubt, he would have tried to improve his tackling—which is enthusiastic enough, but technically is not much better than was my own excuse for the art—but he would have embraced him for all his heart, and for his innate knowledge of how to shape a game from midfield.

I love both his nous and his conviction that he will find a way to win, to make the killer pass or produce the decisive volley with such instant authority and nerve. When a game reaches a vital phase, these qualities seem to come out of his every pore. Long ago he became part of United history, but in the season of 2006–07, when United won their first title in four years, when he came back from career-threatening eye problems, it was as though he became the very heart of Old Trafford.

The more I watched him, the more I thought, 'This lad is Manchester United through and through . . .' He's always on the ball, always turning on goal, always looking to bring other people into the action, and if he loses possession you have to think he must be ill.

I first saw him play in a youth match at Sunderland. He had touched the ball only a few times before I realised the hairs on my neck were standing up. I concluded, 'It doesn't matter how big he is, he has the ability, he has the vision.' Most impressively of all, he had the talent to pass the ball through the eye of a needle, the most vital of assets when you are trying to break down a packed defence. In his maturity, Scholes does it so well that he reminds me of the player who I always thought had mastered the art more completely than anyone I had seen: Michel Platini of France.

Paul is so good now that it is always the greatest disappointment for me when I do not see his name on the team-sheet. His absence makes me despondent as I wonder, 'Who is going to do the clever stuff, the short, acute passing that cuts open a defence?' Young stars like Cristiano Ronaldo and Wayne Rooney have displayed brilliant natural talent in recent seasons, of course, but the key to a great career is a deepening understanding of your own skills, and a consistent ability to produce them at times of maximum pressure. In this, Cristiano and Wayne have the perfect example in Paul Scholes.

His emergence, along with David Beckham, the Neville brothers and Nicky Butt was the most spectacular reward for Ferguson's immediate attention to the scouting department when he first came down from Scotland. He saw what I had seen in that reserve match at Bramall Lane, Sheffield; there had been no planting, so how could we hope for a harvest?

Ryan Giggs, prised away from Manchester City, came on a year earlier than the rest of the pack. I will never forget the first time I saw him. Alex had invited me to the training ground to watch the summer trialists and, when I arrived, I couldn't see the manager. 'Oh, he's down on pitch eleven, watching some kid he really likes the look of,' I was told. As I walked down, I saw from a distance something quite extraordinary. A small, slim, dark-haired boy went on an irresistible run, then provoked a brilliant save from the goalkeeper. When I got to the touchline I asked Ferguson, 'Who is that little lad?' His eyes narrowed and then glinted with a small smile. 'His name is Ryan Wilson—and we signed him this morning.'

Because of family troubles, Ryan Wilson changed his name to Ryan Giggs—but, down the years, nothing else has changed beyond the inevitable loss of a little pace. He is still as fresh and as ambitious to play outstanding football as he was on that summer morning when he made me catch my breath.

The fact that Alex Ferguson was able to show such a hand of youth, one which so quickly won a title under the influence of the talisman Eric Cantona, will maybe prove in the long run to be his supreme achievement. At a time when any other club had every reason to congratulate itself if it brought through an outstanding young player once every two years, here was an explosion. Gary Neville was smart and versatile, his brother Phil a tremendous force wherever you played him, and if Nicky Butt suffered at times from a loss of concentration in his passing, he was tough and aggressive, a fact which he announced to me quite dramatically in a game at Chelsea. On one run he was hit with a series of crunching tackles, but he never gave an inch and he kept hold of the ball.

And then there was David Beckham. When he came to my soccer school, the first thing I thought about him was that I had probably never seen a lad who wanted to be a footballer quite so much. He just couldn't get enough of the ball, and in this he reminded me of myself at his age. He was small and polite and I thought he had special skill—though when I expressed this opinion to one of the staff coaches, who also scouted for a First Division club, he said, 'I don't rate him. He's not big enough, not strong enough.'

I didn't agree, but I could see the point. Though he had good pace, and could always turn a game with a free kick or a spectacular shot on goal, he needed to develop his passing game because it was clear he lacked the capacity of a conventional winger to get by a full back. Really, it was the only flaw in his game, but he compensated marvellously. He learned ways of controlling the ball that were quite exceptional, and as he progressed through the United youth team the range of his talent became increasingly obvious.

His graduation to the first team was natural—and almost immediately he made his splash. His goal against Wimbledon at Selhurst Park announced ambition without limits. When he saw the goalkeeper off his line, he struck the ball home so beautifully, from such a distance, there was no doubt that here was more than a gifted young footballer. He announced an extraordinary presence, and it was something that, I noticed, struck Cantona powerfully. When the Frenchman offered his congratulations, the expression on his face was quite eloquent. It said, 'I wouldn't have minded doing something like that myself.'

David Beckham could do everything in a game, it seemed, except dribble and tackle and be content with the idea of being just another leading footballer. On the field he had demonstrated an ambition to be spectacular—when he scored that goal at Selhurst Park, you had to wonder, 'Where did he get the nerve to try that?'—and off the pitch he was obviously carrying some of the same feeling.

His eventual break with Manchester United was about one basic point of difference between him and Alex Ferguson. Beckham thought that a celebrity lifestyle, being drawn increasingly into the showbiz world of his wife Victoria, was compatible with the regime of a professional footballer. His manager did not.

Towards the end of his time at Old Trafford I found it increasingly difficult to pass comment on his situation. Whatever I said seemed to be magnified hugely, and there was maybe also the problem that I found it impossible to relate to the culture in which the player had grown so huge. 'Well, of course,' someone told me, 'apart from being a great footballer, David is also a fashion icon.' I just wished I knew what that was.

There was never much question that, apart from his wonderful ball skills, he also had another extremely well-developed talent: understanding the way publicity works, how it is that an image is made. This was a skill David Beckham had no doubt honed as he travelled through his wife's celebrity world.

There were two occasions when this knack of his came to my attention. On the first it was pointed out to me; on the second I saw it for myself. Around the time it seemed to me that his lifestyle was beginning to take over from his football, someone leaned over during a game at Old Trafford and whispered in my ear, 'Have you ever noticed what David Beckham does when he scores? He runs to the corner flag all on his own. If someone else scores, he's usually the first one hanging on him. I suppose it means he is always in the picture.'

Maybe he was simply following one of the laws of celebrity, but certainly his awareness of the relationship between action and media response was underlined for me when we were in Singapore for the final campaigning in the London bid for the Olympics of 2012. We were sitting together when

Jacques Rogge, the president of the International Olympic Committee, came to the stage to announce the winning candidate. As Rogge was making his announcement, David turned to me and said, 'Paris have got it, look how the press photographers are all going over to the French delegation.' As I waited for the news, I thought, 'I would never have noticed that.' Of course, London won the vote, to general astonishment, not least mine after the emphatic statement of a companion who seemed to know so much about the world of communications.

The growth of the Beckham image meant that United came under immense pressure when he moved to Real Madrid. It is true that when it happened he wasn't playing his best football, either for United or England, but his talent for public relations meant that there could be only one loser in the huge controversy which enveloped not just the club but all of English football when it was clear he was on his way to Spain.

Even at this late stage I do feel the need to make a basic point about David's departure from Old Trafford. While, as I have said, it is true that the manager had serious problems with the Beckhams' lifestyle, finding it unhelpful, to say the least, to his idea of the proper atmosphere for the smooth running of a football club, there was never any question of the player being driven out of United. This was the impression given by Beckham and his people—and it was quite wrong. Yes, maybe there were issues to be dealt with, but they had not reached the point where the hero of United and so many England fans had been shown the door.

I can say this with great conviction because I saw the contract he rejected when he decided to leave for

Madrid. It would be an invasion of privacy if I gave the precise details of the deal, but I can say that it was an excellent, generous offer. Certainly it did not resemble in the slightest a goodbye note. In reporting this I hope there is no impression that I am discounting David Beckham's great contribution to United, or his place in the history of the club. His was a spectacular talent and there was no question he enhanced hugely the confidence and the aura of a club Alex Ferguson brought back to huge prominence.

However, if am perfectly honest, I have to say we must look elsewhere for the hierarchy of players who did most to shape the years of revival and achievement in the course of Sir Alex Ferguson's building of three quite separate teams. I have already given Paul Scholes and Ryan Giggs their high places in the Ferguson regime. Now it is time for the men who, in their vastly different natures, shared between them all those qualities which make the difference between good, winning teams and great ones. They are the kind of players who have something inside them which announces, from the first moment you see them on the field, that they are subject to special forces.

In the case of Eric Cantona, his spirit and his instinct were rarely less than quirkish; his aura was peculiar to his own rather eccentric view of both himself and the game he played. In the case of Roy Keane and Peter Schmeichel there were no shadows, no mysteries. What you saw was what they were. They were as ferocious as Cantona, in his moods and his inspiration, was unchartable. But in one sense all three were inseparable: they had an extraordinary will to dominate every situation in which they found themselves. It meant that they were the players who underpinned everything Alex Ferguson achieved, as he made good his promise to build again on the foundations laid down by Sir Matt Busby.

I have to start with Keane because his influence was so immense it reached into every corner of the field. He was strong in a way I could not have been, not even with all the passionate urgings of Jimmy Murphy. Keane didn't so much tackle opponents as demolish them; he read points of danger in the way of Nobby Stiles but, unlike Nobby, he was not content with breaking up an attack and giving a simple pass. In one aspect Keane was different too from Bryan Robson, who in terms of leadership and force and ambition was probably the player with whom he could most easily be compared. Robson was so often hit by injuries. Keane seemed capable of overcoming anything.

He played through injury and the controversy which so frequently surrounded his aggressive style on the field. Undoubtedly there were times when he went too far—no one could approve of his notoriously cynical tackle on Alf Inge Haaland, whatever the background, and nor was it uplifting to see him leading the hounding of a referee—but then always there was that commitment which made him such an extraordinary competitor, and arguably the most influential player in the history of the Premiership.

When Keane won a crucial tackle it lifted both his team and the crowd; it was a statement about the course of a game and it produced an authority which touched every aspect of his play. Among all his achievements, at one point there was an extraordinary statistic: his passing accuracy was at 97 per cent. Much of it was short stuff as he moved the ball downfield, but there were also biting passes, born of his deep understanding of how to play in midfield, and at such times the crowd and the opposition seemed to react as one: the crowd gasped and the men facing him fell back. This man was not just a strength in the team, he *was* the team, a force which so often was simply unstoppable.

The essence of Roy Keane was never more visible, never more inspiring, than when he carried United into the 1999 Champions League final after they had conceded two early goals in Turin against Juventus. This, unquestionably, was the ultimate, defining performance of a great player and a great warrior. Unashamedly, but perhaps not in line with the most correct behaviour of the directors' box, I spent much of the match on my feet, deeply moved by the strength of Keane's performance. When he scored the header which put us back in the game, it was as though he was saying, 'Now, let's get back to work—let's get this thing won.' I was standing up and saying to anyone who cared to listen, 'We can win this now—it's our game.' It was a bold statement, even by someone who has always erred on the side of optimism, but my confidence flowed from the sense that Keane had not only lifted us but flattened Juventus.

In my experience, British-based players are better equipped to battle through an unpromising situation than their Continental rivals. It is as though a lot of the Latin teams expect things to go their way all the time, and then when something goes wrong they have problems in putting it right. For me, Steven Gerrard underpinned this theory in 2005, when he led the successful charge against a Milan leading 3–0 in the Champions League final. If it is a basic strength of the English game, no one expressed it more consistently, more significantly, than Roy Keane. He had a single, unswerving obsession: always to win.

It is the tackles that I will always remember most vividly. I used to dream of making tackles like the ones Keane performed so routinely—and I never made one. Sometimes watching him play I would think to myself, 'Oh, to go in to win like that, to make the challenges that change a game.'

When Keane could no longer quite do what he once did on the field, and when his anger and frustration at the lack of success of the team spilled into heavy public criticism of his team-mates, Alex Ferguson didn't need telling it was time to make a break. He knew there would be protests, a sense that part of the soul of the club had been exiled, but there could only be one manager and it was not Roy Keane. So Ferguson had to do the hard thing—something, given all that his captain had contributed, that I know he found one of the toughest decisions of his career.

Eric Cantona was a mystery, an enigma and, perhaps most surprising to anyone measuring his impact at Old Trafford, initially an aside in a conversation between Alex Ferguson and the manager of Leeds United, Howard Wilkinson, as Ferguson asked casually about the possibility of signing a player who, despite obvious talent, had spent a career drifting from one club to another in France and then England. When Cantona crossed the Pennines he brought more than talent. It was an hauteur which lads like Ryan Giggs, Paul Scholes, Nicky Butt and the Neville boys might have spent a whole career attempting to acquire, if it had not been laid before them by a man who gave the impression that he had finally found a place where he could play to the limits of his ability. Ferguson had stumbled upon gold.

Soon after Cantona arrived he talked about being in tune 'with the spirit' of Old Trafford. He said that he felt the presence of old players around him whenever he went on the field. Of course the fans responded as warmly as the young players who so quickly looked up to this wanderer who came among them with so much swagger, almost a strutting belief that he had arrived at his point of destiny.

Amid all the theatre, I analysed Cantona's talent and found it quite exceptional in certain areas. He will always be remembered for the flourish and panache of his goals, so many of them the result of an amazing delicacy in such a big man, but I think his greatest single asset was his ability to run with the ball at speed. In this, I believe he had few rivals, one of them being Diego Maradona. Cantona brought to life brilliantly the old maxim of Jimmy Murphy which I have mentioned often in these pages, and which still holds true: when you have control of the ball and a little space, run directly at the defence, force them into decisions, get them on to the back foot. Then you create so many possibilities for yourself and your team-mates.

Why did his talent work so well at Old Trafford after the nomad years in France and at Sheffield Wednesday and Leeds? I saw it as another triumph for the judgement of the manager. In my opinion he read the player's nature perfectly. Cantona was a natural born rebel, resentful of authority and uniforms, eager to assert his independence and his free will. In the past, I suspected, too many managers had tried to impose themselves on this free spirit, pushed him into corners where he became sullen and resentful.

Ferguson's approach was quite different. If Cantona wanted to fly off to Paris for a few days, he was usually granted his wish. 'Be back on Tuesday,' the manager said, 'and be ready to train and to play.' You could see Cantona grow almost day by day in his new environment.

Of course there was a fine line between the good and the bad of Cantona, always the fear that he might blow like a volcano. He did this while I was on a tour of Africa. An enterprising *Daily Mirror* reporter tracked me down on the phone and told me about Cantona's 'amazing eruption' at Selhurst Park, how he had turned into the crowd and attacked a Palace supporter after being sent off. I told the reporter that I could only imagine there must have been a high degree of provocation; but a professional player couldn't do that and not expect the severe punishment—at least a six-month ban—that would quickly come his way.

There was one other shadow over Eric Cantona. He never produced the best of himself in European or international football for France. In England, however, it was as though he was a great dramatic actor operating on a stage that he found so much to his liking. Alex Ferguson's role in this turbulent life was that of a knowing theatre director. He knew what he could get out of his star performer—and what he couldn't. He said he would take the best of the Frenchman, not the worst; he would only confront and chivvy him whenever it was absolutely essential. He would not be a figure of authority, but a friend and an admirer always ready to celebrate a special, though at times difficult, talent. It was the inspired—and practical—decision that did so much to shape an era.

In the course of these next few pages I intend to do something that is often asked of me privately, and is always a source of some agonised decision-making, partly because of the choices required, partly because in measuring the talent of footballers there are so many different factors to weigh, so many fears that in honouring one player you are doing less than justice to another. I am going to pick the best Manchester United team from all my years as a player and a director (excluding the great players of the 1948 team because although I did play with some of them towards the end of their careers, when their brilliance was shining most brightly on the pitch they were never more than fabled names on our radio back in Ashington).

There is one place that is automatic. It is the one that belongs to Schmeichel.

Schmeichel gave Manchester United the greatest gift at any goalkeeper's disposal. He sent waves of confidence through the team. He even became an arm of the attack, moving the ball to Ryan Giggs or Andrei Kanchelskis in one easy, powerful motion that turned defence into assault so quickly. Twice, against Queens Park Rangers, goals flowed directly from the work of the goalkeeper. In the Champions League final in Barcelona, he unsettled Bayern's defence with a charge down the field before David Beckham sent in the corner that led to Teddy Sheringham's equaliser. No one suggested Schmeichel should do that. It sprang from his refusal to countenance the idea of defeat.

He also, as Cantona did in his prime, embraced the meaning of the club and is still frequently to be seen around Old Trafford, revelling in the aura of the place. He gave an early indication of his commitment while helping Denmark to the European Championship title in

Sweden in 1992. Before the game against England, he was asked if he was aware Gary Lineker was close to scoring a record number of goals for his country. 'Yes, I am,' he said, 'but it's not going to happen against me. That record belongs to Bobby Charlton and my club.'

I hadn't seen him before he arrived at United, but the first time I watched him I realised immediately that he was a sensational goalkeeper. He had everything: command, reflexes, judgement, nerve and powerful accurate kicking. And then there was that final classic quality of a great keeper: if he ever made a mistake, he simply didn't recognise it—someone else got the bollocking. He could not accept the concept of being flawed in the slightest way. None of his team-mates complained. They knew the supreme value of a goalkeeper everyone can trust.

All this means that Peter Schmeichel has no rival as the foundation of my best Manchester United team chosen from the mid-fifties until today. The rest of it, playing 4–4–2, is: Gary Neville, Pallister, Stiles, Irwin; Cantona, Robson, Keane, Edwards; Law, Best.

I never saw the great Johnny Carey play for the '48 team, and Bill Foulkes's greatest strength was as a central defender, so the right back has to be Gary Neville. He has been a marvellously consistent and highly competitive player, confident and tough the strongest of the pack led by Scholes and Beckham. He's quick and he wins his tackles, and when there is a need you can trust him in one of the central defensive positions. My friend Shay Brennan, a European Cup winner, is one rival, but he didn't have Neville's versatility.

Choosing a left back is one of the toughest assignments. How do you pick one from Roger

Byrne, Tony Dunne and Denis Irwin? Byrne was a born leader, an unorthodox defender but one equipped with a personalised radar system. Apart from his talent, he had an aura all of his own. Tony Dunne was possibly the quickest defender I ever saw. His marking ability was quite brilliant, and I recall telling a journalist who had commented on Tony's great form around the time we won the European Cup, 'Well, you know, he's been the best left back in Europe for years. He goes like lightning.' In 539 appearances for United, Dunne scored just two goals—he wasn't a particularly good kicker of the ball—but he did have a kind of genius. He read an opponent so well that, with his speed, he could go out against any winger on earth confident of putting him in his pocket. However, Irwin has to get the vote because, on top of his other qualities of pace and judgement, he scored a lot of goals for a defender. You never worried about Denis Irwin; I remember him once making a mistake, an occasion so rare I found myself thinking, 'Really, I never thought I would see that.'

In the middle of defence I am torn between the twin pillars of Alex Ferguson's first title-winning team, Gary Pallister and Steve Bruce, and the man who brought a wave of reassurance whenever he walked into a dressing room, Nobby Stiles. Between Pallister and Bruce, I have to give the edge to Pallister. They were both defenders of the highest quality, they read attacks with great insight, and they weren't afraid to put their heads in the dangerous places, but Pallister was a little more composed on the ball. Nobby is my friend, one of the great joys of my life, but my affection for him does not influence his selection one iota. Nobby is in because no teams were ever more reassured, or so driven, than those of United and England before such great matches as the semi-finals and final of the European Cup in 1968 and the same stages of the World Cup two years earlier. I know because I was there; I felt the force and strength of Nobby as though he was a band of steel running through everything we did. People used to look at him and say, 'Well, you know he is not the most graceful player,' and they were right—but they missed the point. The higher the pressure, the better Nobby was. If I ever picked a team without Nobby I would expect to be charged with negligence, at the very least.

Bryan Robson goes into my midfield because he was simply a great player, one whose spirit and ability were never diminished by his many serious injuries. You would want Bryan because of the sheer quality of his competitive character; the other skills—the tackling, the goal scoring, the inspiration—were all bonuses which carry him into my team alongside Roy Keane. Between them, they would squeeze the will out of the opposition.

Cantona is not the easiest choice when you think of the ability of men like Dennis Viollet and Liam Whelan who so dazzled the emerging Brazilian masters, but the Frenchman goes in because maybe no one ever seized a time, and an opportunity, at the end of a previously flawed career quite so perfectly as when he set the young Lions of Old Trafford on their way. As I said earlier, for reasons that may have been embedded in his background in French football, he never excelled in Europe, but in England for a while he was both king and puppet-master.

The fans of today may wonder about the absence of such as Paul Scholes, my model footballer, Ryan

Giggs, David Beckham, Wayne Rooney and Cristiano Ronaldo, but they are still playing and, certainly in the case of Rooney and Ronaldo, have time left to define their careers fully. Some accounts, which were closed long ago, just cannot be forgotten—or surpassed. It is why Duncan Edwards, George Best and Denis Law walk into my team.

Now, when I look at the list, and the notes and scratchings in and out that accompanied it, I feel the strongest surge of pride. It comes from the fact that all of them wore the shirt that became the badge of my life—and that on any given day I would back them to beat anyone in the world.

# EPILOGUE

There is, I've always known, a point in every man's story where you cannot escape the truth, and maybe I've reached it now. I'm still looking to the good years that I hope are left to me, but also have to accept, as reluctantly as a boy who never wanted an adventure to end, that so much I have considered valuable, even indispensable, to my happiness has to be let go.

It is not that sensations like playing against Alfredo di Stefano and Ferenc Puskas, and alongside Denis Law and George Best, or feeling the blast of the crowd on a big night at Old Trafford or some other great stadium in Europe with Nobby Stiles chivvying at your back, are in any way disposable. They are too thrilling and timeless for that. But when you consider all that you have seen and experienced since these were the staples of your life, and all the miles you have covered, you have to wonder: hasn't the road gone far enough?

No, I'm not saying I am about to resign from the board of Manchester United, or that suddenly I'm going to find it easy to turn down a request to fly to Nairobi or Sarajevo, Johannesburg or São Paulo, and be able, at least one more time, to marvel at the power of football to enter the spirit and the language of every nation on earth. If you gave me the chance, I would probably argue for ever that in the sweep of its appeal, its ability to touch every corner of humanity, football is the only game that needed to be invented. But a man can make the point only so many times, just as he can get on only so many airplanes. There is surely a moment when he has to see that he should, as the great golfer Walter Hagen once advised, pause and smell the flowers.

This thought came to me quite strongly while locked in a Brazilian traffic jam—always a colourful affair, no doubt, but the kind which makes you think a little about how most sensibly to apportion some of the time left to you.

So much of it is owed to my wife Norma, my daughters, and my three grandchildren: Suzanna's Robert and Andrea's William and Emma; they have all given me a multitude of reasons for pride. Sometimes I think I should spend rather more time displaying this feeling that comes to me in some distant corner of the world and gives me a sudden yearning to be home.

Already I've had young Robert out on the Old Trafford pitch for a few minutes, just for him to get a feeling of the place. However, though he has shown talent for sport, including the display of a good golf swing and tennis stroke, no one will insist more fervently than his grandfather that his life is his own.

Sometimes I'm asked if I ever regret the fact that I never had a son, that there was no Bobby Junior with whom to kick around a ball in the back garden. My reaction is that you have to be rather conceited to think in such terms. I was given two girls and they have been the most precious of gifts. Ask for a lad? No, you do not ask for a boy, any more than you ask for the moon. You get what you are given and you thank God.

Suzanne was always fascinated by the weather. Norma and I sometimes wondered why; maybe it was because she went to school quite near Manchester airport, but who really knew except this determined young girl who announced she wanted to be a meteorologist? This meant, she pointed out, Reading University, which specialised in the subject. She studied pure mathematics and physics, and after joining the Ministry of Defence, which had been in charge of predicting the weather since the Second World War, she was sent on a special course in Germany, where she learned about how the layers of weather affect flying. She came back determined to learn how to fly herself, and though, because her job changed, she didn't take her pilot's licence, she did fly solo from the famous Battle of Britain station Biggin Hill. Eventually, she appeared on television for a while and our pride in her career was never diminished by suggestions that her place in the public eye had something to do with her family connection. Like any indignant father would, I pointed out that my girl was a qualified scientist.

Andrea went to university in Nottingham and then business school in London. She was just as emphatic as Suzanne about what she wanted to do: she wanted to be a high-powered businesswoman, and she landed a good job with Canon, the giant camera and film firm. However, she became frustrated working on budgets that were not always implemented, and wasn't happy with her life, so she decided to do something different. She went to Manchester University and got a second degree. Now she is a qualified physiotherapist and enjoys her work as she never could in a business suit. In the end this, I believe, is what you want most for your children: an understanding that life is not something to submit to, but a challenge you must try to shape by your own efforts in some activity that truly interests you.

I suspect that I have made it clear enough in these pages that in my case football was more than even a vocation—it was a compulsion. Now, when for one last time I try to capture for you the meaning of all that part of my life so strongly interwoven with Manchester United, I see something more clearly than ever before. I see that if football has been my joy and my expression and sometimes my pain, it has also been my vehicle for understanding that other people's lives and achievements do not receive the kind of attention paid to a spectacular goal in a big football match. I have had experiences that have carried me far beyond the boundaries of the games we play. When I say this I think of meeting men like Scotty Lee in Sarajevo and Peter Karanja in the second worst slum in Africa. I think of the commitment they have made to people much less fortunate than themselves, and how they do this day in, day out. In those moments of reflection I am grateful to football because, among all its other gifts, it has enabled me in recent years to help such men at least a little in their efforts to give a chance to young people who, without their efforts, would have nowhere to turn.

Scotty Lee drove a relief truck through the Bosnian mountains at that time when Sarajevo was a shooting gallery for snipers and artillery men whose job was to terrorise the population of a city I knew only as the place where I once played a fierce European Cup tie. Scotty saw a young woman pushing a pram go down under sniper fire, he saw the remnants of massacre, he saw the horror brought to ordinary people who wanted only a decent life. Because of this he stayed behind and did what he could to both heal the wounds and prevent new ones. Through football, Scotty's campaigning is to befriend young people and teach them how to identify and avoid the landmines which are still either ending or wrecking so many young lives. Through the Laureus Sport for Good Foundation, I have been able to help, in the company of the Romanian tennis star Ilie Nastase, to throw a little spotlight on to work which otherwise might go unnoticed. It has been a great privilege, and is one I place alongside getting involved with what might easily be described as the most remarkable football club in the world, Mathere United of Nairobi.

Unaided by the Kenyan Football Association, Mathere has become more than a football club, they have become a symbol of hope for young people across great swathes of Africa brought so low by Aids and hunger and desperate poverty. They won the Kenyan league title, playing exuberant, joyful football, a force rising from the bleakest of possibilities; they pushed into Tanzania and Uganda; last year they were nominated for a Nobel Prize. They have given me images which no one could forget, not least of an immaculately dressed young man emerging from a slum, beaming with pride that he was part of something that brought the real hope of achievement.

Nearer home, the work of Macclesfield Town in holding clinics to fight depression among young people, a terrible scourge which has resulted in so many lost lives through suicides and drug abuse, is another example of how football can be a force for good. Laureus have put some money into the Macclesfield project, which has helped them to employ a group of counsellors. Broken marriage and indebtedness are some of the causes of despair, and where else can a young person go for quick and significant help beyond maybe ten minutes with some overworked GP? At Macclesfield Football

Club that need is being supplied, and when I saw the effect of the effort, how comfortable young people were in going to the local football club, I said to a board meeting at Old Trafford, 'If Macclesfield can do it, I'm sure Manchester United can.' Now we do, and the response has been tremendous.

I do not wish to glorify or exaggerate my role in such magnificent work. My point is that if football has given me so much down all the years, not the least of its gifts has been an ability to put a little back into a world which has often dazzled me with its rewards. When I ran past that stand of mining implements in the primary school in Ashington, in a bright crimson jersey with a miner's helmet under my arm, I couldn't know those dreams I had in my young head would quickly pale into insignificance against the reality of what lay before me. I have met kings and presidents—and Nelson Mandela—for no better reason than that I was able to play football, to do that which was presented as a gift. I've been to every corner of the world and felt the affection, even the love, of those who see in football something that has brought enrichment and thrills to their lives.

So, of course, as long as I'm strong and energetic enough, there will be days when I put aside the slippers and old gardening sweater, and go off to some new assignment, some lingering part of the legacy that I was able to make for myself as a young man on the football field. In the meantime, there will be other days when maybe I take out a bottle of the good wine that Norma has stored away for special occasions, and toast all of those who I have known and loved, and played for and alongside.

Munich, as I have already made plain, will always be included in my recall of the best and the worst of my times; everything that has happened in the last fifty years of my life has been conditioned in some way by that tragedy. It is at the top of the list of all those things that in my memory's eye can never be obscured, any more than the days of glory when Duncan Edwards was so young and powerful and, like the team he inspired, was going to last forever.

Of course no one lasts forever, but if you are very lucky, as I have been, you have a certain duty to remember and cherish all the best of what you have felt and seen. I have tried to write it all down here, and I have to say it has never been a chore. But then how could it be? So much of what I have known and seen has been a feast that I know will nourish me to the last of my days.

Maybe one of the most unforgettable contributions to such a belief came on a rainy day in Manchester in late January 1994. It was the day we buried the Old Man—the day we looked into the eyes of the thousands who crowded the streets and saw in their glistening tears the meaning of the best of what could be achieved by the game in which we had made our lives.

The Old Man always told us that football is more than a game. It has the power to bring happiness to ordinary people. In the sadness and the rain, that belief was the glory of his life—and the unbreakable pride I felt at being part of it. He was Manchester United and, I will always like to think, so am I.

# CLUB STATISTICS

## compiled by Jack Rollin

## BOBBY CHARLTON

| | |
|---|---|
| 11 October 1937 | Born Ashington, Northumberland |
| 6 June 1953 | Joined Manchester United groundstaff |
| 4 October 1954 | Turned professional |
| 6 October 1956 | League debut v Charlton Athletic (scoring twice) |
| May 1966 | FWA Footballer of the Year |
| June 1966 | European Footballer of the Year |
| 1969 | Awarded OBE |
| May 1973 | Appointed manager Preston North End |
| 1974 | Awarded CBE; PFA Merit Award |
| May 1974 | Player-manager of Preston North End |
| 1975–76 | Waterford United player (played 31, scored 18) |
| 1982 | Wigan Athletic director and caretaker manager |
| 1984 | Director of Manchester United |
| 1994 | Knighted |

Bobby Charlton played in 759 first-class matches for Manchester United and 45 with Preston North End.

His United figures break down as follows: 606 League, 79 FA Cup, 24 League Cup, 45 European, 3 Charity Shield, 2 World Club Championship.

At Preston, it was 38 League, 4 FA Cup and 3 League Cup.

His goals at United were 199 League, 19 FA Cup, 7 League Cup, 22 European and 2 Charity Shield.

At Preston, it was 8 League, 1 FA Cup and 1 League Cup for a grand total of 259.

## HONOURS WITH MANCHESTER UNITED

First Division champions: 1957, 1965, 1967
FA Cup winners: 1963
European Cup winners: 1968
FA Youth Cup winners: 1954, 1955, 1956

# MANCHESTER UNITED

## 1956–57

| No. | Competition | Date | | Opponent | Venue | Result | Score | Goals |
|---|---|---|---|---|---|---|---|---|
| 1 | Div 1 | 6 | Oct | Charlton | (h) | W | 4–2 | ⚽⚽ |
| 2 | Div 1 | 20 | Oct | Everton | (h) | L | 2–5 | ⚽ |
| 3 | Div 1 | 3 | Nov | Wolves | (h) | W | 3–0 | |
| 4 | Div 1 | 10 | Nov | Bolton | (a) | L | 0–2 | |
| 5 | Div 1 | 17 | Nov | Leeds | (h) | W | 3–2 | ⚽⚽⚽ |
| 6 | Div 1 | 18 | Feb | Charlton | (a) | W | 5–1 | ⚽ |
| 7 | Div 1 | 23 | Feb | Blackpool | (h) | L | 0–2 | |
| 8 | Div 1 | 9 | Mar | Aston Villa | (h) | D | 1–1 | ⚽ |
| 9 | Div 1 | 16 | Mar | Wolves | (a) | D | 1–1 | ⚽ |
| 10 | FA Cup | 23 | Mar | Birmingham | (a) | W | 2–0 | ⚽ |
| 11 | Div 1 | 25 | Mar | Bolton | (h) | L | 0–2 | |
| 12 | Div 1 | 30 | Mar | Leeds | (a) | W | 2–1 | ⚽ |
| 13 | Div 1 | 13 | Apr | Luton | (a) | W | 2–0 | |
| 14 | Div 1 | 19 | Apr | Burnley | (a) | W | 3–1 | |
| 15 | Div 1 | 20 | Apr | Sunderland | (h) | W | 4–0 | |
| 16 | E Cup | 25 | Apr | Real Madrid | (h) | D | 2–2 | ⚽ |
| 17 | FA Cup | 4 | May | Aston Villa | (n) | L | 1–2 | |

| Games/Goals Season | League | FA Cup | European | Total |
|---|---|---|---|---|
| | 14/10 | 2/1 | 1/1 | 17/12 |

393

1957–58

| | | | | | | | |
|---|---|---|---|---|---|---|---|
| 18 | Div 1 | 28 | Sep | Wolves | (a) | L | 1–3 |
| 19 | Div 1 | 5 | Oct | Aston Villa | (h) | W | 4–1 |
| 20 | Div 1 | 26 | Oct | WBA | (a) | L | 3–4 |
| 21 | Div 1 | 30 | Nov | Tottenham | (h) | L | 3–4 |
| 22 | Div 1 | 21 | Dec | Leicester | (h) | W | 4–0 |
| 23 | Div 1 | 25 | Dec | Luton | (h) | W | 3–0 |
| 24 | Div 1 | 26 | Dec | Luton | (a) | D | 2–2 |
| 25 | Div 1 | 28 | Dec | Man City | (a) | D | 2–2 |
| 26 | FA Cup | 4 | Jan | Workington | (a) | W | 3–1 |
| 27 | Div 1 | 11 | Jan | Leeds | (a) | D | 1–1 |
| 28 | E Cup | 14 | Jan | Red Star B | (h) | W | 2–1 |
| 29 | Div 1 | 18 | Jan | Bolton | (h) | W | 7–2 |
| 30 | FA Cup | 25 | Jan | Ipswich | (h) | W | 2–0 |
| 31 | Div 1 | 1 | Feb | Arsenal | (a) | W | 5–4 |
| 32 | E Cup | 5 | Feb | Red Star B | (a) | D | 3–3 |
| 33 | FA Cup | 1 | Mar | WBA | (a) | D | 2–2 |
| 34 | FA Cup | 5 | Mar | WBA | (h) | W | 1–0 |
| 35 | Div 1 | 8 | Mar | WBA | (h) | L | 0–4 |
| 36 | Div 1 | 15 | Mar | Burnley | (a) | L | 0–3 |

| No. | Competition | Date | | Opponent | Venue | Result | Score | Goals |
|---|---|---|---|---|---|---|---|---|
| 37 | FA Cup | 22 | Mar | Fulham | (n) | D | 2–2 | ⚽⚽ |
| 38 | FA Cup | 26 | Mar | Fulham | (n) | W | 5–3 | ⚽ |
| 39 | Div 1 | 29 | Mar | Sheffield W | (a) | L | 0–1 | |
| 40 | Div 1 | 31 | Mar | Aston Villa | (a) | L | 2–3 | |
| 41 | Div 1 | 4 | Apr | Sunderland | (h) | D | 2–2 | |
| 42 | Div 1 | 5 | Apr | Preston | (h) | D | 0–0 | |
| 43 | Div 1 | 7 | Apr | Sunderland | (a) | W | 2–1 | ⚽ |
| 44 | Div 1 | 12 | Apr | Tottenham | (a) | L | 0–1 | |
| 45 | Div 1 | 23 | Apr | Newcastle | (h) | D | 1–1 | |
| 46 | Div 1 | 26 | Apr | Chelsea | (a) | L | 1–2 | |
| 47 | FA Cup | 3 | May | Bolton | (n) | L | 0–2 | |

| Games/Goals | League | FA Cup | European | Total |
|---|---|---|---|---|
| Season | 21/8 | 7/5 | 2/3 | 30/16 |
| Summary | 35/18 | 9/6 | 3/4 | 47/28 |

1958–59

| No. | Competition | Date | | Opponent | Venue | Result | Score | Goals |
|---|---|---|---|---|---|---|---|---|
| 48 | Div 1 | 23 | Aug | Chelsea | (h) | W | 5–2 | ⚽⚽⚽ |
| 49 | Div 1 | 27 | Aug | Nottm F | (a) | W | 3–0 | ⚽⚽ |

| | | | | | | | |
|---|---|---|---|---|---|---|---|
| 50 | Div 1 | 30 Aug | Blackpool | (a) | L | 1–2 | |
| 51 | Div 1 | 3 Sep | Nottm F | (h) | D | 1–1 | ⚽⚽⚽ |
| 52 | Div 1 | 6 Sep | Blackburn | (h) | W | 6–1 | |
| 53 | Div 1 | 8 Sep | West Ham | (a) | L | 2–3 | |
| 54 | Div 1 | 13 Sep | Newcastle | (a) | D | 1–1 | ⚽ |
| 55 | Div 1 | 17 Sep | West Ham | (h) | W | 4–1 | |
| 56 | Div 1 | 20 Sep | Tottenham | (h) | D | 2–2 | |
| 57 | Div 1 | 27 Sep | Man City | (a) | D | 1–1 | ⚽ |
| 58 | Div 1 | 8 Oct | Preston | (h) | L | 0–2 | |
| 59 | Div 1 | 11 Oct | Arsenal | (h) | D | 1–1 | |
| 60 | Div 1 | 18 Oct | Everton | (a) | L | 2–3 | |
| 61 | Div 1 | 25 Oct | WBA | (h) | L | 1–2 | |
| 62 | Div 1 | 1 Nov | Leeds | (a) | W | 2–1 | |
| 63 | Div 1 | 8 Nov | Burnley | (h) | L | 1–3 | |
| 64 | Div 1 | 15 Nov | Bolton | (a) | L | 3–6 | ⚽ |
| 65 | Div 1 | 22 Nov | Luton | (h) | W | 2–1 | ⚽ |
| 66 | Div 1 | 29 Nov | Birmingham | (a) | W | 4–0 | ⚽⚽ |
| 67 | Div 1 | 6 Dec | Leicester | (h) | W | 4–1 | ⚽ |
| 68 | Div 1 | 13 Dec | Preston | (a) | W | 4–3 | ⚽ |
| 69 | Div 1 | 20 Dec | Chelsea | (a) | W | 3–2 | ⚽ |
| 70 | Div 1 | 3 Jan | Blackpool | (h) | W | 3–1 | ⚽ |

| No. | Comp | Date | Opponent | Venue | Result | Score | Goals |
|---|---|---|---|---|---|---|---|
| 71 | FA Cup | 10 Jan | Norwich | (a) | L | 0–3 | |
| 72 | Div 1 | 31 Jan | Newcastle | (h) | D | 4–4 | ⚽⚽⚽ |
| 73 | Div 1 | 7 Feb | Tottenham | (a) | W | 3–1 | ⚽⚽ |
| 74 | Div 1 | 16 Feb | Man City | (h) | W | 4–1 | |
| 75 | Div 1 | 21 Feb | Wolves | (h) | W | 2–1 | ⚽ |
| 76 | Div 1 | 28 Feb | Arsenal | (a) | L | 2–3 | |
| 77 | Div 1 | 2 Mar | Blackburn | (a) | W | 3–1 | |
| 78 | Div 1 | 7 Mar | Everton | (h) | W | 2–1 | |
| 79 | Div 1 | 14 Mar | WBA | (a) | W | 3–1 | |
| 80 | Div 1 | 21 Mar | Leeds | (h) | W | 4–0 | ⚽⚽ |
| 81 | Div 1 | 27 Mar | Portsmouth | (h) | W | 6–1 | ⚽⚽⚽ |
| 82 | Div 1 | 28 Mar | Burnley | (a) | L | 2–4 | |
| 83 | Div 1 | 30 Mar | Portsmouth | (a) | W | 3–1 | ⚽⚽ |
| 84 | Div 1 | 4 Apr | Bolton | (h) | W | 3–0 | ⚽⚽ |
| 85 | Div 1 | 18 Apr | Birmingham | (h) | W | 1–0 | |
| 86 | Div 1 | 25 Apr | Leicester | (a) | L | 1–2 | |

| Games/Goals | League | FA Cup | European | Total |
|---|---|---|---|---|
| Season | 38/29 | 1 | — | 39/29 |
| Summary | 73/47 | 10/6 | 3/4 | 86/57 |

## 1959–60

| No. | Div | Date | Opponent | Venue | Result | Score | Goals |
|---|---|---|---|---|---|---|---|
| 87 | Div 1 | 22 Aug | WBA | (a) | L | 2–3 | |
| 88 | Div 1 | 26 Aug | Chelsea | (h) | L | 0–1 | ⚽⚽ |
| 89 | Div 1 | 29 Aug | Newcastle | (h) | W | 3–2 | |
| 90 | Div 1 | 2 Sep | Chelsea | (a) | W | 6–3 | ⚽⚽ |
| 91 | Div 1 | 5 Sep | Birmingham | (a) | D | 1–1 | ⚽ |
| 92 | Div 1 | 9 Sep | Leeds | (h) | W | 6–0 | |
| 93 | Div 1 | 12 Sep | Tottenham | (h) | L | 1–5 | |
| 94 | Div 1 | 16 Sep | Leeds | (a) | D | 2–2 | |
| 95 | Div 1 | 19 Sep | Man City | (a) | L | 0–3 | ⚽⚽ |
| 96 | Div 1 | 26 Sep | Preston | (a) | L | 0–4 | |
| 97 | Div 1 | 3 Oct | Leicester | (h) | W | 4–1 | |
| 98 | Div 1 | 10 Oct | Arsenal | (h) | W | 4–2 | ⚽ |
| 99 | Div 1 | 24 Oct | Sheffield W | (h) | W | 3–1 | |
| 100 | Div 1 | 31 Oct | Blackburn | (a) | D | 1–1 | |
| 101 | Div 1 | 7 Nov | Fulham | (h) | D | 3–3 | |
| 102 | Div 1 | 14 Nov | Bolton | (a) | D | 1–1 | |
| 103 | Div 1 | 21 Nov | Luton | (h) | W | 4–1 | |
| 104 | Div 1 | 28 Nov | Everton | (a) | L | 1–2 | |
| 105 | Div 1 | 26 Dec | Burnley | (h) | L | 1–2 | |

| 106 | Div 1 | 28 Dec | Burnley | (a) | W | 4–1 | |
| 107 | Div 1 | 2 Jan | Newcastle | (a) | L | 3–7 | |
| 108 | FA Cup | 9 Jan | Derby | (a) | W | 4–2 | |
| 109 | Div 1 | 16 Jan | Birmingham | (h) | W | 2–1 | ⚽ |
| 110 | Div 1 | 23 Jan | Tottenham | (a) | L | 1–2 | |
| 111 | FA Cup | 30 Jan | Liverpool | (a) | W | 3–1 | ⚽⚽ |
| 112 | Div 1 | 6 Feb | Man C | (h) | D | 0–0 | |
| 113 | Div 1 | 13 Feb | Preston | (h) | D | 1–1 | |
| 114 | FA Cup | 20 Feb | Sheffield W | (h) | L | 0–1 | |
| 115 | Div 1 | 24 Feb | Leicester | (a) | L | 1–3 | |
| 116 | Div 1 | 27 Feb | Blackpool | (a) | W | 6–0 | ⚽⚽⚽ |
| 117 | Div 1 | 5 Mar | Wolves | (h) | L | 0–2 | ⚽⚽ |
| 118 | Div 1 | 19 Mar | Nottm F | (h) | W | 3–1 | |
| 119 | Div 1 | 26 Mar | Fulham | (a) | W | 5–0 | ⚽⚽ |
| 120 | Div 1 | 30 Mar | Sheffield W | (a) | L | 2–4 | |
| 121 | Div 1 | 2 Apr | Bolton | (h) | W | 2–0 | ⚽⚽ |
| 122 | Div 1 | 15 Apr | West Ham | (a) | L | 1–2 | |
| 123 | Div 1 | 16 Apr | Blackburn | (h) | W | 1–0 | |
| 124 | Div 1 | 18 Apr | West Ham | (h) | W | 5–3 | ⚽⚽ |
| 125 | Div 1 | 23 Apr | Arsenal | (a) | L | 2–5 | |
| 126 | Div 1 | 30 Apr | Everton | (h) | W | 5–0 | |

| Games/Goals | League | FA Cup | European | Total |
|---|---|---|---|---|
| *Season Summary* | 37/18 | 3/3 | — | 40/21 |
| | 110/65 | 13/9 | 3/4 | 126/78 |

## 1960–61

| | | | | | | | |
|---|---|---|---|---|---|---|---|
| 127 | Div 1 | 20 Aug | Blackburn | (h) | L | 1–3 | |
| 128 | Div 1 | 24 Aug | Everton | (a) | L | 0–4 | |
| 129 | Div 1 | 31 Aug | Everton | (h) | W | 4–0 | ⚽ |
| 130 | Div 1 | 3 Sep | Tottenham | (a) | L | 1–4 | |
| 131 | Div 1 | 5 Sep | West Ham | (a) | L | 1–2 | |
| 132 | Div 1 | 10 Sep | Aston Villa | (h) | D | 1–1 | ⚽ |
| 133 | Div 1 | 14 Sep | West Ham | (h) | W | 6–1 | ⚽⚽ |
| 134 | Div 1 | 17 Sep | Leicester | (a) | L | 1–3 | |
| 135 | Div 1 | 24 Sep | Wolves | (h) | L | 1–3 | ⚽ |
| 136 | Div 1 | 1 Oct | Bolton | (a) | D | 1–1 | |
| 137 | Div 1 | 15 Oct | Burnley | (a) | L | 3–5 | |
| 138 | Div 1 | 22 Oct | Newcastle | (h) | W | 3–2 | |
| 139 | Div 1 | 29 Oct | Arsenal | (a) | L | 1–2 | |
| 140 | Div 1 | 5 Nov | Sheffield W | (h) | D | 0–0 | |

| No. | Comp | Date | | Opponent | Venue | Result | Score | |
|---|---|---|---|---|---|---|---|---|
| 141 | Div 1 | 12 | Nov | Birmingham | (a) | L | 1–3 | ⚽ |
| 142 | Div 1 | 19 | Nov | WBA | (h) | W | 3–0 | |
| 143 | Div 1 | 26 | Nov | Cardiff | (a) | L | 0–3 | |
| 144 | Div 1 | 3 | Dec | Preston | (h) | W | 1–0 | ⚽ |
| 145 | Div 1 | 10 | Dec | Fulham | (a) | D | 4–4 | ⚽⚽ |
| 146 | Div 1 | 17 | Dec | Blackburn | (a) | W | 2–1 | ⚽ |
| 147 | Div 1 | 24 | Dec | Chelsea | (a) | W | 2–1 | |
| 148 | Div 1 | 26 | Dec | Chelsea | (h) | W | 6–0 | ⚽⚽⚽ |
| 149 | Div 1 | 31 | Dec | Man C | (h) | W | 5–1 | |
| 150 | FA Cup | 7 | Jan | Middlesbrough | (h) | W | 3–0 | |
| 151 | Div 1 | 14 | Jan | Tottenham | (h) | W | 2–0 | |
| 152 | Div 1 | 21 | Jan | Leicester | (a) | L | 0–6 | |
| 153 | FA Cup | 28 | Jan | Sheffield W | (a) | D | 1–1 | |
| 154 | FA Cup | 1 | Feb | Sheffield W | (h) | L | 2–7 | ⚽ |
| 155 | Div 1 | 4 | Feb | Aston Villa | (h) | D | 1–1 | |
| 156 | Div 1 | 11 | Feb | Wolves | (a) | L | 1–2 | ⚽⚽ |
| 157 | Div 1 | 18 | Feb | Bolton | (h) | W | 3–1 | |
| 158 | Div 1 | 25 | Feb | Nottm F | (a) | L | 2–3 | ⚽ |
| 159 | Div 1 | 4 | Mar | Man City | (a) | W | 3–1 | |
| 160 | Div 1 | 11 | Mar | Newcastle | (a) | D | 1–1 | |
| 161 | Div 1 | 18 | Mar | Arsenal | (h) | D | 1–1 | |

| No. | Div | Date | | Opponent | Venue | Result | Score | Goals |
|---|---|---|---|---|---|---|---|---|
| 162 | Div 1 | 25 | Mar | Sheffield W | (a) | L | 1–5 | ⚽ |
| 163 | Div 1 | 31 | Mar | Blackpool | (a) | L | 0–2 | |
| 164 | Div 1 | 1 | Apr | Fulham | (h) | W | 3–1 | ⚽ |
| 165 | Div 1 | 3 | Apr | Blackpool | (h) | W | 2–0 | |
| 166 | Div 1 | 8 | Apr | WBA | (a) | D | 1–1 | |
| 167 | Div 1 | 22 | Apr | Preston | (a) | W | 4–2 | ⚽⚽ |
| 168 | Div 1 | 29 | Apr | Cardiff | (h) | D | 3–3 | ⚽⚽ |

| | League | FA Cup | European | Total |
|---|---|---|---|---|
| Games/Goals | 39/21 | 3 | — | 42/21 |
| *Season*<br>*Summary* | 149/86 | 16/9 | 3/4 | 168/99 |

## 1961–62

| No. | Div | Date | | Opponent | Venue | Result | Score | Goals |
|---|---|---|---|---|---|---|---|---|
| 169 | Div 1 | 19 | Aug | West Ham | (a) | D | 1–1 | |
| 170 | Div 1 | 23 | Aug | Chelsea | (h) | W | 3–2 | |
| 171 | Div 1 | 26 | Aug | Blackburn | (h) | W | 6–1 | ⚽ |
| 172 | Div 1 | 30 | Aug | Chelsea | (a) | L | 0–2 | |
| 173 | Div 1 | 2 | Sep | Blackpool | (a) | W | 3–2 | ⚽ |
| 174 | Div 1 | 9 | Sep | Tottenham | (h) | W | 1–0 | |

| No. | Comp | Date | Opponent | Venue | Result | Score |
|---|---|---|---|---|---|---|
| 175 | Div 1 | 16 Sep | Cardiff | (a) | W | 2–1 |
| 176 | Div 1 | 18 Sep | Aston Villa | (a) | D | 1–1 |
| 177 | Div 1 | 23 Sep | Man City | (h) | W | 3–2 |
| 178 | Div 1 | 30 Sep | Wolves | (h) | L | 0–2 |
| 179 | Div 1 | 7 Oct | WBA | (a) | D | 1–1 |
| 180 | Div 1 | 21 Oct | Arsenal | (a) | L | 1–5 |
| 181 | Div 1 | 28 Oct | Bolton | (h) | L | 0–3 |
| 182 | Div 1 | 4 Nov | Sheffield W | (a) | L | 1–3 |
| 183 | Div 1 | 11 Nov | Leicester | (h) | D | 2–2 |
| 184 | Div 1 | 18 Nov | Ipswich | (a) | L | 1–4 |
| 185 | Div 1 | 25 Nov | Burnley | (h) | L | 1–4 |
| 186 | Div 1 | 2 Dec | Everton | (a) | L | 1–5 |
| 187 | Div 1 | 9 Dec | Fulham | (h) | W | 3–0 |
| 188 | Div 1 | 16 Dec | West Ham | (h) | L | 1–2 |
| 189 | Div 1 | 26 Dec | Nottm F | (h) | W | 6–3 |
| 190 | FA Cup | 6 Jan | Bolton | (h) | W | 2–1 |
| 191 | Div 1 | 13 Jan | Blackpool | (h) | L | 0–1 |
| 192 | Div 1 | 15 Jan | Aston Villa | (h) | W | 2–0 |
| 193 | Div 1 | 20 Jan | Tottenham | (a) | D | 2–2 |
| 194 | FA Cup | 31 Jan | Arsenal | (h) | W | 1–0 |
| 195 | Div 1 | 3 Feb | Cardiff | (h) | W | 3–0 |

| No. | Comp | Date | Opponent | Venue | Res | Score | Goals |
|---|---|---|---|---|---|---|---|
| 196 | Div 1 | 10 Feb | Man City | (a) | W | 2–0 | ⚽⚽⚽ |
| 197 | FA Cup | 17 Feb | Sheffield W | (h) | D | 0–0 | |
| 198 | FA Cup | 21 Feb | Sheffield W | (a) | W | 2–0 | |
| 199 | Div 1 | 24 Feb | WBA | (h) | W | 4–1 | |
| 200 | Div 1 | 28 Feb | Wolves | (a) | D | 2–2 | |
| 201 | Div 1 | 3 Mar | Birmingham | (a) | D | 1–1 | |
| 202 | FA Cup | 10 Mar | Preston | (a) | D | 0–0 | |
| 203 | FA Cup | 14 Mar | Preston | (h) | W | 2–1 | ⚽ |
| 204 | Div 1 | 17 Mar | Bolton | (a) | L | 0–1 | |
| 205 | Div 1 | 24 Mar | Sheffield W | (h) | D | 1–1 | |
| 206 | FA Cup | 31 Mar | Tottenham | (n) | L | 1–3 | ⚽ |
| 207 | Div 1 | 7 Apr | Ipswich | (h) | W | 5–0 | |
| 208 | Div 1 | 16 Apr | Arsenal | (h) | L | 2–3 | |
| 209 | Div 1 | 21 Apr | Everton | (h) | D | 1–1 | |
| 210 | Div 1 | 23 Apr | Sheffield U | (h) | L | 0–1 | |
| 211 | Div 1 | 24 Apr | Sheffield U | (a) | W | 3–2 | |
| 212 | Div 1 | 28 Apr | Fulham | (a) | L | 0–2 | |

| Games/Goals | League | FA Cup | European | Total |
|---|---|---|---|---|
| Season | 37/8 | 7/2 | — | 44/10 |
| Summary | 186/94 | 23/11 | 3/4 | 212/109 |

| No. | Comp | Date | Opponent | Venue | Result | Score | ⚽ |
|---|---|---|---|---|---|---|---|
| 213 | Div 1 | 13 Oct | Blackburn | (h) | L | 0–3 | |
| 214 | Div 1 | 20 Oct | Tottenham | (a) | L | 2–6 | |
| 215 | Div 1 | 27 Oct | West Ham | (h) | W | 3–1 | |
| 216 | Div 1 | 3 Nov | Ipswich | (a) | W | 5–3 | |
| 217 | Div 1 | 10 Nov | Liverpool | (h) | D | 3–3 | |
| 218 | Div 1 | 17 Nov | Wolves | (a) | W | 3–2 | |
| 219 | Div 1 | 24 Nov | Aston Villa | (h) | D | 2–2 | |
| 220 | Div 1 | 3 Dec | Sheffield U | (a) | D | 1–1 | |
| 221 | Div 1 | 8 Dec | Nottm F | (h) | W | 5–1 | |
| 222 | Div 1 | 26 Dec | Fulham | (a) | W | 1–0 | ⚽ |
| 223 | Div 1 | 23 Feb | Blackpool | (h) | D | 1–1 | ⚽ |
| 224 | Div 1 | 2 Mar | Blackburn | (a) | D | 2–2 | ⚽ |
| 225 | FA Cup | 4 Mar | Huddersfield | (h) | W | 5–0 | ⚽ |
| 226 | Div 1 | 9 Mar | Tottenham | (h) | L | 0–2 | |
| 227 | FA Cup | 11 Mar | Aston Villa | (h) | W | 1–0 | |
| 228 | FA Cup | 16 Mar | Chelsea | (h) | W | 2–1 | |
| 229 | Div 1 | 18 Mar | West Ham | (a) | L | 1–3 | |
| 230 | Div 1 | 23 Mar | Ipswich | (h) | L | 0–1 | |
| 231 | FA Cup | 30 Mar | Coventry | (a) | W | 3–1 | ⚽⚽ |

| No. | Comp. | Date | Opponent | | Result | Score |
|---|---|---|---|---|---|---|
| 232 | Div 1 | 1 Apr | Fulham | (h) | L | 0–2 |
| 233 | Div 1 | 9 Apr | Aston Villa | (a) | W | 2–1 |
| 234 | Div 1 | 13 Apr | Liverpool | (a) | L | 0–1 |
| 235 | Div 1 | 15 Apr | Leicester | (h) | D | 2–2 |
| 236 | Div 1 | 16 Apr | Leicester | (a) | L | 3–4 |
| 237 | Div 1 | 20 Apr | Sheffield U | (h) | D | 1–1 |
| 238 | Div 1 | 22 Apr | Wolves | (h) | W | 2–1 |
| 239 | FA Cup | 27 Apr | Southampton | (n) | W | 1–0 |
| 240 | Div 1 | 1 May | Sheffield W | (h) | L | 1–3 |
| 241 | Div 1 | 4 May | Burnley | (a) | W | 1–0 |
| 242 | Div 1 | 6 May | Arsenal | (h) | L | 2–3 |
| 243 | Div 1 | 10 May | Birmingham | (a) | L | 1–2 |
| 244 | Div 1 | 15 May | Man City | (a) | D | 1–1 |
| 245 | Div 1 | 18 May | Orient | (h) | W | 3–1 |
| 246 | FA Cup | 25 May | Leicester | (n) | W | 3–1 |

| Games/Goals | League | FA Cup | European | Total |
|---|---|---|---|---|
| Season | 28/7 | 6/2 | — | 34/9 |
| Summary | 214/101 | 29/13 | 3/4 | 246/118 |

| | | | | | | | | |
|---|---|---|---|---|---|---|---|---|
| 247 | C Shd | 17 Aug | Everton | (a) | L | 0–4 | ⚽⚽ |
| 248 | Div 1 | 24 Aug | Sheffield W | (a) | D | 3–3 | |
| 249 | Div 1 | 28 Aug | Ipswich | (h) | W | 2–0 | |
| 250 | Div 1 | 31 Aug | Everton | (h) | W | 5–1 | |
| 251 | Div 1 | 3 Sep | Ipswich | (a) | W | 7–2 | ⚽⚽ |
| 252 | Div 1 | 7 Sep | Birmingham | (a) | D | 1–1 | |
| 253 | Div 1 | 11 Sep | Blackpool | (h) | W | 3–2 | |
| 254 | Div 1 | 14 Sep | WBA | (h) | W | 1–0 | |
| 255 | Div 1 | 16 Sep | Blackpool | (a) | L | 0–1 | |
| 256 | Div 1 | 21 Sep | Arsenal | (a) | L | 1–2 | |
| 257 | ECWC | 25 Sep | Willem II | (a) | D | 1–1 | |
| 258 | Div 1 | 28 Sep | Leicester | (h) | W | 3–2 | |
| 259 | Div 1 | 2 Oct | Chelsea | (a) | D | 1–1 | |
| 260 | Div 1 | 5 Oct | Bolton W | (a) | W | 1–0 | |
| 261 | ECWC | 15 Oct | Willem II | (h) | W | 6–1 | ⚽ |
| 262 | Div 1 | 19 Oct | Nottm F | (a) | W | 2–1 | |
| 263 | Div 1 | 26 Oct | West Ham | (h) | L | 0–1 | |
| 264 | Div 1 | 28 Oct | Blackburn | (h) | D | 2–2 | |
| 265 | Div 1 | 2 Nov | Wolves | (a) | L | 0–2 | |

| No. | Competition | Date | Opponent | Venue | Result | Score | |
|---|---|---|---|---|---|---|---|
| 266 | Div 1 | 9 Nov | Tottenham | (h) | W | 4–1 | |
| 267 | Div 1 | 16 Nov | Aston Villa | (a) | L | 0–4 | |
| 268 | Div 1 | 23 Nov | Liverpool | (h) | L | 0–1 | |
| 269 | Div 1 | 30 Nov | Sheffield U | (a) | W | 2–1 | |
| 270 | ECWC | 3 Dec | Tottenham | (a) | L | 0–2 | ⚽⚽ |
| 271 | Div 1 | 7 Dec | Stoke | (h) | W | 5–2 | |
| 272 | ECWC | 10 Dec | Tottenham | (h) | W | 4–1 | |
| 273 | Div 1 | 14 Dec | Sheffield W | (h) | W | 3–1 | |
| 274 | Div 1 | 21 Dec | Everton | (a) | L | 0–4 | |
| 275 | Div 1 | 26 Dec | Burnley | (a) | L | 1–6 | |
| 276 | Div 1 | 28 Dec | Burnley | (h) | W | 5–1 | |
| 277 | FA Cup | 4 Jan | Southampton | (a) | W | 3–2 | ⚽ |
| 278 | Div 1 | 18 Jan | WBA | (a) | W | 4–1 | |
| 279 | FA Cup | 25 Jan | Bristol R | (h) | W | 4–1 | |
| 280 | Div 1 | 1 Feb | Arsenal | (h) | W | 3–1 | |
| 281 | Div 1 | 8 Feb | Leicester | (a) | L | 2–3 | |
| 282 | FA Cup | 15 Feb | Barnsley | (a) | W | 4–0 | |
| 283 | Div 1 | 19 Feb | Bolton | (h) | W | 5–0 | ⚽ |
| 284 | Div 1 | 22 Feb | Blackburn | (a) | W | 3–1 | ⚽ |
| 285 | ECWC | 26 Feb | Sporting Lisbon | (h) | W | 4–1 | ⚽⚽ |
| 286 | FA Cup | 29 Feb | Sunderland | (h) | D | 3–3 | |

| No. | Comp | Date | Opponent | | Result | | |
|---|---|---|---|---|---|---|---|
| 287 | FA Cup | 4 Mar | Sunderland | (a) | D | 2-2 | |
| 288 | FA Cup | 9 Mar | Sunderland | (n) | W | 5-1 | ⚽ |
| 289 | FA Cup | 14 Mar | West Ham | (n) | L | 1-3 | |
| 290 | ECWC | 18 Mar | Sporting Lisbon | (a) | L | 0-5 | |
| 291 | Div 1 | 21 Mar | Tottenham | (a) | W | 3-2 | ⚽ |
| 292 | Div 1 | 23 Mar | Chelsea | (h) | D | 1-1 | |
| 293 | Div 1 | 27 Mar | Fulham | (a) | D | 2-2 | |
| 294 | Div 1 | 28 Mar | Wolves | (h) | D | 2-2 | ⚽ |
| 295 | Div 1 | 30 Mar | Fulham | (h) | W | 3-0 | |
| 296 | Div 1 | 4 Apr | Liverpool | (a) | L | 0-3 | |
| 297 | Div 1 | 6 Apr | Aston Villa | (h) | W | 1-0 | |
| 298 | Div 1 | 13 Apr | Sheffield U | (h) | W | 2-1 | |
| 299 | Div 1 | 18 Apr | Stoke | (a) | L | 1-3 | ⚽ |
| 300 | Div 1 | 25 Apr | Nottm F | (h) | W | 3-1 | |

| Games/Goals | League | FA Cup | European | C Shd | Total |
|---|---|---|---|---|---|
| Season | 40/9 | 7/2 | 6/4 | 1 | 54/15 |
| Summary | 254/110 | 36/15 | 9/8 | 1 | 300/133 |

1964–65

| No. | Comp | Date | | Opponent | Venue | Result | Score | |
|---|---|---|---|---|---|---|---|---|
| 301 | Div 1 | 22 | Aug | WBA | (h) | D | 2–2 | ⚽ |
| 302 | Div 1 | 24 | Aug | West Ham | (a) | L | 1–3 | |
| 303 | Div 1 | 29 | Aug | Leicester | (a) | D | 2–2 | |
| 304 | Div 1 | 2 | Sep | West Ham | (h) | W | 3–1 | |
| 305 | Div 1 | 5 | Sep | Fulham | (a) | L | 1–2 | |
| 306 | Div 1 | 8 | Sep | Everton | (a) | D | 3–3 | |
| 307 | Div 1 | 12 | Sep | Nottm F | (h) | W | 3–0 | |
| 308 | Div 1 | 16 | Sep | Everton | (h) | W | 2–1 | |
| 309 | Div 1 | 19 | Sep | Stoke | (a) | W | 2–1 | |
| 310 | Fairs | 23 | Sep | Djurgaarden | (a) | D | 1–1 | |
| 311 | Div 1 | 26 | Sep | Tottenham | (h) | W | 4–1 | |
| 312 | Div 1 | 30 | Sep | Chelsea | (a) | W | 2–0 | |
| 313 | Div 1 | 6 | Oct | Burnley | (a) | D | 0–0 | |
| 314 | Div 1 | 10 | Oct | Sunderland | (h) | W | 1–0 | |
| 315 | Div 1 | 17 | Oct | Wolves | (a) | W | 4–2 | |
| 316 | Fairs | 27 | Oct | Djurgaarden | (h) | W | 6–1 | ⚽⚽ |
| 317 | Div 1 | 31 | Oct | Liverpool | (a) | W | 2–0 | ⚽⚽ |
| 318 | Div 1 | 7 | Nov | Sheffield W | (h) | W | 1–0 | |
| 319 | Fairs | 11 | Nov | B Dortmund | (a) | W | 6–1 | ⚽⚽⚽ |

| No. | Comp. | Date | Opponent | | Result | Score | |
|---|---|---|---|---|---|---|---|
| 320 | Div 1 | 14 Nov | Blackpool | (a) | W | 2-1 | |
| 321 | Div 1 | 21 Nov | Blackburn | (h) | W | 3-0 | |
| 322 | Div 1 | 28 Nov | Arsenal | (a) | W | 3-2 | |
| 323 | Fairs | 2 Dec | B Dortmund | (h) | W | 4-0 | ⚽⚽ |
| 324 | Div 1 | 5 Dec | Leeds | (h) | L | 0-1 | |
| 325 | Div 1 | 12 Dec | WBA | (a) | D | 1-1 | |
| 326 | Div 1 | 16 Dec | Birmingham | (h) | D | 1-1 | ⚽ |
| 327 | Div 1 | 26 Dec | Sheffield U | (a) | W | 1-0 | |
| 328 | Div 1 | 28 Dec | Sheffield U | (h) | D | 1-1 | |
| 329 | FA Cup | 9 Jan | Chester | (h) | W | 2-1 | |
| 330 | Div 1 | 16 Jan | Nottm F | (a) | D | 2-2 | |
| 331 | Fairs | 20 Jan | Everton | (h) | D | 1-1 | |
| 332 | Div 1 | 23 Jan | Stoke | (h) | D | 1-1 | |
| 333 | FA Cup | 30 Jan | Stoke | (a) | D | 0-0 | |
| 334 | FA Cup | 3 Feb | Stoke | (h) | W | 1-0 | |
| 335 | Div 1 | 6 Feb | Tottenham | (a) | L | 0-1 | ⚽ |
| 336 | Fairs | 9 Feb | Everton | (a) | W | 2-1 | |
| 337 | Div 1 | 13 Feb | Burnley | (h) | W | 3-2 | |
| 338 | FA Cup | 20 Feb | Burnley | (h) | W | 2-1 | |
| 339 | Div 1 | 24 Feb | Sunderland | (a) | L | 0-1 | |
| 340 | Div 1 | 27 Feb | Wolves | (h) | W | 3-0 | ⚽⚽ |

411

| No. | Competition | Date | Opponent | Venue | Result | Score | Goals |
|---|---|---|---|---|---|---|---|
| 341 | FA Cup | 10 Mar | Wolves | (a) | W | 5–3 | ⚽⚽⚽ |
| 342 | Div 1 | 13 Mar | Chelsea | (h) | W | 4–0 | |
| 343 | Div 1 | 15 Mar | Fulham | (h) | W | 4–1 | |
| 344 | Div 1 | 20 Mar | Sheffield W | (a) | L | 0–1 | |
| 345 | Div 1 | 22 Mar | Blackpool | (h) | W | 2–0 | |
| 346 | FA Cup | 27 Mar | Leeds | (n) | D | 0–0 | |
| 347 | FA Cup | 31 Mar | Leeds | (n) | L | 0–1 | |
| 348 | Div 1 | 3 Apr | Blackburn | (a) | W | 5–0 | ⚽ |
| 349 | Div 1 | 12 Apr | Leicester | (h) | W | 1–0 | |
| 350 | Div 1 | 17 Apr | Leeds | (a) | W | 1–0 | |
| 351 | Div 1 | 19 Apr | Birmingham | (a) | W | 4–2 | ⚽⚽ |
| 352 | Div 1 | 24 Apr | Liverpool | (h) | W | 3–0 | |
| 353 | Div 1 | 26 Apr | Arsenal | (h) | W | 3–1 | |
| 354 | Div 1 | 28 Apr | Aston Villa | (a) | L | 1–2 | |
| 355 | Fairs | 12 May | Strasbourg | (a) | W | 5–0 | |
| 356 | Fairs | 19 May | Strasbourg | (h) | D | 0–0 | |
| 357 | Fairs | 31 May | Ferencváros | (h) | W | 3–2 | |
| 358 | Fairs | 6 Jun | Ferencváros | (a) | L | 0–1 | |
| 359 | Fairs | 16 Jun | Ferencváros | (a) | L | 1–2 | |

| Games/Goals | League | FA Cup | European | C Shd | Total |
|---|---|---|---|---|---|
| Season | 41/10 | 7 | 11/8 | — | 59/18 |
| Summary | 295/120 | 43/15 | 20/16 | 1 | 359/151 |

| No. | Comp | Date | | Opponent | Venue | Result | Score | Goals |
|---|---|---|---|---|---|---|---|---|
| 360 | C Shd | 14 | Aug | Liverpool | (h) | D | 2–2 | ⚽ |
| 361 | Div 1 | 21 | Aug | Sheffield W | (h) | W | 1–0 | |
| 362 | Div 1 | 24 | Aug | Nottm F | (a) | L | 2–4 | |
| 363 | Div 1 | 28 | Aug | Northampton | (a) | D | 1–1 | |
| 364 | Div 1 | 1 | Sep | Nottm F | (h) | D | 0–0 | |
| 365 | Div 1 | 4 | Sep | Stoke | (h) | D | 1–1 | |
| 366 | Div 1 | 8 | Sep | Newcastle | (a) | W | 2–1 | |
| 367 | Div 1 | 11 | Sep | Burnley | (a) | L | 0–3 | |
| 368 | Div 1 | 15 | Sep | Newcastle | (h) | D | 1–1 | |
| 369 | Div 1 | 18 | Sep | Chelsea | (h) | W | 4–1 | ⚽⚽ |
| 370 | E Cup | 22 | Sep | HJK Helsinki | (a) | W | 3–2 | |
| 371 | Div 1 | 25 | Sep | Arsenal | (a) | L | 2–4 | |
| 372 | E Cup | 6 | Oct | HJK Helsinki | (h) | W | 6–0 | ⚽⚽ |
| 373 | Div 1 | 9 | Oct | Liverpool | (h) | W | 2–0 | |
| 374 | Div 1 | 16 | Oct | Tottenham | (a) | L | 1–5 | |
| 375 | Div 1 | 23 | Oct | Fulham | (h) | W | 4–1 | ⚽⚽ |
| 376 | Div 1 | 30 | Oct | Blackpool | (a) | W | 2–1 | |
| 377 | Div 1 | 6 | Nov | Blackburn | (h) | D | 2–2 | |
| 378 | Div 1 | 13 | Nov | Leicester | (a) | W | 5–0 | |

| No. | Comp | Date | Opponent | Venue | Result | Score | Goals |
|---|---|---|---|---|---|---|---|
| 379 | E Cup | 17 Nov | Vorwaerts | (a) | W | 2–0 | |
| 380 | Div 1 | 20 Nov | Sheffield U | (h) | W | 3–1 | |
| 381 | E Cup | 1 Dec | Vorwaerts | (h) | W | 3–1 | |
| 382 | Div 1 | 4 Dec | West Ham | (h) | D | 0–0 | |
| 383 | Div 1 | 11 Dec | Sunderland | (a) | W | 3–2 | |
| 384 | Div 1 | 15 Dec | Everton | (h) | W | 3–0 | ⚽ |
| 385 | Div 1 | 18 Dec | Tottenham | (h) | W | 5–1 | ⚽ |
| 386 | Div 1 | 27 Dec | WBA | (h) | D | 1–1 | |
| 387 | Div 1 | 1 Jan | Liverpool | (a) | L | 1–2 | |
| 388 | Div 1 | 8 Jan | Sunderland | (h) | D | 1–1 | |
| 389 | Div 1 | 12 Jan | Leeds | (a) | D | 1–1 | |
| 390 | Div 1 | 15 Jan | Fulham | (a) | W | 1–0 | ⚽ |
| 391 | FA Cup | 22 Jan | Derby | (a) | W | 5–2 | |
| 392 | Div 1 | 29 Jan | Sheffield W | (a) | D | 0–0 | |
| 393 | E Cup | 2 Feb | Benfica | (h) | W | 3–2 | |
| 394 | Div 1 | 5 Feb | Northampton | (h) | W | 6–2 | ⚽⚽⚽ |
| 395 | FA Cup | 12 Feb | Rotherham | (h) | D | 0–0 | |
| 396 | FA Cup | 15 Feb | Rotherham | (a) | W | 1–0 | |
| 397 | Div 1 | 19 Feb | Stoke | (a) | D | 2–2 | |
| 398 | Div 1 | 26 Feb | Burnley | (h) | W | 4–2 | ⚽ |
| 399 | FA Cup | 5 Mar | Wolves | (a) | W | 4–2 | |

| No. | Comp | Opponent | Date | | Result | | Goals |
|---|---|---|---|---|---|---|---|
| 400 | E Cup | Benfica | 9 Mar | (a) | W | 5–1 | ⚽ |
| 401 | Div 1 | Chelsea | 12 Mar | (a) | L | 0–2 | |
| 402 | Div 1 | Arsenal | 19 Mar | (h) | W | 2–1 | |
| 403 | FA Cup | Preston | 26 Mar | (a) | D | 1–1 | |
| 404 | FA Cup | Preston | 30 Mar | (h) | W | 3–1 | |
| 405 | Div 1 | Leicester | 9 Apr | (h) | L | 1–2 | |
| 406 | E Cup | Partizan | 13 Apr | (a) | L | 0–2 | |
| 407 | E Cup | Partizan | 20 Apr | (h) | W | 1–0 | |
| 408 | FA Cup | Everton | 23 Apr | (n) | L | 0–1 | |
| 409 | Div 1 | Everton | 25 Apr | (a) | D | 0–0 | |
| 410 | Div 1 | Blackpool | 27 Apr | (h) | W | 2–1 | ⚽ |
| 411 | Div 1 | West Ham | 30 Apr | (a) | L | 2–3 | ⚽ |
| 412 | Div 1 | Blackburn | 7 May | (a) | W | 4–1 | ⚽⚽ |
| 413 | Div 1 | Aston Villa | 9 May | (h) | W | 6–1 | ⚽⚽ |

| Games/Goals | League | FA Cup | European | C Shd | Total |
|---|---|---|---|---|---|
| Season | 38/16 | 7 | 8/2 | 1 | 54/18 |
| Summary | 333/136 | 50/15 | 28/18 | 2 | 413/169 |

| | | | | | | | |
|---|---|---|---|---|---|---|---|
| 414 | Div 1 | 20 Aug | WBA | (h) | W | 5–3 | |
| 415 | Div 1 | 23 Aug | Everton | (a) | W | 2–1 | |
| 416 | Div 1 | 27 Aug | Leeds | (a) | L | 1–3 | |
| 417 | Div 1 | 31 Aug | Everton | (h) | W | 3–0 | |
| 418 | Div 1 | 3 Sep | Newcastle | (h) | W | 3–2 | |
| 419 | Div 1 | 7 Sep | Stoke | (a) | L | 3–0 | |
| 420 | Div 1 | 10 Sep | Tottenham | (a) | L | 1–2 | |
| 421 | Div 1 | 17 Sep | Man City | (h) | W | 1–0 | |
| 422 | Div 1 | 24 Sep | Burnley | (h) | W | 4–1 | ⚽ |
| 423 | Div 1 | 1 Oct | Nottm F | (a) | L | 1–4 | |
| 424 | Div 1 | 8 Oct | Blackpool | (a) | W | 2–1 | |
| 425 | Div 1 | 15 Oct | Chelsea | (h) | D | 1–1 | |
| 426 | Div 1 | 29 Oct | Arsenal | (h) | W | 1–0 | |
| 427 | Div 1 | 5 Nov | Chelsea | (a) | W | 3–1 | |
| 428 | Div 1 | 12 Nov | Sheffield W | (h) | W | 2–0 | ⚽ |
| 429 | Div 1 | 19 Nov | Southampton | (a) | W | 2–1 | ⚽⚽ |
| 430 | Div 1 | 26 Nov | Sunderland | (h) | W | 5–0 | |
| 431 | Div 1 | 30 Nov | Leicester | (a) | W | 2–1 | |
| 432 | Div 1 | 3 Dec | Aston Villa | (a) | L | 1–2 | |

| | | | | | | |
|---|---|---|---|---|---|---|
| 433 | Div 1 | 10 Dec | Liverpool | (h) | D | 2–2 |
| 434 | Div 1 | 17 Dec | WBA | (a) | W | 4–3 |
| 435 | Div 1 | 26 Dec | Sheffield U | (a) | L | 1–2 |
| 436 | Div 1 | 27 Dec | Sheffield U | (h) | W | 2–0 |
| 437 | Div 1 | 31 Dec | Leeds | (h) | D | 0–0 |
| 438 | Div 1 | 14 Jan | Tottenham | (h) | W | 1–0 |
| 439 | Div 1 | 21 Jan | Man City | (a) | D | 1–1 |
| 440 | FA Cup | 28 Jan | Stoke | (h) | W | 2–0 |
| 441 | Div 1 | 4 Feb | Burnley | (a) | D | 1–1 |
| 442 | Div 1 | 11 Feb | Nottm F | (h) | W | 1–0 |
| 443 | FA Cup | 18 Feb | Norwich | (h) | L | 1–2 |
| 444 | Div 1 | 25 Feb | Blackpool | (h) | W | 4–0 |
| 445 | Div 1 | 3 Mar | Arsenal | (a) | D | 1–1 |
| 446 | Div 1 | 11 Mar | Newcastle | (a) | D | 0–0 |
| 447 | Div 1 | 18 Mar | Leicester | (h) | W | 5–2 |
| 448 | Div 1 | 25 Mar | Liverpool | (a) | D | 0–0 |
| 449 | Div 1 | 27 Mar | Fulham | (a) | D | 2–2 |
| 450 | Div 1 | 28 Mar | Fulham | (h) | W | 2–1 |
| 451 | Div 1 | 1 Apr | West Ham | (h) | W | 3–0 |
| 452 | Div 1 | 10 Apr | Sheffield W | (a) | D | 2–2 |
| 453 | Div 1 | 18 Apr | Southampton | (h) | W | 3–0 |

| No. | Comp | Date | | Opponent | | Result | Goals |
|---|---|---|---|---|---|---|---|
| 454 | Div 1 | 22 | Apr | Sunderland | (a) | D | 0–0 |
| 455 | Div 1 | 29 | Apr | Aston Villa | (h) | W | 3–1 |
| 456 | Div 1 | 6 | May | West Ham | (a) | W | 6–1 ⚽ |
| 457 | Div 1 | 13 | May | Stoke | (h) | D | 0–0 |

| Games/Goals | League | FA Cup | European | C Shd | Total |
|---|---|---|---|---|---|
| Season | 42/12 | 2 | — | — | 44/12 |
| Summary | 375/148 | 52/15 | 28/18 | 2 | 457/181 |

## 1967–68

| No. | Comp | Date | | Opponent | | Result | Goals |
|---|---|---|---|---|---|---|---|
| 458 | C Shd | 12 | Aug | Tottenham | (h) | D | 3–3 ⚽⚽ |
| 459 | Div 1 | 19 | Aug | Everton | (a) | L | 1–3 |
| 460 | Div 1 | 23 | Aug | Leeds | (h) | W | 1–0 ⚽ |
| 461 | Div 1 | 26 | Aug | Leicester | (h) | D | 1–1 |
| 462 | Div 1 | 2 | Sep | West Ham | (a) | W | 3–1 ⚽⚽ |
| 463 | Div 1 | 6 | Sep | Sunderland | (a) | D | 1–1 |
| 464 | Div 1 | 9 | Sep | Burnley | (h) | D | 2–2 |
| 465 | Div 1 | 16 | Sep | Sheffield W | (a) | D | 1–1 |
| 466 | E Cup | 20 | Sep | Hibernians | (h) | W | 4–0 |

| No. | Comp. | Date | | Opponent | Venue | Result | Score | |
|---|---|---|---|---|---|---|---|---|
| 467 | Div 1 | 23 | Sep | Tottenham | (h) | W | 3-1 | |
| 468 | E Cup | 27 | Sep | Hibernians | (a) | D | 0-0 | ⚽⚽ |
| 469 | Div 1 | 30 | Sep | Man City | (a) | W | 2-1 | |
| 470 | Div 1 | 7 | Oct | Arsenal | (h) | W | 1-0 | |
| 471 | Div 1 | 14 | Oct | Sheffield U | (a) | W | 3-0 | ⚽ |
| 472 | Div 1 | 25 | Oct | Coventry | (h) | W | 4-0 | ⚽ |
| 473 | Div 1 | 28 | Oct | Nottm F | (a) | L | 1-3 | |
| 474 | Div 1 | 4 | Nov | Stoke | (h) | W | 1-0 | ⚽ |
| 475 | Div 1 | 8 | Nov | Leeds | (a) | L | 0-1 | |
| 476 | Div 1 | 11 | Nov | Liverpool | (a) | W | 2-1 | |
| 477 | E Cup | 15 | Nov | Sarajevo | (a) | D | 0-0 | ⚽ |
| 478 | Div 1 | 18 | Nov | Southampton | (h) | W | 3-2 | |
| 479 | Div 1 | 25 | Nov | Chelsea | (a) | D | 1-1 | |
| 480 | E Cup | 29 | Nov | Sarajevo | (h) | W | 2-1 | |
| 481 | Div 1 | 2 | Dec | WBA | (h) | W | 2-1 | |
| 482 | Div 1 | 9 | Dec | Newcastle | (a) | D | 2-2 | |
| 483 | Div 1 | 16 | Dec | Everton | (h) | W | 3-1 | |
| 484 | Div 1 | 23 | Dec | Leicester | (a) | D | 2-2 | |
| 485 | Div 1 | 26 | Dec | Wolves | (h) | W | 4-0 | ⚽⚽ |
| 486 | Div 1 | 30 | Dec | Wolves | (a) | W | 3-2 | ⚽⚽ |
| 487 | Div 1 | 6 | Jan | West Ham | (h) | W | 3-1 | ⚽⚽ |

| No. | Competition | Date | Opponent | Venue | Result | Score | |
|---|---|---|---|---|---|---|---|
| 488 | Div 1 | 20 Jan | Sheffield W | (h) | W | 4–2 | ⚽ |
| 489 | FA Cup | 27 Jan | Tottenham | (h) | D | 2–2 | ⚽⚽ |
| 490 | FA Cup | 31 Jan | Tottenham | (a) | L | 0–1 | |
| 491 | Div 1 | 3 Feb | Tottenham | (a) | W | 2–1 | ⚽ |
| 492 | Div 1 | 17 Feb | Burnley | (a) | L | 1–2 | |
| 493 | E Cup | 28 Feb | Gornik Zabrze | (h) | W | 2–0 | |
| 494 | Div 1 | 2 Mar | Chelsea | (h) | L | 1–3 | |
| 495 | E Cup | 13 Mar | Gornik Zabrze | (a) | L | 0–1 | |
| 496 | Div 1 | 16 Mar | Coventry | (a) | L | 0–2 | |
| 497 | Div 1 | 23 Mar | Nottm F | (h) | W | 3–0 | |
| 498 | Div 1 | 27 Mar | Man City | (h) | L | 1–3 | |
| 499 | Div 1 | 30 Mar | Stoke | (a) | W | 4–2 | |
| 500 | Div 1 | 6 Apr | Liverpool | (h) | L | 1–2 | |
| 501 | Div 1 | 12 Apr | Fulham | (a) | W | 4–0 | |
| 502 | Div 1 | 13 Apr | Southampton | (a) | D | 2–2 | |
| 503 | Div 1 | 15 Apr | Fulham | (h) | W | 3–0 | |
| 504 | Div 1 | 20 Apr | Sheffield U | (h) | W | 1–0 | |
| 505 | E Cup | 24 Apr | Real Madrid | (h) | W | 1–0 | ⚽⚽ |
| 506 | Div 1 | 27 Apr | WBA | (a) | L | 3–6 | |
| 507 | Div 1 | 4 May | Newcastle | (h) | W | 6–0 | |
| 508 | Div 1 | 11 May | Sunderland | (h) | L | 1–2 | |

| No. | Comp | Date | | Opponent | Venue | Result | Score | Goals |
|---|---|---|---|---|---|---|---|---|
| 509 | E Cup | 15 | May | Real Madrid | (a) | D | 3–3 | |
| 510 | E Cup | 29 | May | Benfica | (n) | W | 4–1 | ⚽⚽ |

Games/Goals

*Season Summary*

| | League | FA Cup | European | C Shd | Total |
|---|---|---|---|---|---|
| | 41/15 | 2/1 | 9/2 | 1/2 | 53/20 |
| | 416/163 | 54/16 | 37/20 | 3/2 | 510/201 |

### 1968–69

| No. | Comp | Date | | Opponent | Venue | Result | Score | Goals |
|---|---|---|---|---|---|---|---|---|
| 511 | Div 1 | 10 | Aug | Everton | (h) | W | 2–1 | |
| 512 | Div 1 | 14 | Aug | WBA | (a) | L | 1–2 | |
| 513 | Div 1 | 17 | Aug | Man City | (a) | D | 0–0 | |
| 514 | Div 1 | 21 | Aug | Coventry | (h) | W | 1–0 | |
| 515 | Div 1 | 24 | Aug | Chelsea | (h) | L | 0–4 | |
| 516 | Div 1 | 28 | Aug | Tottenham | (h) | W | 3–1 | ⚽⚽ |
| 517 | Div 1 | 31 | Aug | Sheffield W | (a) | L | 4–5 | ⚽⚽ |
| 518 | Div 1 | 7 | Sep | West Ham | (h) | D | 1–1 | |
| 519 | Div 1 | 14 | Sep | Burnley | (a) | L | 0–1 | |
| 520 | E Cup | 18 | Sep | Waterford | (a) | W | 3–1 | ⚽ |
| 521 | Div 1 | 21 | Sep | Newcastle | (h) | W | 3–1 | |

| | | | | Opponent | | | |
|---|---|---|---|---|---|---|---|
| 522 | WCC | 25 | Sep | Estudiantes | (a) | L | 0–1 |
| 523 | E Cup | 2 | Oct | Waterford | (h) | W | 7–1 |
| 524 | Div 1 | 5 | Oct | Arsenal | (h) | D | 0–0 |
| 525 | Div 1 | 9 | Oct | Tottenham | (a) | D | 2–2 |
| 526 | Div 1 | 12 | Oct | Liverpool | (a) | L | 0–2 |
| 527 | WCC | 16 | Oct | Estudiantes | (h) | D | 1–1 |
| 528 | Div 1 | 19 | Oct | Southampton | (h) | L | 1–2 |
| 529 | Div 1 | 26 | Oct | QPR | (a) | W | 3–2 |
| 530 | Div 1 | 2 | Nov | Leeds | (h) | D | 0–0 |
| 531 | Div 1 | 9 | Nov | Sunderland | (a) | D | 1–1 |
| 532 | E Cup | 13 | Nov | Anderlecht | (h) | W | 3–0 |
| 533 | Div 1 | 16 | Nov | Ipswich | (h) | D | 0–0 |
| 534 | Div 1 | 23 | Nov | Stoke | (a) | D | 0–0 |
| 535 | E Cup | 27 | Nov | Anderlecht | (a) | L | 1–3 |
| 536 | Div 1 | 30 | Nov | Wolves | (h) | W | 2–0 |
| 537 | Div 1 | 7 | Dec | Leicester | (a) | L | 1–2 |
| 538 | Div 1 | 14 | Dec | Liverpool | (h) | W | 1–0 |
| 539 | Div 1 | 21 | Dec | Southampton | (a) | L | 0–2 |
| 540 | Div 1 | 26 | Dec | Arsenal | (a) | L | 0–3 |
| 541 | FA Cup | 4 | Jan | Exeter | (a) | W | 3–1 |
| 542 | Div 1 | 11 | Jan | Leeds | (a) | L | 1–2 |

| No. | Competition | Date | | Opponent | Venue | Result | Score | |
|---|---|---|---|---|---|---|---|---|
| 543 | Div 1 | 18 | Jan | Sunderland | (h) | W | 4–1 | |
| 544 | FA Cup | 25 | Jan | Watford | (h) | D | 1–1 | |
| 545 | Div 1 | 1 | Feb | Ipswich | (a) | L | 0–1 | |
| 546 | FA Cup | 3 | Feb | Watford | (a) | W | 2–0 | |
| 547 | FA Cup | 8 | Feb | Birmingham | (a) | D | 2–2 | |
| 548 | Div 1 | 15 | Feb | Wolves | (a) | D | 2–2 | ⚽ |
| 549 | FA Cup | 24 | Feb | Birmingham | (h) | W | 6–2 | |
| 550 | E Cup | 26 | Feb | Rapid Vienna | (h) | W | 3–0 | |
| 551 | FA Cup | 1 | Mar | Everton | (h) | L | 0–1 | |
| 552 | E Cup | 5 | Mar | Rapid Vienna | (a) | D | 0–0 | |
| 553 | Div 1 | 8 | Mar | Man C | (h) | L | 0–1 | |
| 554 | Div 1 | 8 | Apr | Coventry | (a) | L | 1–2 | |
| 555 | Div 1 | 12 | Apr | Newcastle | (a) | L | 0–2 | |
| 556 | E Cup | 23 | Apr | AC Milan | (a) | L | 0–2 | |
| 557 | E Cup | 15 | May | AC Milan | (h) | W | 1–0 | ⚽ |
| 558 | Div 1 | 17 | May | Leicester | (h) | W | 3–2 | |

| | League | FA Cup | European | C Shd | WCC | Total |
|---|---|---|---|---|---|---|
| Games/Goals Season Summary | 32/5 | 6 | 8/2 | — | 2 | 48/7 |
| | 448/168 | 60/16 | 45/22 | 3/2 | 2 | 558/208 |

## 1969–70

| | | | | | | |
|---|---|---|---|---|---|---|
| 559 | Div 1 | 9 Aug | Crystal Palace | (a) | D | 2–2 |
| 560 | Div 1 | 13 Aug | Everton | (h) | L | 0–2 |
| 561 | Div 1 | 16 Aug | Southampton | (h) | L | 1–4 |
| 562 | Div 1 | 23 Aug | Wolves | (a) | D | 0–0 |
| 563 | Div 1 | 27 Aug | Newcastle | (h) | D | 0–0 |
| 564 | Div 1 | 30 Aug | Sunderland | (h) | W | 3–1 |
| 565 | L Cup | 3 Sep | Middlesbrough | (h) | W | 1–0 |
| 566 | Div 1 | 6 Sep | Leeds | (a) | D | 2–2 |
| 567 | Div 1 | 13 Sep | Liverpool | (h) | W | 1–0 |
| 568 | Div 1 | 17 Sep | Sheffield W | (a) | W | 3–1 |
| 569 | Div 1 | 20 Sep | Arsenal | (a) | D | 2–2 |
| 570 | L Cup | 23 Sep | Wrexham | (h) | W | 2–0 |
| 571 | Div 1 | 27 Sep | West Ham | (h) | W | 5–2 |
| 572 | Div 1 | 4 Oct | Derby | (a) | L | 0–2 |
| 573 | Div 1 | 8 Oct | Southampton | (a) | W | 3–0 |
| 574 | Div 1 | 11 Oct | Ipswich | (h) | W | 2–1 |
| 575 | L Cup | 14 Oct | Burnley | (a) | D | 0–0 |
| 576 | Div 1 | 18 Oct | Nottm F | (h) | D | 1–1 |
| 577 | L Cup | 20 Oct | Burnley | (h) | W | 1–0 |

| No. | Comp | Date | | Opponent | Venue | Res | Score | |
|---|---|---|---|---|---|---|---|---|
| 578 | Div 1 | 25 | Oct | WBA | (a) | L | 1–2 | |
| 579 | Div 1 | 1 | Nov | Stoke | (h) | D | 1–1 | ⚽ |
| 580 | Div 1 | 8 | Nov | Coventry | (a) | W | 2–1 | |
| 581 | L Cup | 12 | Nov | Derby | (a) | D | 0–0 | |
| 582 | Div 1 | 15 | Nov | Man City | (a) | L | 0–4 | |
| 583 | L Cup | 19 | Nov | Derby | (h) | W | 1–0 | ⚽⚽ |
| 584 | Div 1 | 22 | Nov | Tottenham | (h) | W | 3–1 | |
| 585 | Div 1 | 29 | Nov | Burnley | (a) | D | 1–1 | ⚽ |
| 586 | L Cup | 3 | Dec | Man City | (a) | L | 1–2 | |
| 587 | Div 1 | 6 | Dec | Chelsea | (h) | L | 0–2 | ⚽ |
| 588 | Div 1 | 13 | Dec | Liverpool | (a) | W | 4–1 | |
| 589 | L Cup | 17 | Dec | Man City | (h) | D | 2–2 | |
| 590 | Div 1 | 26 | Dec | Wolves | (h) | D | 0–0 | |
| 591 | Div 1 | 27 | Dec | Sunderland | (a) | D | 1–1 | |
| 592 | FA Cup | 3 | Jan | Ipswich | (a) | W | 1–0 | |
| 593 | Div 1 | 10 | Jan | Arsenal | (h) | W | 2–1 | |
| 594 | Div 1 | 17 | Jan | West Ham | (a) | D | 0–0 | |
| 595 | FA Cup | 24 | Jan | Man City | (h) | W | 3–0 | |
| 596 | Div 1 | 26 | Jan | Leeds | (h) | D | 2–2 | |
| 597 | Div 1 | 31 | Jan | Derby | (h) | W | 1–0 | ⚽ |
| 598 | FA Cup | 7 | Feb | Northampton | (a) | W | 8–2 | |

| | | | | | | | |
|---|---|---|---|---|---|---|---|
| 599 | Div 1 | 10 Feb | Ipswich | (a) | W | 1–0 | |
| 600 | Div 1 | 14 Feb | Crystal Palace | (h) | D | 1–1 | |
| 601 | FA Cup | 21 Feb | Middlesbrough | (a) | D | 1–1 | |
| 602 | FA Cup | 25 Feb | Middlesbrough | (h) | W | 2–1 | |
| 603 | Div 1 | 28 Feb | Stoke | (a) | D | 2–2 | ⚽ |
| 604 | FA Cup | 14 Mar | Leeds | (n) | D | 0–0 | |
| 605 | Div 1 | 17 Mar | Burnley | (h) | D | 3–3 | |
| 606 | Div 1 | 21 Mar | Chelsea | (a) | L | 1–2 | |
| 607 | FA Cup | 23 Mar | Leeds | (n) | D | 0–0 | |
| 608 | FA Cup | 26 Mar | Leeds | (n) | L | 0–1 | |
| 609 | Div 1 | 28 Mar | Man City | (h) | L | 1–2 | |
| 610 | Div 1 | 31 Mar | Nottm F | (a) | W | 2–1 | |
| 611 | Div 1 | 4 Apr | Newcastle | (a) | L | 1–5 | ⚽⚽ |
| 612 | Div 1 | 8 Apr | WBA | (h) | W | 7–0 | ⚽⚽⚽ |
| 613 | FA Cup | 10 Apr | Watford | (n) | W | 2–0 | ⚽⚽ |
| 614 | Div 1 | 13 Apr | Tottenham | (a) | L | 1–2 | |
| 615 | Div 1 | 15 Apr | Sheffield W | (h) | D | 2–2 | ⚽ |

| Games/Goals | League | FA Cup | L Cup | European | C Shd | WCC | Total |
|---|---|---|---|---|---|---|---|
| Season | 40/12 | 9/1 | 8/1 | — | — | — | 57/14 |
| Summary | 488/180 | 69/17 | 8/1 | 45/22 | 3/2 | 2 | 615/222 |

| | | | | | | | | |
|---|---|---|---|---|---|---|---|---|
| 616 | Div 1 | 15 Aug | Leeds | (h) | L | 0–1 | | |
| 617 | Div 1 | 19 Aug | Chelsea | (h) | D | 0–0 | | |
| 618 | Div 1 | 22 Aug | Arsenal | (a) | L | 0–4 | | |
| 619 | Div 1 | 25 Aug | Burnley | (a) | W | 2–0 | ⚽ | |
| 620 | Div 1 | 29 Aug | West Ham | (h) | D | 1–1 | | |
| 621 | Div 1 | 2 Sep | Everton | (h) | W | 2–0 | ⚽ | |
| 622 | Div 1 | 5 Sep | Liverpool | (a) | D | 1–1 | | |
| 623 | L Cup | 9 Sep | Aldershot | (a) | W | 3–1 | | |
| 624 | Div 1 | 12 Sep | Coventry | (h) | W | 2–0 | ⚽ | |
| 625 | Div 1 | 19 Sep | Ipswich | (a) | L | 0–4 | | |
| 626 | Div 1 | 26 Sep | Blackpool | (h) | D | 1–1 | | |
| 627 | Div 1 | 3 Oct | Wolves | (a) | L | 2–3 | | |
| 628 | L Cup | 7 Oct | Portsmouth | (h) | W | 1–0 | ⚽ | |
| 629 | Div 1 | 10 Oct | Crystal Palace | (h) | L | 0–1 | | |
| 630 | Div 1 | 17 Oct | Leeds | (a) | D | 2–2 | ⚽ | |
| 631 | Div 1 | 24 Oct | WBA | (h) | W | 2–1 | ⚽ | |
| 632 | L Cup | 28 Oct | Chelsea | (h) | W | 2–1 | | |
| 633 | Div 1 | 31 Oct | Newcastle | (a) | L | 0–1 | | |
| 634 | Div 1 | 7 Nov | Stoke | (h) | D | 2–2 | | |

| | | | | | | |
|---|---|---|---|---|---|---|
| 635 | Div 1 | 14 Nov | Nottm F | (a) | W | 2-1 |
| 636 | L Cup | 18 Nov | Crystal Palace | (h) | W | 4-2 |
| 637 | Div 1 | 21 Nov | Southampton | (a) | L | 0-1 |
| 638 | Div 1 | 28 Nov | Huddersfield | (h) | D | 1-1 |
| 639 | Div 1 | 5 Dec | Tottenham | (a) | D | 2-2 |
| 640 | Div 1 | 12 Dec | Man City | (h) | L | 1-4 |
| 641 | L Cup | 16 Dec | Aston Villa | (h) | D | 1-1 |
| 642 | Div 1 | 19 Dec | Arsenal | (h) | L | 1-3 |
| 643 | L Cup | 23 Dec | Aston Villa | (a) | L | 1-2 |
| 644 | Div 1 | 26 Dec | Derby | (a) | D | 4-4 |
| 645 | FA Cup | 2 Jan | Middlesbrough | (h) | D | 0-0 |
| 646 | FA Cup | 5 Jan | Middlesbrough | (a) | L | 1-2 |
| 647 | Div 1 | 9 Jan | Chelsea | (a) | W | 2-1 |
| 648 | Div 1 | 16 Jan | Burnley | (h) | D | 1-1 |
| 649 | Div 1 | 30 Jan | Huddersfield | (a) | W | 2-1 |
| 650 | Div 1 | 6 Feb | Tottenham | (h) | W | 2-1 |
| 651 | Div 1 | 20 Feb | Southampton | (h) | W | 5-1 |
| 652 | Div 1 | 23 Feb | Everton | (a) | L | 0-1 |
| 653 | Div 1 | 27 Feb | Newcastle | (h) | W | 1-0 |
| 654 | Div 1 | 6 Mar | WBA | (a) | L | 3-4 |
| 655 | Div 1 | 13 Mar | Nottm F | (h) | W | 2-0 |

| No. | Div | Date | Opponent | | Result | | Score | |
|---|---|---|---|---|---|---|---|---|
| 656 | Div 1 | 20 Mar | Stoke | (a) | W | | 2–1 | |
| 657 | Div 1 | 3 Apr | West Ham | (a) | L | | 1–2 | |
| 658 | Div 1 | 10 Apr | Derby | (h) | L | | 1–2 | |
| 659 | Div 1 | 12 Apr | Wolves | (h) | W | | 1–0 | |
| 660 | Div 1 | 13 Apr | Coventry | (a) | L | | 1–2 | |
| 661 | Div 1 | 17 Apr | Crystal Palace | (a) | W | | 5–3 | |
| 662 | Div 1 | 19 Apr | Liverpool | (h) | L | | 0–2 | |
| 663 | Div 1 | 24 Apr | Ipswich | (h) | W | | 3–2 | ⚽ |
| 664 | Div 1 | 1 May | Blackpool | (a) | D | | 0–0 | |
| 665 | Div 1 | 5 May | Man City | (a) | W | | 4–3 | ⚽ |

| Games/Goals | League | FA Cup | L Cup | European | C Shd | WCC | Total |
|---|---|---|---|---|---|---|---|
| Season | 42/5 | 2 | 6/3 | — | — | — | 50/8 |
| Summary | 530/185 | 71/17 | 14/4 | 45/22 | 3/2 | 2 | 665/230 |

(Total column goal markers: ⚽ ⚽)

## 1971–72

| No. | Div | Date | Opponent | | Result | | Score | |
|---|---|---|---|---|---|---|---|---|
| 666 | Div 1 | 14 Aug | Derby | (a) | D | | 2–2 | |
| 667 | Div 1 | 18 Aug | Chelsea | (a) | W | | 3–2 | ⚽ |
| 668 | Div 1 | 20 Aug | Arsenal | (h) | W | | 3–1 | ⚽ |

| | | | | | | |
|---|---|---|---|---|---|---|
| 669 | Div 1 | 23 Aug | WBA | (h) | W | 3–1 |
| 670 | Div 1 | 28 Aug | Wolves | (a) | D | 1–1 |
| 671 | Div 1 | 31 Aug | Everton | (a) | L | 0–1 |
| 672 | Div 1 | 4 Sep | Ipswich | (h) | W | 1–0 |
| 673 | L Cup | 7 Sep | Ipswich | (a) | W | 3–1 |
| 674 | Div 1 | 11 Sep | Crystal Palace | (a) | W | 3–1 |
| 675 | Div 1 | 18 Sep | West Ham | (h) | W | 4–2 |
| 676 | Div 1 | 25 Sep | Liverpool | (a) | D | 2–2 |
| 677 | Div 1 | 2 Oct | Sheffield U | (h) | W | 2–0 |
| 678 | L Cup | 6 Oct | Burnley | (h) | D | 1–1 |
| 679 | Div 1 | 9 Oct | Huddersfield | (a) | W | 3–0 |
| 680 | Div 1 | 16 Oct | Derby | (h) | W | 1–0 |
| 681 | L Cup | 18 Oct | Burnley | (a) | W | 1–0 |
| 682 | Div 1 | 23 Oct | Newcastle | (a) | W | 1–0 |
| 683 | L Cup | 27 Oct | Stoke | (h) | D | 1–1 |
| 684 | Div 1 | 30 Oct | Leeds | (h) | L | 0–1 |
| 685 | Div 1 | 6 Nov | Man City | (a) | D | 3–3 |
| 686 | L Cup | 8 Nov | Stoke | (a) | D | 0–0 |
| 687 | Div 1 | 13 Nov | Tottenham | (h) | W | 3–1 |
| 688 | L Cup | 15 Nov | Stoke | (a) | L | 1–2 |
| 689 | Div 1 | 20 Nov | Leicester | (h) | W | 3–2 |

⚽⚽ ⚽ ⚽⚽ ⚽

| No. | Competition | Date | | Opponent | Venue | Result | Score |
|---|---|---|---|---|---|---|---|
| 690 | Div 1 | 27 | Nov | Southampton | (a) | W | 5–2 |
| 691 | Div 1 | 4 | Dec | Nottm F | (h) | W | 3–2 |
| 692 | Div 1 | 11 | Dec | Stoke | (a) | D | 1–1 |
| 693 | Div 1 | 18 | Dec | Ipswich | (a) | D | 0–0 |
| 694 | Div 1 | 27 | Dec | Coventry | (h) | D | 2–2 |
| 695 | Div 1 | 1 | Jan | West Ham | (a) | L | 0–3 |
| 696 | Div 1 | 8 | Jan | Wolves | (h) | L | 1–3 |
| 697 | FA Cup | 15 | Jan | Southampton | (a) | D | 1–1 |
| 698 | FA Cup | 19 | Jan | Southampton | (h) | W | 4–1 |
| 699 | Div 1 | 22 | Jan | Chelsea | (h) | L | 0–1 |
| 700 | Div 1 | 29 | Jan | WBA | (a) | L | 1–2 |
| 701 | FA Cup | 5 | Feb | Preston | (a) | W | 2–0 |
| 702 | Div 1 | 12 | Feb | Newcastle | (h) | L | 0–2 |
| 703 | Div 1 | 19 | Feb | Leeds | (a) | L | 1–5 |
| 704 | FA Cup | 26 | Feb | Middlesbrough | (h) | D | 0–0 |
| 705 | FA Cup | 29 | Feb | Middlesbrough | (a) | W | 3–0 |
| 706 | Div 1 | 4 | Mar | Tottenham | (a) | L | 0–2 |
| 707 | Div 1 | 11 | Mar | Huddersfield | (h) | W | 2–0 |
| 708 | FA Cup | 18 | Mar | Stoke | (h) | D | 1–1 |
| 709 | FA Cup | 22 | Mar | Stoke | (a) | L | 1–2 |
| 710 | Div 1 | 25 | Mar | Crystal Palace | (h) | W | 4–0 |

| | | | | | | |
|---|---|---|---|---|---|---|
| 711 | Div 1 | 1 Apr | Coventry | (a) | W | 3–2 |
| 712 | Div 1 | 3 Apr | Liverpool | (h) | L | 0–3 |
| 713 | Div 1 | 4 Apr | Sheffield U | (a) | D | 1–1 |
| 714 | Div 1 | 8 Apr | Leicester | (a) | L | 0–2 |
| 715 | Div 1 | 12 Apr | Man City | (h) | L | 1–3 |
| 716 | Div 1 | 22 Apr | Nottm F | (a) | D | 0–0 |
| 717 | Div 1 | 25 Apr | Arsenal | (a) | L | 0–3 |
| 718 | Div 1 | 29 Apr | Stoke | (h) | W | 3–0 |

| Games/Goals | League | FA Cup | L Cup | European | C Shd | WCC | Total |
|---|---|---|---|---|---|---|---|
| Season | 40/8 | 7/2 | 6/2 | — | 3/2 | — | 53/12 |
| Summary | 570/193 | 78/19 | 20/6 | 45/22 | 3/2 | 2 | 718/242 |

1972–73

| | | | | | | |
|---|---|---|---|---|---|---|
| 719 | Div 1 | 12 Aug | Ipswich | (h) | L | 1–2 |
| 720 | Div 1 | 15 Aug | Liverpool | (a) | L | 0–2 |
| 721 | Div 1 | 30 Aug | Chelsea | (h) | D | 0–0 |
| 722 | Div 1 | 2 Sep | West Ham | (a) | D | 2–2 |
| 723 | L Cup | 6 Sep | Oxford | (a) | D | 2–2 |

| No. | Competition | Date | Opponent | Venue | Result | Score |
|-----|-------------|------|----------|-------|--------|-------|
| 724 | Div 1 | 9 Sep | Coventry | (h) | L | 0–1 |
| 725 | L Cup | 12 Sep | Oxford | (h) | W | 3–1 |
| 726 | Div 1 | 16 Sep | Wolves | (a) | L | 0–2 |
| 727 | Div 1 | 23 Sep | Derby | (h) | W | 3–0 |
| 728 | Div 1 | 30 Sep | Sheffield U | (a) | L | 0–1 |
| 729 | L Cup | 3 Oct | Bristol R | (a) | D | 1–1 |
| 730 | L Cup | 11 Oct | Bristol R | (h) | L | 1–2 |
| 731 | Div 1 | 21 Oct | Newcastle | (a) | L | 1–2 |
| 732 | Div 1 | 28 Oct | Tottenham | (h) | L | 1–4 |
| 733 | Div 1 | 4 Nov | Leicester | (a) | D | 2–2 |
| 734 | Div 1 | 11 Nov | Liverpool | (h) | W | 2–0 |
| 735 | Div 1 | 18 Nov | Man City | (a) | L | 0–3 |
| 736 | Div 1 | 25 Nov | Southampton | (h) | W | 2–1 |
| 737 | Div 1 | 2 Dec | Norwich | (a) | W | 2–0 |
| 738 | Div 1 | 9 Dec | Stoke | (h) | L | 0–2 |
| 739 | Div 1 | 23 Dec | Leeds | (h) | D | 1–1 |
| 740 | Div 1 | 26 Dec | Derby | (a) | L | 1–3 |
| 741 | Div 1 | 6 Jan | Arsenal | (a) | L | 1–3 |
| 742 | FA Cup | 13 Jan | Wolves | (a) | L | 0–1 |
| 743 | Div 1 | 20 Jan | West Ham | (h) | D | 2–2 |
| 744 | Div 1 | 24 Jan | Everton | (h) | D | 0–0 |

| | | | | | | | |
|---|---|---|---|---|---|---|---|
| 745 | Div 1 | 27 Jan | Coventry | (a) | D | 1–1 | |
| 746 | Div 1 | 10 Feb | Wolves | (h) | W | 2–1 | ⚽⚽ |
| 747 | Div 1 | 17 Feb | Ipswich | (a) | L | 1–4 | |
| 748 | Div 1 | 3 Mar | WBA | (h) | W | 2–1 | |
| 749 | Div 1 | 10 Mar | Birmingham | (a) | L | 1–3 | |
| 750 | Div 1 | 17 Mar | Newcastle | (h) | W | 2–1 | |
| 751 | Div 1 | 24 Mar | Tottenham | (a) | D | 1–1 | |
| 752 | Div 1 | 31 Mar | Southampton | (a) | W | 2–0 | ⚽ |
| 753 | Div 1 | 7 Apr | Norwich | (h) | W | 1–0 | |
| 754 | Div 1 | 11 Apr | Crystal Palace | (h) | W | 2–0 | |
| 755 | Div 1 | 14 Apr | Stoke | (a) | D | 2–2 | |
| 756 | Div 1 | 18 Apr | Leeds | (a) | W | 1–0 | |
| 757 | Div 1 | 21 Apr | Man City | (h) | D | 0–0 | |
| 758 | Div 1 | 23 Apr | Sheffield U | (h) | L | 1–2 | |
| 759 | Div 1 | 28 Apr | Chelsea | (a) | L | 0–1 | |

| Games/Goals | League | FA Cup | L Cup | European | C Shd | WCC | Total |
|---|---|---|---|---|---|---|---|
| Season | 36/6 | 1 | 4/1 | — | — | — | 41/7 |
| Summary | 606/199 | 79/19 | 24/7 | 45/22 | 3/2 | 2 | 759/249 |

*Other cup competitions:* 1970–71 Watney Cup 3 games, 2 goals; 1971–72 Watney Cup 1 game; 1972–73 Anglo–Italian Cup 3 games, 2 goals.

# PRESTON NORTH END

## 1973–74 / MANAGER

### 1974–75

| # | Comp | Date | | Opponent | Venue | Result | Score | |
|---|---|---|---|---|---|---|---|---|
| 1 | Div 3 | 17 | Aug | Plymouth | (h) | W | 1–0 | ⚽⚽ |
| 2 | L Cup | 20 | Aug | Rochdale | (h) | W | 1–0 | |
| 3 | Div 3 | 24 | Aug | Watford | (a) | L | 2–3 | ⚽ |
| 4 | Div 3 | 31 | Aug | Walsall | (h) | W | 3–2 | |
| 5 | Div 3 | 3 | Sep | Bury | (h) | W | 3–0 | |
| 6 | Div 3 | 7 | Sep | Aldershot | (a) | W | 2–1 | |
| 7 | L Cup | 10 | Sep | Sunderland | (h) | W | 2–0 | ⚽ |
| 8 | Div 3 | 14 | Sep | Blackburn | (h) | D | 0–0 | |
| 9 | Div 3 | 17 | Sep | Charlton | (h) | W | 2–0 | |
| 10 | Div 3 | 21 | Sep | Peterborough | (a) | D | 0–0 | |
| 11 | Div 3 | 24 | Sep | Crystal Palace | (a) | L | 0–1 | |
| 12 | Div 3 | 28 | Sep | Bournemouth | (h) | W | 5–2 | |
| 13 | Div 3 | 1 | Oct | Bury | (a) | L | 0–2 | |
| 14 | Div 3 | 5 | Oct | Hereford | (a) | D | 2–2 | |
| 15 | L Cup | 9 | Oct | Chester | (a) | L | 0–1 | |

| # | Comp | Date | | Opponent | | Result | Score | |
|---|---|---|---|---|---|---|---|---|
| 16 | Div 3 | 12 | Oct | Colchester | (h) | L | 0–2 | |
| 17 | Div 3 | 19 | Oct | Brighton | (a) | W | 4–0 | ⚽ |
| 18 | Div 3 | 22 | Oct | Gillingham | (h) | W | 1–0 | |
| 19 | Div 3 | 26 | Oct | Grimsby | (h) | W | 2–0 | |
| 20 | Div 3 | 2 | Nov | Halifax | (a) | L | 0–3 | |
| 21 | Div 3 | 6 | Nov | Gillingham | (a) | L | 1–2 | |
| 22 | Div 3 | 9 | Nov | Southend | (h) | L | 1–4 | |
| 23 | Div 3 | 15 | Nov | Tranmere | (a) | L | 1–3 | |
| 24 | FA Cup | 23 | Nov | Blyth | (a) | D | 1–1 | |
| 25 | FA Cup | 26 | Nov | Blyth | (h) | W | 5–1 | ⚽ |
| 26 | Div 3 | 30 | Nov | Huddersfield | (h) | W | 4–0 | ⚽ |
| 27 | Div 3 | 7 | Dec | Wrexham | (a) | D | 1–1 | |
| 28 | FA Cup | 14 | Dec | B Auckland | (a) | W | 2–0 | ⚽ |
| 29 | Div 3 | 21 | Dec | Port Vale | (h) | W | 1–0 | |
| 30 | Div 3 | 26 | Dec | Blackburn | (a) | L | 0–3 | |
| 31 | Div 3 | 28 | Dec | Chesterfield | (h) | W | 2–1 | |
| 32 | FA Cup | 4 | Jan | Carlisle | (h) | L | 0–1 | |
| 33 | Div 3 | 11 | Jan | Wrexham | (h) | W | 3–1 | ⚽ |
| 34 | Div 3 | 18 | Jan | Huddersfield | (a) | W | 1–0 | |
| 35 | Div 3 | 1 | Feb | Southend | (a) | D | 1–1 | |
| 36 | Div 3 | 8 | Feb | Halifax | (h) | W | 1–0 | |

| 37 | Div 3 | 15 Feb | Swindon | (a) | L | 0–1 |
| 38 | Div 3 | 18 Feb | Swindon | (h) | W | 2–0 |
| 39 | Div 3 | 22 Feb | Tranmere | (h) | W | 1–0 |
| 40 | Div 3 | 28 Feb | Walsall | (a) | L | 0–2 |
| 41 | Div 3 | 8 Mar | Crystal Palace | (h) | D | 1–1 |
| 42 | Div 3 | 15 Mar | Bournemouth | (a) | L | 0–1 |
| 43 | Div 3 | 18 Mar | Plymouth | (a) | L | 1–2 |
| 44 | Div 3 | 22 Mar | Aldershot | (h) | W | 3–1 |
| 45 | Div 3 | 29 Mar | Port Vale | (a) | L | 1–3 |

| Games/Goals | League | FA Cup | L Cup | Total |
|---|---|---|---|---|
| *Season* | 38/8 | 4/1 | 3/1 | 45/10 |

*Competitions*: Football League Divisions 1 and 3; FA Cup; League Cup; Fairs Cup; European Cup-Winners' Cup; European Cup; World Club Championship; Charity Shield.

# PICTURE CREDITS

All photographs that courtesy of Sir Bobby Charlton.